AF622476

Renewable Energy from Wind and Solar Power

Renewable Energy from Wind and Solar Power

Law and Regulation

William Webster

WS
&H

Wildy, Simmonds & Hill Publishing

© William Webster, 2021

Contains public sector information licensed under the Open Government Licence v3.0

ISBN: 9780854902866

British Library Cataloguing in Publication Data

A catalogue record for this book is available from the British Library

The right of the author to be identified as the author of this Work has been asserted by him in accordance with sections 77 and 78 of the Copyright, Designs and Patents Act 1988.

All rights reserved. No part of this book may be reproduced, stored in a retrieval system, or transmitted, in any form or by any means, electronic, mechanical, photocopying, recording or otherwise, without the consent of the copyright owners, application for which should be addressed to the publisher. Such a written permission must also be obtained before any part of this publication is stored in a retrieval system of any nature.

All reasonable care was taken in the preparation of this book, but any person relying on any of the statements, express or implied, in this book does so entirely at his or her own risk and without liability on the part of either the author or the publisher.

First published in 2021 by

Wildy, Simmonds & Hill Publishing
Wildy & Sons Ltd
Lincoln's Inn Archway
Carey Street
London WC2A 2JD
www.wildy.com

Typeset by Heather Jones, North Petherton, Somerset.
Printed and bound by CPI Group (UK) Ltd, Croydon, CR0 4YY

Contents

Preface

This book was written in the 6-month period before the first lockdown in March 2020. At that point, the legal publishing world went into a state of hibernation. The instruction from my publisher was to keep the book up to date. In the event, the book was largely rewritten and by the time it went into production in September 2020 I was satisfied that it was as up to date as I could make it, particularly when it came to the extensive case and appeal studies (with added commentaries) contained in Chapter 8 (wind power projects) and Chapter 10 (solar power development), which I consider to be the main highlights of the book.

In 2019, electricity generation in the UK from low carbon and renewable sources (LCRS) was 37.1%, whereas only a decade ago electricity generated from fossil fuels provided around 80% of the UK's electricity needs (split between gas and coal). Although oil still forms a key part of the UK's energy mix (40%), there has been a steep decline in oil production with the UK becoming a net importer in 2005. By 2019, coal accounted for less than 1% of the UK's electricity, whereas as recently as 2013 it had been as much as 18%. The real winners in all this are wind and solar. Indeed, on a windy Boxing Day 2020, a record 50.7% of the UK's electricity was derived from wind power, with wind and solar contributing 29% across the year, up from 23% in 2019.

Production of energy from LCRS is expected to intensify. The government has made the expansion of offshore wind production one of the main opportunities for achieving net zero emissions. On 27 June 2019, the Climate Change Act 2008 (2050 Target Amendment) Order 2019 (SI 2019/1056) came into force. Under this provision the previous target to cut emissions by 80% by 2050 was changed to 100%. The push is therefore on to target *net-zero* greenhouse gas emissions by 2050. The current Prime Minister has chosen to go even further by pledging that offshore wind farms would generate enough electricity to power every home in the UK by 2030.

Many in the industry would point to the need for a better balance between onshore and offshore wind energy. Onshore wind energy is still held back by the constraints of local development plans, whereas offshore production is characterised by its very high cost, difficulties with connectivity to the grid and the harm which can be caused to sensitive marine habitats. The UK clearly needs a reliable mix of carbon-free sources of energy supply, and in view of recent trends it seems highly likely that the day will come when wind, solar and nuclear will become the main contributors of electricity supply as the UK plays its role in the shift towards a greener world.

The book begins with an analysis of what is meant by climate change and the UK's record in the generation of electricity from LCRS in recent years. It then moves into an overview of the regulatory framework affecting wind and solar developments, with separate chapters dealing with nationally significant infrastructure projects, environmental impact assessment, habitats regulations and national planning guidance relevant to wind and solar developments. The final chapters deal with wind and solar farms and are followed by a large number of recent case studies and commentaries.

I am indebted to the Right Honourable Lord Justice Lindblom (Senior President of Tribunals) for kindly providing me with a generous Foreword. I am also grateful to Andrew Riddoch of Wildy, Simmonds & Hill for his wise advice and support throughout. My thanks also goes to my clerks at 3 Paper Buildings, most notably to Mark Heath and Joe Townsend, both of whom helped me cope with the daily demands of my practice in tandem with book writing. Lastly, I thank my wife as I struggled to complete and update the text in the final months.

All errors and omissions in this book are my own. I do though encourage readers to get in touch with me directly (or with the publishers) if they spot any mistakes or wish to offer suggestions for the next edition.

William Webster
3 Paper Buildings
Temple
January 2021

Foreword

William Webster has taken on, and performed, a formidable task. In describing and explaining the complex framework of regulation for electricity generation by the two principal sources of renewable energy in this country – solar and wind power – and in presenting a vast amount of law, policy and decision-making, he has filled an expanding gap in the literature on environmental and energy law. Indeed, he has produced the first comprehensive and authoritative coverage of the subject in a legal textbook.

Rightly, the book places its examination of the relevant law and policy in the wider context of the United Kingdom's efforts to reduce reliance on fossil fuels, the legally binding targets for greenhouse gas emissions in the Climate Change Act 2008, the international obligations under the Paris Agreement of 2015, the IPCC's *Special Report on Global Warming of 1.5°C* of October 2018, and the reports of the Committee on Climate Change in 2018 and 2019.

The book explores the arrangements for the approval of wind and solar energy projects in the planning legislation and the process of gaining consent under section 36 of the Electricity Act 1989. It connects that discussion to the legislative regimes for the protection of the environment, including the legislation for Environmental Impact Assessment, with a particular focus on habitats and the historic environment. It illuminates the law on nationally significant infrastructure projects. It brings together the national policy and guidance bearing on wind and solar energy projects. And it devotes full chapters specifically to the development of wind farms, both onshore and offshore, and to the development of solar energy. All of this is lucid and thorough.

A feature of the book likely to be welcomed by practitioners is the series of case studies in Chapters 8 and 10, which analyse recent decisions of the courts and of the Secretary of State, or an inspector or reporter, and draw out the salient principles – for example, on wind power or solar power development proposed in the Green Belt; or affecting an important landscape, or a heritage asset or its setting, or biodiversity; or likely to harm the living conditions of local residents; or offering 'community benefits'; or of a scale requiring a development consent order, with a wide range of implications for the local environment, and requiring powers for the compulsory acquisition of land. Here again the approach is both practical and meticulous.

William Webster's experience as a practitioner in this area of the law, the care he has taken in organising his material and the clarity of his text will, I am sure, bring this book the success it deserves.

The Rt Hon Lord Justice Lindblom
August 2020

List of Abbreviations

AEoI	adverse effects on integrity
ALARP	As Low As Reasonably Practicable
ALC	Agricultural Land Classification
AONB	Area of Outstanding Natural Beauty
BMV	best and most versatile
CantCC	Canterbury City Council
CCC	Committee on Climate Change
CCTV	closed-circuit television
CfD	Contracts for Difference
CHP	combined heat and power
CIL Regulations	Community Infrastructure Levy Regulations 2010 (SI 2010/948)
CO_2	carbon dioxide
dB	decibel
DBEIS	Department for Business, Energy & Industrial Strategy
DCO	development consent order
DECC	Department of Energy and Climate Change
DEFRA	Department for Environment, Food and Rural Affairs
DNS	Developments of National Significance
DUKES	*Digest of United Kingdom Energy Statistics 2020*
EIA	Environmental Impact Assessment
EIA Directive	Directive 2011/92/EU of the European Parliament and of the Council of 13 December 2011 on the assessment of the effects of certain public and private projects on the environment
EMF	electric and magnetic field
ES	Environmental Statement
EU	European Union
ExA	Examining Authority
FEPA licence	Food and Environment Protection Act 1985 licence
FiT	feed-in tariff

GPDO	Town and Country Planning (General Permitted Development) (England) Order 2015 (SI 2015/596)
GREAT	Graveney Rural Environment Action Team
GW	gigawatt
GWh	gigawatt hour
Habitats Directive	Council Directive 92/43/EEC of 21 May 1992 on the conservation of natural habitats and of wild fauna and flora
Habitats Regulations 2017	Conservation of Habitats and Species Regulations 2017 (SI 2017/1012)
HGV	heavy goods vehicle
Hornsea Project Three	Hornsea Project Three Offshore Wind Farm
HRA	Habitats Regulations 2017 Assessment
ICNIRP	International Commission on Non-Ionizing Radiation Protection
IPCC	Intergovernmental Panel on Climate Change
KCC	Kent County Council
KJ	kilojoule
km	kilometre
km^2	square kilometre
kV	kilovolt
kW	kilowatt
kWh	kilowatt hour
KWT	Kent Wildlife Trust
LBD	limits to built development
LCA	Landscape Character Area
LCRS	low carbon and renewable sources
LCT	Landscape Character Type
LP	South Downs Local Plan 2014–2033
LPA	local planning authority
m	metre
m^2	square metre
mm	millimetre
MBC	Maidstone Borough Council
MBLP	Maidstone Borough-Wide Local Plan
MCS	Microgeneration Certification Scheme
MMO	Marine Management Organisation
MW	megawatt
MWh	megawatt hour
NATS	National Air Traffic Services
NFDC	New Forest District Council

NFFO	National Federation of Fishermen's Organisations
NIA	National Infrastructure Assessment
NIC	National Infrastructure Commission
NPPF	National Planning Policy Framework
NPPG	National Planning Practice Guidance
NPS	National Policy Statement
NPS EN-1	Overarching National Policy Statement for Energy
NPS EN-3	National Policy Statement for Renewable Energy Infrastructure
NPS EN-5	National Policy Statement for Electricity Networks Infrastructure
NPSP	NPS Ports
NSIP	nationally significant infrastructure project
Offshore Regulations	Conservation of Offshore Marine Habitats and Species Regulations 2017 (SI 2017/1013)
PA 2008	Planning Act 2008 (as amended by the Localism Act 2011)
PD rights	permitted development rights
PES	protected European sites
PINS	Planning Inspectorate
PMP	South Downs National Park Partnership Management Plan 2014–2019
PPA	planning performance agreement
PPW	Planning Policy Wales
PSR	Primary Surveillance Radar
PV	photovoltaics
RHI	Renewable Heat Incentive
RHPP	Renewable Heat Premium Payment
RSPB	Royal Society for the Protection of Birds
RTFO	Renewable Transport Fuel Obligation
SAC	Special Area of Conservation
SAM	Scheduled Ancient Monument
SBC	Swale Borough Council
SEG	smart export guarantee
SLA	Special Landscape Area
SNCB	statutory nature conservation body
SoS	Secretary of State
SPA	Special Protection Area
SPD	supplementary planning document
SSSI	Site of Special Scientific Interest
STC	Standard Test Condition
TCE	The Crown Estate

TCPA 1990	Town and Country Planning Act 1990
UK	United Kingdom
UNFCC	United Nations Framework Convention on Climate Change
Water Framework Directive	Directive 2000/60/EC of the European Parliament and of the Council of 23 October 2000 establishing a framework for Community action in the field of water policy
WMS	Written Ministerial Statement
2011 Regulations	Town and Country Planning (Environmental Impact Assessment) Regulations 2011 (SI 2011/1824)
2017 Infrastructure Regulations	Infrastructure Planning (Environmental Impact Assessment) Regulations 2017 (SI 2017/572)
2017 T&C Regulations	Town and Country Planning (Environmental Impact Assessment) Regulations 2017 (SI 2017/1012)
°C	degree centigrade

Table of Cases

References are to page numbers.

Table of Statutes

References are to page numbers.

Table of Statutory Instruments

References are to page numbers.

Table of EU Material

References are to page numbers.

Table of Other Material

References are to page numbers.

Chapter 1

Introduction

SCOPE OF INTRODUCTION

1.1 This book is concerned with the law and regulation of electricity generation of the two most popular sources of energy collected from renewable resources. The scope of this chapter is essentially to provide a wider context for the United Kingdom's (UK's) record in generating renewable electricity from solar and wind power. The chapter starts with an overview on climate change and the UK's record in dealing with this in recent years. Key issues addressed include UK energy policy, the sources of energy that are available to the UK from fossil fuels and renewables, and the national and international efforts intended to bring about a progressive shift from fossil fuels to low carbon electricity.

CLIMATE CHANGE

1.2 The obvious driver for the rapid growth of electricity generated from renewable sources is climate change. It is not the function of this book to delve into the science of global warming, but experts now recognise that unless urgent steps are taken to limit greenhouse gas emissions[1] global warming could cause the Earth's surface temperature to give rise to potentially harmful effects on ecosystems, biodiversity and human livelihoods.

1.3 At current emission rates, global warming is predicted to rise to 1.5°C above pre-industrial levels between 2030 and 2052. This is the conclusion of the *Special Report on Global Warming of 1.5°C* published on 8 October 2018 by the Intergovernmental Panel on Climate Change (IPCC) ('the report'). The report includes over 6,000 scientific references and was prepared by 91 authors from

---

[1] The primary greenhouse gases are carbon dioxide (CO_2), methane (CH_4), nitrous oxide (N_20) and trospheric ozone (O_3). Without greenhouse gases, the average temperature of the Earth's surface would be about –18°C rather than the present average of 15°C.

40 countries. The report was called for at the United Nations Climate Change Conference in 2015 and was delivered at the United Nations' 48th session of the IPCC to provide an authoritative, scientific guide for governments to deal with climate change.

1.4 According to the IPCC report, even if global warming was limited to 1.5°C there would still be increased risks to health, livelihoods, food security, water supply, human security and economic growth. Impacts would include reduction in crop yields and nutritional quality. Livestock would also be affected with rising temperatures through changes in feed quality, spread of diseases and water resource availability. Risks from some diseases, such as malaria and dengue fever, are also projected to increase. The report suggests that limiting global warming to 1.5°C, compared to 2°C, could reduce the number of people exposed to climate-related risks and susceptibility to poverty by up to several hundred million by 2050. Even if global warming is limited to 1.5°C global sea levels are still expected to rise. Should it exceed this the report suggests that irreversible instabilities could be triggered in the Antarctic and Greenland ice sheets resulting in a rise in sea levels by several metres. Limiting global warming to 1.5°C is also projected to prevent the thawing over centuries of a permafrost area in the range of 1.5 to 2.5 million km^2. The report's predictions also extend to wholesale damage to ecosystems, including to fisheries, coral reefs, insects, plants and vertebrates. For instance, approximately 4% or 13% of global terrestrial land area is projected to undergo a transformation of its ecosystems of one kind or another at temperature rises of 1°C or 2°C respectively. The report's key finding is that steps should be taken to limit global warming below or close to a target of 1.5°C, which would require a reduction in greenhouse gas emissions of around 45% by 2030 and reach *net-zero* emissions by 2050. However, even just for limiting global warming to below 2°C, emissions would still have to decline by 25% by 2030 and by 100% by 2075.

1.5 The principal attack on greenhouse gas emissions comes from the shift away from fossil fuels in the generation of electricity.[2] By January 2020 the UK had cut its emissions by around two-fifths since 1990 with almost all of its recent progress coming from the electricity sector. Emissions from electricity generation have fallen rapidly in the decade since 2010 as coal power has been almost phased out and even gas output has declined. Fossil fuels have been displaced by falling

---

2 The National Grid announced in May 2020 that wind and solar power was producing 28% of the UK's power generation, which was only just behind gas-fired power generation which made up 30% of the UK's energy mix. Since April 2020 the UK's electricity system has run without its last remaining coal plants for 54 consecutive days, which had helped the carbon intensity of the electricity grid to fall to 143 grams of CO_2 per kWh. The lowest carbon intensity ever was recorded at 46 grams of CO_2 per kWh on 24 May. It was reported by the head of the National Grid's control centre that May was the first calendar month of electricity generation without coal 'since the Industrial Revolution'.

demand and by renewables, such as wind, solar and biomass. What is most noteworthy, however, is that the UK's wind farms overtook nuclear for the first time ever in 2019, becoming the country's second-largest source of electricity generation.

THE UK'S RECORD ON CLIMATE CHANGE

1.6 The UK has a moderate to good record when it comes to climate change. Under the Climate Change Act 2008 legally binding targets were set to cut emissions of greenhouse gases. The key provision was the commitment to cut emissions by at least 34% by 2020 and by 80% by 2050 compared with 1990 levels. The Act also requires the government to publish carbon targets setting five-yearly caps on greenhouse gas emissions. To achieve such targets the government had to take immediate steps to decarbonise electricity generation by introducing a strategy of shifting progressively from fossil fuels to low carbon electricity. This has been the clear achievement of the last decade with around 75% of emissions' reductions since 2012 coming from the power sector. Indeed, such is their growing popularity, onshore wind and solar power developments are likely to be cheaper than gas plants by the 2020s. Another key provision of the Climate Change Act 2008 was the establishment of the Committee on Climate Change (CCC) to advise the government and to report annually to Parliament on the UK's efforts to reduce emissions.

1.7 The National Planning Policy Framework (NPPF) was introduced by the government in 2012 and contained extensive planning policy on climate change at Part 10 to inform plan-making and decision-making. The current revision of the NPPF (issued in 2019) (to which extensive reference is made later) deals with climate change at Part 14 at paragraphs 149–154.[3] In terms of the implications of the revised NPPF for planning for climate change, these are the areas of interest:

(a) The revised NPPF retains the link between planning policy and the Planning Act 2008 (PA 2008), which means that all local plans must set a carbon dioxide (CO_2) emissions reduction target and lay out clear ways of measuring progress on CO_2 emissions reduction.[4]

---

3 Special mention should be made of the report of the Royal Town Planning Institute, *Rising to the Climate Crisis – A Guide for Local Authorities on Planning for Climate Change* (2nd edn) (December 2018).

4 PA 2008, s.18D, concerns development plan documents and climate change policies. The section provides that in Planning and Compulsory Purchase Act 2004, s.19 (preparation of local development plan documents) after subs.(1) the following section should be inserted: '(1A) Development plan documents must (taken as a whole) include policies designed to secure that the development and use of land in the local planning authority's area contribute to the mitigation of, and adaptation to, climate change.'

(b) Guidance on viability testing has been rebalanced, creating more opportunity for policy that might address climate change.
(c) There is still confusion about the scope of planning authorities to set ambitious targets beyond the Building Regulations on energy efficiency.
(d) There is nothing to stop local plans adopting requirements for on-site renewable energy generation.

1.8 The Paris Agreement involved the United Nations Framework Convention on Climate Change (UNFCCC) which dealt with greenhouse gas emissions mitigation, adaptation and finance. The agreement was negotiated by representatives of 196 state parties at the 21st Conference of representatives of the UNFCCC at Le Bourget, near Paris and was adopted on 12 December 2015. As of March 2019, 195 UNFCCC members had signed the agreement. The Paris Agreement's long-term goal was to keep the increase in global average temperature to well below 2°C above pre-industrial levels and to pursue efforts to limit the increase to 1.5°C in recognition of the fact that this would substantially reduce the risks and impacts of climate change. The objective was that each country would determine, plan and regularly report on the contribution which it had made to mitigate global warming.[5] In June 2017 President Trump announced his intention to withdraw the United States from the Paris Agreement. The earliest effective date of withdrawal for the United States under the agreement would be 4 November 2020 (coincidentally one day after the presidential election). In practice, however, changes in policy that are contrary to the Paris Agreement have already been put in place in the United States, which is the world's second-largest emitter of greenhouse gases.

1.9 In its annual report to Parliament in June 2018 (*Reducing UK emissions – 2018 Progress Report to Parliament*) the CCC set out various messages to government to put emissions reductions on track. The report, whilst indicating that emissions were down 43% compared to the 1990 baseline, went on to state that most of this was down to the excellent progress which had taken place in reducing emissions from electricity generation, whereas reductions in other sectors of the market had stalled. For instance, withdrawal of incentives had cut home insulation installations to 5% of their 2012 level and woodland creation fell short of stated government ambition in all areas of the UK. The CCC also

---

5 Mention should be made of *R (Plan B Earth) v Secretary of State for Transport* [2020] EWCA Civ 214, where the Court of Appeal ruled unlawful the Secretary of State's (SoS's) National Policy Statement (NPS) on Airports designating a third runway at Heathrow on the ground that it failed to take into account the 2015 Paris Agreement. In other words, the government had failed to take into account its own policy commitments on climate change under the Paris Agreement. The decision did not decide that there should be no third runway at Heathrow, merely that the NPS on Airports supporting the project was incompatible with the UK's commitment to reducing carbon emissions and mitigating climate change under the Paris Agreement.

advised that low-cost, low-risk options to reduce emissions were not being supported by government.

1.10 Looked at in the round, however, it is plain that wind and solar will not solve all of the UK's energy problems, and research and development into battery storage, carbon capture and renewable power projects of all kinds are still urgently needed. The government must also ensure that all new housing and construction projects are compatible with climate goals.

1.11 In October 2018 the government wrote to the CCC asking for advice about a roadmap to a *net-zero* economy, including how emissions might be reduced and the expected costs and benefits of doing so.

1.12 In May 2019 the CCC published a watershed report suggesting that the UK could end its contribution to global warming by setting a target to reduce greenhouse gas emissions to zero by 2050 – the UK's contribution to stopping global warming was requested by the UK, Scottish and Welsh governments in light of the Paris Agreement and the IPCC's report in 2018. The target is referred to as *net zero* as it would be met by some sources of emissions being offset by removal of CO_2 from the atmosphere, such as by growing trees. The report suggested: (a) that the foundations were in place to implement the policy throughout the UK; (b) that policies would have to ramp up significantly for a *net-zero* emissions target to be credible; and (c) that the overall costs of the transition to a *net-zero* economy were manageable.

1.13 On 12 June 2019 the then Prime Minister, Theresa May, announced that the UK would 'eradicate' its net contribution to climate change by 2050. On 27 June 2019 the statutory instrument, the Climate Change Act 2008 (2050 Target Amendment) Order 2019 (SI 2019/1056) came into force. Under this provision the previous target to cut emissions by 80% by 2050 was changed to 100%. The UK is the first major economy to target *net-zero* greenhouse gas emissions by 2050.

1.14 Despite the confidence of the foregoing measures, on 10 July 2019 the CCC published a damning assessment of progress in preparing for climate change in the UK. The report suggested that the priority given to climate adaptation had been eroded over the past ten years and that the UK was still not prepared for even a 2°C rise in global temperature, let alone the more extreme levels of global warming.

THE UK'S SOURCES OF ENERGY

1.15 The energy used in the UK may be classified by whether its source is from fossil fuels, low carbon sources or other. The main sources of fossil fuels in the UK are coal, gas and oil. The low carbon sources include nuclear and renewables such as wind, hydro, solar photovoltaics (PV) and biofuels. Fossil fuels remain the dominant source of energy supply.

1.16 Electricity generated from low carbon and renewable sources include onshore and offshore wind, shoreline wave and tidal, solar PV, hydro and bioenergy (vis: energy from landfill gas, sewage gas, and from biodegradable waste, animal biomass, anaerobic digestion and plant biomass). The largest of these sources are wind and solar PV. Active solar, heat pumps and deep geothermal are also used in heat generation.

BRIEF STATISTICAL OVERVIEW (FOSSIL FUELS AND RENEWABLES)[6]

1.17 The year 2019 saw a continuation of the switch away in the main sources of electricity generation from coal and gas to low carbon and renewable sources. In 2019 electricity generation in the UK from low carbon and renewable sources was 37.1%, up from 33.1% in 2018 (wind generation represented 71% of this increase in generation). Since 2004, the renewables share of UK electricity generation has increased tenfold (in 2004 it had been only 3.6%). The broad picture is that of an inexorable increase in electricity generation from low carbon and renewable sources, whereas a decade ago electricity generated from fossil fuels provided around 80% of the UK's electricity needs (split between gas and coal).

1.18 In 2019 UK net emissions of CO_2 were provisionally estimated to be 351.5 million tonnes, some 3.9% per cent lower than in 2018, which is mainly due to the changes in the mix of sources used for electricity generation.

1.19 In 2019 coal comprised 2.8% of the UK's energy generation, down from 4% in 2018. It is thought that coal-fired power now accounts for less than 1% of the UK's electricity,[7] whereas it had been as much as 18% in 2013.

6 Figures come from the *Digest of United Kingdom Energy Statistics 2020* (DUKES) produced by the Department for Business, Energy & Industrial Strategy (DBEIS) (latest edition published on 30/07/2020).

7 *The Guardian* newspaper reported on 14 October 2019 that the latest analysis by Carbon Brief showed that coal-fire power was less than 1%. British coal plants are shutting down ahead of the 2025 ban. By the spring of 2020 just four remain: West Burton A and Ratcliffe-on-Soar in

1.20 Oil still forms a key part of the UK's energy mix. Over 40% of the UK's total energy production in 2019 was from crude oil. There has, however, been a steep decline in UK oil production. From its peak of 137 million tonnes in 1999, production has dropped by nearly two-thirds to 52 million tonnes, with the UK becoming a net importer in 2005.

1.21 Gas accounts for 29% of the UK's energy production and is second only to oil. UK gas production fell in 2019 and is now 65% below the peak recorded in 2000. The long-term pattern is one of gradual decline.

1.22 As previously indicated, in 2019 low carbon and renewables' share of electricity generation was 37.1%, whereas in 2018 it had been 33.3%. Offshore and onshore wind was the largest component of renewable generation in 2019 at approximately 54% (with the share of each being 26.7% of total generation).

1.23 In 2019 solar PV accounted for 11% of the UK's electricity generation from low carbon and renewables. By 2023, when the UK's largest solar farm at Cleve Hill on the north Kent coast is predicted to come online (see Chapter 10, Case Study X), this percentage is likely to rise.

1.24 Electricity generation from other renewable sources included renewable heat (by wood, plant biomass, heat pumps, sewage gas and anaerobic digestion), which increased by 2.4% in 2019 (primarily due to increases in plant biomass and wood fuel) and accounted for 22% of all renewable use (with domestic wood combustion retaining the largest share of renewable heat at 44%). Total electricity generation from bioenergy (including landfill gas and waste) amounted to 28%. Hydro generation was 5% in 2019 with no increase in capacity.

1.25 In 2019 nuclear generation fell to 17.3% of electricity generation (a reduction of 2.3% from 2018), which was the lowest level of nuclear generation since 2008. In December 2018 construction began on Hinkley Point C nuclear power station. On completion in 2027 it is forecast that it will provide 7% of the UK's generating needs for around 60 years. This is the first nuclear power station to be built for 20 years and has been financed mainly by the state-owned EDF of France and by the state-owned General Nuclear Power Group CGN of China. In contrast to the much lower cost of generating electricity from renewable sources, according to December 2017 estimates, Hinkley Point C was to be built for £20.3 billion by 2025. However, by September 2019 the estimated total cost had risen to £22.9 billion.

Nottinghamshire, Kilroot in Northern Ireland and two units at the Drax site in North Yorkshire, which are earmarked for conversion to gas.

1.26 It should also be noted that imports of electricity via high-voltage power cables linking the UK to European energy markets rose to almost 7% of the UK's total demand for electricity in 2019, a figure which is expected to increase. In 2019 net imports via interconnectors amounted to 21,170GWh, whereas it had been only 14,760GWh in 2017.

SITES GENERATING RENEWABLE ELECTRICITY AT THE END OF DECEMBER 2019[8]

1.27

Type	*FiT supported*[9]	*Total*
Solar PV	857,770	1,023,824
Onshore wind	7,602	9,817
Hydro	1,175	1,520
Anaerobic digestion	421	657
Landfill gas		456
Plant biomass		435
Sewage sludge digestion		194
Energy from waste		62
Offshore wind		44
Marine energy		20
Animal biomass (non-anaerobic digestion)		6

EUROPEAN ENERGY POLICY

1.28 Production and consumption of energy from renewable sources in the UK has been steadily increasing since 2000. The rise has also been driven by the 2009 European Union (EU) Renewable Energy Directive (Directive 2009/28/EC), which establishes an overall policy for the production and promotion of energy from renewable sources in the EU. It required the EU to fulfil at least 20% of its total energy needs with renewables by 2020 – to be achieved through the attainment of individual national targets. The UK's target was set at 15% whereas, of course, by 2019 the UK obtained 37% of its electricity from renewable sources.

8 Excluding co-firing (co-firing is the combustion of two (or more) different types of materials at the same time). Further, the number of sites is subject to revision due to lags in data sources. This particularly affects solar PV, where more sites may have come online since the information was compiled for the latest edition of DUKES.

9 See 1.36–1.37.

1.29 The revised EU Renewable Energy Directive (Directive 2018/2001/EU) came into force in December 2018 and is required to be incorporated into the national law of member states by 30 June 2021. However, as the UK left the EU on 31 March 2020 the revised EU Directive is only of academic interest. It is though noteworthy that it establishes a binding renewable energy target for the EU for 2030 of at least 32% from renewable sources.

UK RENEWABLES' POLICIES

Overview

1.30 The UK's low carbon policies have seen renewable electricity capacity increase by more than three times since 2010. As renewables now provide between one-third and 40% of the UK's electricity generation it means that the UK has comfortably exceeded its domestic 2020–21 target of 30%. One notable staple on the energy landscape are the promises made by politicians to phase out the sale of diesel and petrol cars. For instance, Scotland wants to phase out the sale of petrol and diesel cars by 2032, whereas the Labour Party is currently proposing that sales should end by 2030. For its part, the UK government announced in 2017 that a ban would be in force by 2040. In practice, of course, any halt in the sale of non-electric cars will have to go hand in hand with improvements in the necessary infrastructure intended to bring about such a change in the buying habits of motorists, such as more wind farms, mass production of new battery technology, super rapid charging points and many more power stations to cope with the electric revolution and usage at peak times of the day (which one might suppose would be in the early evenings and/or overnight for battery-driven vehicles). According to a National Grid report[10] peak demand for electricity could, by 2040, add around 30GW annually (which is said to be the equivalent of almost ten times the total predicted output of the new Hinkley Point C nuclear power station being built in Somerset) to the current electricity usage at peak times which currently stands at around 61GW per year. It is suggested that to produce the extra 30GW needed per year to power electric cars the UK would need to build either an additional 10,000 new wind turbines or 9.6 Hinkley Point C power stations at, of course, vast cost in either case (quite apart from the ordinary planning hurdles). It is, then, hardly surprising that the National Grid is predicting that the UK will become increasingly reliant on imported electricity to around one-third of total demand, raising questions about energy security.

---

10 This item comes from an online article by Steven Swinford in *The Daily Telegraph* on 27 July 2017 who was reporting on the National Grid's *Future Energy Scenarios* report (July 2017).

AVAILABILITY OF FINANCIAL ASSISTANCE FOR THE GENERATION AND EXPORT OF RENEWABLE ENERGY TO THE GRID

Contracts for Difference

1.31 The Contracts for Difference (CfD) scheme is the government's main mechanism for supporting low carbon electricity generation. CfDs incentivise investment in renewable energy by providing developers of projects with high upfront costs and long lifetimes with direct protection from volatile wholesale prices, and they protect consumers from paying increased support costs when electricity prices are high. Renewable generators located in the UK that meet the eligibility requirements can apply for a CfD by submitting what is a form of 'sealed bid'. There have been three auctions, or allocation rounds, to date, which have seen a range of different renewable technologies competing directly against each other for a contract. Successful operators of renewable projects enter into a contract with the Low Carbon Contracts Company, a government-owned company. Operators are paid a flat (indexed) rate for the electricity they produce over a 15-year period. This is the difference between the so-called 'strike price' (a price for electricity reflecting the cost of investing in a particular low carbon technology) and the 'reference price' (a measure of the average market price for electricity in the UK market). Delivery partners are: (a) the Low Carbon Contracts Company, which is a party to the contracts awarded in CfD allocation rounds (auctions) and its primary role is to issue the contracts, manage them during the construction and delivery phase and make CfD payments; (b) the National Grid, which is the delivery body for the CfD scheme, responsible for running the CfD allocation process; and (c) Ofgem, which is responsible for hearing certain appeals.

1.32 The government has recently decided to re-open CfD for onshore wind, which ceased in 2016 (subject to a period of grace for projects that already had planning permission). A consultation was recently released on a CfD scheme (where the deadline for responses closed on 22 May 2020), which proposes to bring back the so-called 'Pot 1' auction for onshore wind (capped at 5MW capacity) in the next planned auction round in 2021. It is proposed that offshore wind will be separated in a new 'Pot 3'.

1.33 The proposals are a positive signal that government policy on renewable power is shifting in response to the UK's *net-zero* commitment. There are, however, plenty of issues for developers and investors to consider in a world where the consultation expects CfD Pot 1 bids to be below the wholesale price of power. What is not clear is what caps there will be on each pot or across the auction as a whole. If there is a significant volume of Pot 1 auction bids below the wholesale price then the government is likely to want a capacity cap as well as a budget cap. The level this cap is set at is key – in the last auction round the cap for offshore wind was set at 6GW. The consultation makes clear the government expects Pot 1 auction bids below the wholesale price of power. Round 3 of the CfD auction cleared at £39.65 (2012 prices) for remote island onshore wind. Price competition between solar and wind, as well as within other technologies, seems likely to be fierce and operators will need to think carefully about the value of the contracts *vs* forecast power prices which could mean some operators exiting earlier in the process, leaving CfD auctions to investors with large portfolios.

1.34 However, nothing in the proposals addresses the difficult planning environment for onshore wind in England which could mean that proposals find favour with local communities with proposals which are compliant with current planning practice for onshore winds. This is particularly important when the government's climate advisers are apparently saying that onshore wind power capacity will need to triple in 15 years if the UK is to meet its target of *net-zero* emissions by 2050.[11]

1.35 The consultation is also seeking views on the opportunities of storage co-locating with CfD sites. There is also a proposal to end payments for generators when prices are negative – potentially reducing the business case for storage at times of high generation.

Feed-in tariffs

1.36 The feed-in tariff (FiT) scheme was designed to support investment in small-scale renewable and low carbon electricity generation projects up to 5MW capacity. It offered long-term support to projects and provided tariffs based on the costs of generation for each technology – those supported being solar PV, onshore wind power, hydropower, anaerobic digestion and micro (<2kW) combined heat and power (micro-CHP). Under the scheme, generators receive three sources of income/savings: (a) a generation tariff – a payment for every kilowatt hour generated, dependent on the technology and capacity of the installation and the date installed; (b) an export tariff – an additional payment for every kilowatt hour exported to the grid; and (c) bill savings – additional benefit from usage of electricity 'on site' as opposed to paying the retail price for importing that energy from the grid. The FiT scheme was hugely successful in

11 Reported in *The Guardian* on 3 March 2020.

attracting investment.[12] However, a review of the scheme took place in 2015 and new measures were introduced in early 2016 to ensure that the scheme's costs were effectively controlled, providing value for money for the consumers who funded it through their electricity bills. Unfortunately, the FiT scheme closed to new applications on 31 March 2019 subject to a grace period and a number of time-limited extensions. Existing generating stations under the FiT scheme will continue to receive support for up to 25 years.

Feed-in tariffs supported capacity

1.37 Much small-scale (up to 5MW capacity) renewable electricity in the UK is supported by, and has increased as a result of, the FiT scheme. During the first nine months (April to December 2010) of the FiT scheme, a total of 106MW of renewable capacity was installed and subsequently confirmed on it. During 2011 a further 954MW of FiT-supported renewable capacity was installed. For 2012, 855MW of capacity was added and in 2013, 613MW. In 2014, 980MW of capacity was added while in 2015 a further 1,709MW of FiT capacity was installed, with 83% of this new capacity coming from solar PV. A further 677MW capacity was installed in 2016, of which 69% came from solar PV. In 2017, 181MW of new capacity was installed, with solar PV accounting for 87% of this. In 2018, 155MW of new capacity was installed in FiTs, of which 85% was solar PV.

1.38 FiTs closed to new entrants at the end of March 2019 although 96MW was installed on FiTs in the first three months of 2019 ahead of the deadline. Solar PV accounted for 94% of this new capacity. Total FiTs capacity stood at 6,340MW at the end of March 2019 although this number is still subject to revision. Not all small-scale generators are accredited on FiTs. The number of sub-50kW installations that are registered with the Microgeneration Certification Scheme (MCS) but not accredited on FiTs grew by 32,000 in 2019, accounting for around 102MW. The number of installations registered on the MCS continues to grow.

Smart export guarantee

1.39 Following the closure of the FiT scheme to new installations, with effect from 1 January 2020 the government has introduced a new supplier-led smart export guarantee (SEG) in the UK. Under the SEG licensed electrical suppliers

---

[12] There were over 1.01 million small-scale installations (less than 5MW) installed at the end of 2019, with a total capacity of 6,677MW, which accounts for 14% of total renewable capacity. Solar PV represents a significant majority of small-scale installations and installed small-scale capacity, with respectively 99% and 81% of the total. 931,000 of these installations are sub-4kW retrofitted solar schemes. These account for nearly 40% of total small-scale capacity.

(with 150,000 domestic customers or more) are required to offer small-scale low carbon generators a price per kilowatt hour for electricity exported to the grid. Remuneration would be available to solar PV, wind, anaerobic digestion and hydro all up to 5MW in capacity and micro-CHP up to 50kW. Mandated suppliers are required to provide at least one SEG-compliant tariff. They are free to determine the price and length of the contract with the proviso that remuneration must be greater than zero at all times. The export must be metered (with a meter capable of reporting exports on a half-hourly basis) and registered for settlement – typically smart meters will provide this functionality. The SEG will ensure that homes and businesses supplying their own low carbon electricity will be able to receive payment for the excess electricity which they export to the grid from their own energy suppliers. It complements the move to a smart energy system where consumers can make some of their own electricity and increasingly control when they use power (for example to charge electric cars) to minimise costs.

Renewable Heat Incentive and Premium Payment

1.40 The Renewable Heat Incentive (RHI) scheme is a government incentive scheme introduced to encourage a switch to renewable heating systems in place of fossil fuels. The tariff based on the scheme is split into two parts: (a) the non-domestic RHI scheme, which has been open to commercial, industrial, public sector, not for profit and community generators of renewable heat since November 2011; and (b) the domestic RHI scheme, which opened on 9 April 2014 and is still available to homeowners, private and social landlords and people who build their own homes (as at 31 December 2019 there were, under the domestic scheme, 75,847 accreditations with 4,400 Gwh of heat generated and paid for). The Renewable Heat Premium Payment (RHPP) voucher scheme launched in August 2011 made one-off payments to householders to help them buy renewable heating technologies. This scheme closed on 31 March 2014 prior to the introduction of the domestic RHI scheme.

Renewable Transport Fuel Obligation

1.41 The Renewable Transport Fuel Obligation (RTFO) was introduced in April 2008. It places a legal requirement on road transport fuel suppliers (who supply more than 450,000 litres of fossil petrol, diesel or renewable fuel per annum to the UK market) to ensure that 4.75% (by volume) of their overall fuel sales were from a renewable source by 2013/14 and in subsequent years. Under the RTFO all obligated companies are required to submit data to the RTFO administrator on volumes of fossil and renewable fuel they supply. Renewable Transport Fuel certificates are issued in proportion to the quantity of biofuels registered. The Renewable Transport Fuel Obligation (Amendment) Order 2011 (SI 2011/2937) introduced mandatory carbon and sustainability criteria for all renewable fuel and double rewards for some fuel types, including those made from waste and residue materials. From April 2013 the end uses covered by the RTFO were amended to include non-road mobile machinery, agriculture and forestry tractors and recreational craft when not at sea. The Renewable Transport Fuels and Greenhouse Gas Emissions Regulations 2018 (SI 2018/374) have introduced an increase in the obligation to ensure that 7.25% by volume of fuel comes from a renewable source in 2018, rising incrementally through 9.75% in 2020 to 12.4% in 2032. The Regulations also aim to increase the supply of the fuels of the greatest future strategic importance to the UK, through the introduction of an obligation to provide a proportion of 'development' fuels and by setting a maximum limit for the supply of fuels made from crops.

COMMENT – SHOULD THE PLANNING BALANCE CHANGE WHEN IT COMES TO RENEWABLE ENERGY APPLICATIONS?

1.42 The government's recent change of policy in allowing onshore wind schemes to compete for subsidies through the CfD scheme follows hard on the government's pledge to target *net-zero* greenhouse gas emissions by 2050. However, onshore wind and solar is still problematic in view of the need for applicants to act within the constraints of development plan and national policies if they are to obtain planning permission for such developments.

1.43 Some argue that decision-makers may be overly inclined to find that the economic or general environmental benefits associated with the generation of renewable energy and climate change considerations are insufficient to outweigh adverse impacts in terms of landscape and visual effects which cannot be satisfactorily mitigated. Decision-makers correctly point out, of course, that, as the law stands, when it comes to energy needs and the need to decarbonise electricity generation a balance has to be struck with environmental impacts. It is argued by some, however, that a perception exists that the general approach by decision-makers is predominantly landscape-led. On the other hand, supporters of renewable energy will no doubt claim that insufficient weight is being given, not just to the critical importance of reducing carbon emissions, but to the fact that wind and solar energy developments are invariably time-limited and involve restoring the land to its former condition. In other words, that proposals for wind and solar farms should not be treated in the same way as proposals for built development in the countryside which, it must be conceded, are bound to give rise to unacceptable impacts in many sensitive locations. At any rate, a tension exists between those who place adverse landscape and visual impacts ahead of the national need for secure and reliable supplies of electricity as part of the transition to a low carbon economy.

1.44 The current approach is still reflected in the need to undertake an assessment of the balance between environmental benefits and dis-benefits on a case-by-case basis which, for the time being, until the government alters the planning balance to place greater weight on environmental benefits and critical energy targets as against adverse landscape/visual impacts, is still based on the pre-eminence of the development plan in arriving at planning decisions (i.e. should still reflect local policies).

1.45 Planning applications are frequently being rejected because, although decision-makers find that the proposal in question would be of benefit in contributing towards government targets for the generation of electricity from renewable sources, these benefits do not outweigh unacceptable (and necessarily time-limited) environmental impacts. Many people now think that there should be a shift in the planning balance when it comes to renewable energy proposals, notwithstanding conflicts with landscape policies, if the government's green agenda is to stand any realistic chance of being delivered in practice.

1.46 One might also ask whether a greener world is now more, rather than less, likely as a result of the collapse of global market prices for fossil-fuel assets (with no guarantee that demand will return once a global economic recovery takes hold) and the collapse of the UK's fracking industry. There are also the unexpected environmental benefits from Covid-19 such as cleaner air, lower carbon emissions and a respite for wildlife. On any reckoning, the government has much to do if it is to meet its target of *net-zero* greenhouse gas emissions by 2050. It is the view of the author that changes to current planning practice must be on the cards in view of plummeting technology costs and the growing momentum for investment in renewable energy where, in 2019, applications for clean energy projects are reported to have reached a four-year high.[13] For instance, might it not be possible for the government, in its pursuit of cutting greenhouse emissions, to: (a) introduce greater flexibility when it comes to the grant of permission for onshore wind farms; and (b) halt the trend away from large-scale solar farms where the scope for using previously developed land and large buildings in the countryside is usually very limited in practice?

1.47 Readers are encouraged to consider the case studies at Chapter 8 (wind power projects) and at Chapter 10 (solar power projects) where a number of important legal authorities and recent planning appeals have been assembled. A detailed review of the decision letter dated 28 May 2020 of the Secretary of State in relation to the development consent order made in relation to Cleve Hill Solar

---

[13] Reported in *The Guardian* on 16 March 2020. There are reputed to have been 269 planning applications for new wind, solar and bioenergy projects in 2019, up from 204 in 2018, according to an analysis of government data by the energy consultancy PX Group. There were also reported to have been 154 applications in 2016 and 185 in 2017.

Park in Kent (which will be the UK's largest solar farm when it comes into operation in 2023) can be found in Chapter 10, Case Study X.

Chapter 2

Overview of the Regulatory Framework affecting Wind and Solar Energy Developments

ONSHORE ENERGY

2.1 In England onshore energy projects with a generating capacity of 50MW or less[1] are considered by local planning authorities (LPAs) under the Town and Country Planning Act 1990 (TCPA 1990) within the remit of local and national planning policies which look to encourage delivery in locations where local environmental impacts are acceptable.[2] Following statutory instruments laid before Parliament on 14 July 2020 (which come into force 28 days after they have been approved by Parliament) the primary consenting route for electricity storage projects[3] above 50MW (except pumped hydro where the planning impacts are much greater) in England will also be under the TCPA 1990.[4] In Wales planning

1 On the basis of indicative sources online, the output of a wind turbine depends on the turbine's size and the wind's speed through the rotor. An average onshore wind turbine might have a capacity of 2.5–3MW from which it follows that with onshore wind turbines of average size, one might be looking at developments of roughly 20 wind turbines being subject to control by LPAs. In the case of solar power, a generating capacity of 50MW is likely to involve a very large area. For instance, it is possible that the total land area required for only a 1MW conventional solar PV power plant would be as much as 4 acres.

2 Planning and Energy Act 2008, s.1, empowers LPAs in England and Wales to include policies in their development plan documents imposing reasonable requirements for a proportion of energy used in development in their area to be energy from renewable sources in their area or to be from low carbon energy from sources within their area and for development to comply with efficiency standards that exceed the energy requirements of building regulations.

3 Electrical batteries are commonly used in wind and solar energy applications. Wind turbines also use excess power to compress air which is usually stored in large above-ground tanks. Hydrogen fuel cells can also be used to store excess energy.

4 These changes will make it simpler for large storage facilities to apply for planning permission. The 50MW threshold meant that there was a clustering of energy storage projects below the 50MW to avoid the nationally significant infrastructure project (NSIP) regime with some providers choosing to develop multiple projects with batteries of less than 50MW rather than one larger battery.

decisions for electricity storage (except pumped hydro) of any size will also be under the 1990 regime although currently this is only the case for storage below 350MW. In determining applications to build onshore wind farms in their local areas it is government policy to give local people much greater say.

PERMITTED DEVELOPMENT

2.2 Permitted development rights (PD rights) exist which allow development for small-scale renewable energy development (referred to as 'microgeneration') associated with dwelling houses and within the curtilage of a dwelling house.[5] There are, however, designations which could affect whether or not PD rights apply which include whether the property: (a) is subject to a direction under article 4 of the GDPO removing certain PD rights; (b) is situated in a National Park, Area of Outstanding Natural Beauty (AONB) or Conservation Area; or (c) is listed as being of Special Architectural or Historic Interest.

PLANNING ACT 2008

2.3 Renewable and low carbon development over 50MW is normally considered under the Planning Act 2008 (as amended by the Localism Act 2011) (PA 2008) which passes responsibility for dealing with development consent applications for what are termed 'nationally significant infrastructure projects' (NSIPs) to the Planning Inspectorate (PINS) which examines applications and makes recommendations to the SoS at the Department for Business, Energy & Industrial Strategy (DBEIS) for development consent (as opposed to planning consent) on energy applications and associated development (NSIPs are addressed in more detail in Chapter 3, including NSIPs in Wales). This includes offshore generation stations with a capacity of over 100MW in English and Welsh territorial waters and in relation to the renewable energy zone,[6] except any part of the zone in relation to which Scottish Ministers have functions. When processing

5 Town and Country Planning (General Permitted Development) (England) Order 2015 (SI 2015/596) (GPDO), Pt.14 (Classes A–I were previously found in the Town and Country Planning (General Permitted Development) Order 1995 (SI 1995/418), Sch.2, Pt.1 and provide PD rights for the installation, alteration and replacement of a wide variety of renewable energy generating equipment on domestic premises; Classes J–O were previously found in the 1995 Order, Sch.2, Pt.3 and provides rights relating to non-domestic premises).

6 An area of sea outside the UK territorial sea over which the UK claims exclusive rights for production of energy from water and wind under Energy Act 2004, s.84. Energy Act 2004, s.95 and Sch.16 set out the requirements for applying to the SoS for a safety zone to be placed around or adjacent to an offshore renewable energy installation. The Electricity (Offshore Generating Stations) (Safety Zones) (Applications Procedures and Control of Access) Regulations 2007 (SI 2007/1948) set out the requirements for applying for a safety zone and advertising.

development applications DBEIS considers the environmental consequences of proposals involving NSIPs, applying European requirements for Environmental Impact Assessments (EIAs).

2.4 NSIPs dealt with by PINS under the PA 2008 include projects within the field of energy and include overhead lines. In relation to electricity generating stations, section 15 (which extends to Wales) is complex and imposes thresholds by reference to the capacity of the generating station. In 2016 onshore wind farms with a capacity of over 50MW were removed from the NSIP regime.[7]

ELECTRICITY ACT 1989: SECTION 36 CONSENTS FOR ONSHORE AND OFFSHORE ELECTRICITY GENERATION

2.5 Section 36 consents granted by the SoS for the DBEIS are concerned with the construction, extension or operation of a generating station (which was disapplied by the PA 2008).[8] Section 36 applies to proposals for onshore generating stations whose capacity exceeds 50MW. Section 36 also applies to proposals for offshore wind farms exceeding 50MW although the threshold is reduced to 1MW for a wind farm within UK territorial waters.[9] Section 36 covers all generating technologies including coal, gas, nuclear, energy from waste and renewable forms of energy.[10]

2.6 In cases involving offshore installations in English and Welsh territorial waters with a generating capacity above 1MW and below 100MW, responsibility for the grant of a section 36 consent rests with the Marine Management Organisation (MMO),[11] to which body certain functions of the SoS for the DBEIS were transferred by Marine and Coastal Access Act 2009, section 12. Section 36

---

7 The Infrastructure Planning (Onshore Wind Generating Stations) Order 2016 (SI 2016/306) removed onshore wind farms of over 50MW in size from the NSIP regime from 5 March 2016.

8 The procedures prescribed for applications for s.36 consent required for the construction etc. of generating stations are contained in Electricity Act 1989, Sch.8. They also apply to applications for consent under s.37 for the installation of overhead lines.

9 The Electricity Act 1989 (Requirement of Consent for Offshore Wind and Water Driven Generating Stations) (England and Wales) Order 2001 (SI 2001/3642) reduces permitted capacity to 1MW in the case of offshore generating stations wholly or mainly driven by wind or water (provided the waters are not within an area in which development requires planning permission under the TCPA 1990).

10 See the guidance note issued by the Department of Energy and Climate Change (DECC) in October 2007 on s.36: 'The consenting process for onshore generating stations above 50MW in England and Wales'.

11 The MMO is **an executive non-departmental public body** in the UK established under the Marine and Coastal Access Act 2009.

consents for offshore generating stations which have a capacity of more than 100MW still rests with the SoS under the PA 2008 and with Scottish Ministers for proposals in Scotland.

2.7 Conditions can also be attached to the section 36 consent itself, essentially for energy policy reasons, covering what the energy development is, how much time the applicant has to start the development and, more recently (for non-CHP fossil fuelled generating stations), requiring the development to have enough land for carbon capture and storage.

2.8 Applicants may seek clarification from DBEIS concerning the scope of the application for a section 36 consent at the same time as they request a 'scoping opinion' from the SoS for the purposes of the EIA.

VARYING SECTION 36 CONSENTS

2.9 Section 36 consents granted by the SoS for the Department of Energy and Climate Change (DECC) (now the SoS for the DBEIS) or their predecessors or the MMO can be varied. By applying to vary a section 36 consent it may be possible to obtain consent for a generating station to be constructed, extended and/or operated in a way that would not have been consistent with the existing consent.[12]

ENVIRONMENTAL STANDARDS

2.10 In formulating any proposals for the construction or extension of a generating capacity, applications under section 36 involving generating stations of a capacity of not less than 10MW subject a licence holder to environmental duties imposed by Schedule 9, paragraph 1 to the Electricity Act 1989 which require that he:

(a) shall have regard to the desirability of preserving natural beauty, of conserving flora, fauna and geological or physiographical features of special interest and of protecting sites, buildings and objects of architectural, historic or archaeological interest; and
(b) shall do what he reasonably can to mitigate any effect which the proposals would have on the natural beauty of the countryside or on any such flora, fauna, features, sites, buildings or objects.

---

12 Electricity Generating Stations (Applications for Variation of Consent) Regulations 2013 (SI 2013/1570).

2.11 The SoS, in considering any application for a section 36 consent, is required to have regard to the desirability of the matters mentioned in (a) above, and to the extent to which the applicant for consent had complied with his duty under (b) above. EIA development is addressed in more detail in Chapter 4.

EUROPEAN SITES

2.12 By virtue of regulation 89 of the Conservation of Habitats and Species Regulations 2017 (SI 2017/1012), the requirements of regulations 63 and 64 (duty to consider effect on a European site) apply to the granting of a section 36 consent, and there is a duty and procedure under regulations 89 to 92 to review past consents. This part is addressed in more detail in Chapter 4.

ENVIRONMENTAL ASSESSMENT

2.13 Assessment is mandatory in the case of all applications for section 36 consents by virtue of the Electricity Works (Environmental Impact Assessment) (England and Wales) Regulations 2017 (SI 2017/580).

EXEMPTION FROM CONSENT REQUIREMENT

2.14 The SoS is empowered by section 36(4) to direct that the consent requirement should not apply to particular classes or descriptions of generating stations. By virtue of the Offshore Generating Stations (Exemption) Order 1990 (SI 1990/443), section 36(1) does not apply to a generating station which is located on an offshore station and is used solely for the purpose of supplying electricity to that offshore installation or to that and any other offshore station.

DEEMED PLANNING PERMISSION

2.15 Alongside a section 36 consent applicants will also require planning permission for development. This is usually obtained by also applying to the SoS for what is known as a 'deemed' planning permission in relation to so much of the operation or change of use to which the consent relates as constitutes development and for any development which may be ancillary to such development or change of use.[13] The provisions of the TCPA 1990, except

[13] TCPA 1990, s.90(2)(a) and (b).

Part XII, then apply to the planning permission as if it had been granted by the SoS on an application called in by him for decision under section 77 of that Act.[14] Planning permission provides the conditions by which the development is controlled and mitigated and is enforced by the LPA. Even if an applicant applies directly to the relevant planning authority for planning permission under the TCPA 1990, section 36 consent will still be required from the SoS.

FEPA LICENCE

2.16 For offshore consents, a Food and Environment Protection Act 1985 licence (FEPA licence) is required from the Marine and Fisheries Agency, an executive agency of the Department for Environment, Food and Rural Affairs (DEFRA), for depositing articles or materials in the sea/tidal waters, including the placement of construction material or disposal of waste dredgings.[15]

OVERHEAD ELECTRICITY LINES

2.17 Section 36 does not include consent for connections to the electricity grid system, which are dealt with under section 37 of the Electricity Act 1989 and which is required when the connection is to be installed above ground and is in excess of 20kV (kilovolts) or is less than 20kV but supplies more than one customer.[16] In the case of NSIPs, the threshold set in the PA 2008 for overhead lines is for applications for lines with a capacity greater than 132kV or which are more than 2km in length. The DBEIS also administers applications under section 37 of the Electricity Act 1989 in England and Wales for overhead lines' consents below the PA 2008 threshold of 132kV or which are less than 2km in length and for associated permissions (i.e. necessary wayleaves over third party land, tree lopping and felling and compulsory purchase orders).[17] In practice, section 37 consent is required for all but the most minor overhead lines in England and Wales and is expressly disapplied in the cases mentioned in regulation 3 of

---

14 *R (Ecogen Developments Ltd) v Secretary of State for Trade and Industry* [2002] EWHC 996 (Admin) and *R (Little) v Secretary of State for Trade and Industry* [2002] EWHC 3001 (Admin).

15 Food and Environment Protection Act (Part II) 1985; s.5 is concerned with licences for the deposit of substances and articles in the sea or under the sea bed). A FEPA licence is granted by the SoS for DEFRA or, in Wales, by the Welsh Assembly Government.

16 Underground connections and overhead lines supplying less than a single consumer with less than 20kV need to be considered through the planning regulations and may be classed as permitted development.

17 Applications for s.37 consent to keep or install an overhead line must comply with the procedures prescribed by Electricity Act 1989, Sch.8.

the Overhead Lines (Exemption) (England and Wales) Regulations 2009 (SI 2009/640), albeit subject to the limitations imposed upon them by regulation 4.

2.18 There is helpful section 37 guidance which was issued by the DECC in July 2014.[18] By virtue of regulation 89 of the Conservation of Habitats and Species Regulations 2017 (SI 2017/1012), the requirements of regulations 63–64 (duty to consider the effect on a European site) also apply to the granting of a section 37 consent. There is also a duty and procedure under regulations 89–92 to review past consents. Section 37 is disapplied in the several cases mentioned in regulation 3 of the Overhead Lines (Exemption) (England and Wales) Regulations 2009 (SI 2009/640) subject to the limitations imposed by regulation 4.

DEEMED PLANNING PERMISSION FOR OVERHEAD LINES

2.19 Alongside a section 37 consent, applicants will, as in the case of section 36 consents, also require planning permission for development (see 2.15).

PUBLIC INQUIRIES WHERE THERE ARE OBJECTIONS TO SECTION 36 AND SECTION 37 APPLICATIONS

2.20 Applications under section 36 (consents for generating stations) and section 37 (consents for overhead power lines) must always take into account the views of the LPA, local people, statutory bodies (such as the Environment Agency) and other interested parties. Where there is an objection to an application by the LPA the SoS must hold a public inquiry before granting consent (which may be held concurrently with an inquiry into a related compulsory purchase order).[19] Current policy on electric and magnetic fields (EMFs) is that power lines should comply with the 1998 International Commission on Non-Ionizing Radiation Protection Guidelines on exposure to EMFs in terms of the 1999 EU Recommendation. Codes of Practice have been developed and agreed with the Energy Networks Association and government and apply to England, Wales, Scotland and Northern Ireland.

---

18 'The Statutory Consents Regime for Overhead Power Lines in England and Wales under Section 37 of the Electricity Act 1989'.

19 Electricity Generating Stations and Overhead Lines (Inquiries Procedure) (England and Wales) Rules 2007 (SI 2007/841). Where an objection cannot be overcome by agreement or addressed by an appropriate condition, the SoS is obliged to arrange for a public inquiry to be held.

ANCILLARY OR SUPPORTING FACILITIES

2.21 By virtue of section 90(2)(b) of the TCPA 1990, section 36 and section 37 consents may include any development which is ancillary to the operation or change of use to which the consent relates.[20] This might well include transformers, substations and associated cabling.[21]

COMPULSORY PURCHASE POWERS

2.22 Compulsory purchase powers can be used by statutory undertakers to acquire land or rights over land for the installation and retention of electric lines. Compulsory purchase is intended as a last resort to secure the assembly of all the land needed for the implementation of projects. Compulsory purchase orders should only be made where there is a compelling case in the public interest to do so. In such cases developers (acting as acquiring authorities) will make the Order and then seek confirmation of that Order from the SoS. Where statutory objections are raised (i.e. objections from owners, lessees and occupiers) the SoS is required to hold a public inquiry[22] before a decision can be made on the Order.

---

20 *R (Redcar & Cleveland BC) v Secretary of State & EDF Energy* [2008] EWHC 1847 (Admin).

21 See also guidance for s.36 consents issued by the DECC in October 2007 ('The consenting process for onshore generating stations above 50MW in England and Wales') which was adopted by the DBEIS. The following is stated in the guidance: 'As a rule of thumb, ancillary facilities which are on-site or very localised may be included, for example electricity switching and transforming substations, whereas, for example, pipelines or railway lines stretching for some miles, or jetties remote from a generating station, may not be included. It is also important that any ancillary development is properly considered – i.e. acknowledged and if part of the application properly covered – in the Environmental Impact Assessment'. In the result, separate planning applications will be required, in the case of onshore and offshore wind farms, for long-distance connections and other essential infrastructure to link up to the National Grid and for UK–continental interconnectors at a time, of course, when the UK is set to become more reliant upon them.

22 Public inquiries in England and Wales relating to electricity infrastructure are held in accordance with the Acquisition of Land Act 1981 and the Compulsory Purchase (Inquiries Procedure) Rules 2007 (SI 2007/3617) or, in circumstances where the SoS considers it is more appropriate for the Inquiry to be conducted by the written representations procedure, the Compulsory Purchase of Land (Written Representations Procedure) (Ministers) Regulations 2004 (SI 2004/2594), which will be engaged if the objector(s) to the Compulsory Purchase Order have provided their permission to the SoS for the Inquiry to proceed in this way. Where the Compulsory Purchase Order relates to statutory undertakers' land it is necessary to refer to Acquisition of Land Act 1981, s.16 or s.31. The Department for Communities and Local Government produced new guidance on compulsory purchase procedures in October 2015 for England only.

POSITION IN WALES

2.23 The Wales Act 2017 contains provisions to devolve functions for onshore and offshore generating stations up to 350MW to Welsh Ministers. Similar functions in Scotland and Northern Ireland under the PA 2008 and the Electricity Act 1989 are fully devolved. In Wales, NSIPs, which include onshore generating stations between 10MW and 50MW, are dealt with by PINS on behalf of the Welsh government.

KEY ELEMENTS OF PLANNING LAW

2.24 The core elements of modern planning law are these:

- the concept of development;
- the requirement of planning permission;
- the control over the grant of planning permission which derives from national and local policy frameworks;
- that in dealing with an application for planning permission, the LPA must always have regard to the provisions of the development plan unless material considerations indicate otherwise.[23]

DEVELOPMENT

2.25 'Development', for these purposes, means 'the carrying out of building, engineering, mining or other operations in, on, over or under land,[24] or the making of any material change[25] in the use of any buildings of other land'.[26] This provision is important as it defines the scope of planning control.

---

23 TCPA 1990, s.70(2); Planning and Compulsory Purchase Act 2004, s.38(6). The s.38(6) duty to have regard to the development plan unless material considerations indicate otherwise drives the 'plan-led' system of development control. It embodies a 'presumption in favour of the development plan' as Lord Hope described it in his speech in *City of Edinburgh Council v Secretary of State for Scotland* [1997] 1 WLR 1447 (at 1449H).

24 Which is termed 'operational development'.

25 Which is termed 'change of use'. A material change in the use of land has to be the result of a definable change in the character of the use made of the land (*Hertfordshire CC v Secretary of State for Communities and Local Government* [2012] EWHC 277 (Admin)).

26 TCPA 1990, s.55(1). Although there are exceptions: see s.55(2).

PLANNING PERMISSION

2.26 Planning permission is required for the carrying out of any development. Permission may be the result of a specific application to an LPA and may relate to proposed or past development and, in the case of the latter, may retrospectively validate development which has already taken place without the requisite planning permission. Sometimes permission may be granted by a development order made by the SoS (known as PD rights)[27] or by virtue of a local development order made by the LPA. As previously indicated, planning applications for energy infrastructure projects with a generating capacity of up to 50MW are considered by LPAs under the TCPA 1990.

NATIONAL PLANNING POLICY FRAMEWORK IN ENGLAND

2.27 In England and Wales[28] the current planning system is underpinned by policy considerations at both national and local levels. At national level most policy is now contained in the NPPF which, in its original form, was issued in March 2012 and was revised most recently in February 2019 and sets out the government's planning policies for England and how these are expected to be applied. Although the guidance within the NPPF must now be taken into account in the preparation of local and neighbourhood plans, and is a material consideration in planning decisions,[29] it does not change the statutory primacy of the development plan as the starting point for decision-taking.[30] In the circumstances, proposed development that accords with an up-to-date local plan should be approved and proposed development that conflicts with it should be refused unless other material considerations indicate otherwise. It is, therefore, obviously desirable that LPAs should have an up-to-date plan in place.[31]

2.28 The following extracts from the NPPF are most likely to impact on plan-making and decision-taking in the case of wind and solar energy generation under the TCPA 1990.

---

27 The GPDO grants permission for a number of minor forms of development. If a person is dissatisfied with the scope of his PD rights, he should obtain an express planning permission.

28 National planning policy in Wales is contained in *Planning Policy Wales,* Edition 10 (December 2018). Scottish planning policy is set out in the Scottish Planning Policy statement (2014) and in Scotland's *National Planning Framework 3* statement (June 2014). Planning policy In Northern Ireland is found in *The Strategic Planning Policy Statement* (September 2015) and in a number of Planning Policy Statements.

29 NPPF, para.2.

30 Planning and Compulsory Purchase Act 2004, ss.19(2)(a) and 38(6), and TCPA 1990, s.70(2).

31 NPPF, para.15.

SUSTAINABLE DEVELOPMENT

2.29 At the heart of the NPPF is a presumption in favour of sustainable development.[32]

2.30 The following paragraphs are taken from NPPF, Part 2 ('Achieving sustainable development'):

> 11. ...
>
> For **plan-making** this means that:
>
> a) plans should positively seek opportunities to meet the development needs of their area, and be sufficiently flexible to adapt to rapid change;
>
> b) strategic policies should, as a minimum, provide for objectively assessed needs for housing and other uses as well as any needs that cannot be met within neighbouring areas,[33] unless:
>
> i. the application of policies in this Framework that protect areas or assets of particular importance provides a strong reason for restricting the overall scale, type or distribution of development in the plan area;[34] or
>
> ii. any adverse impacts of doing so would significantly and demonstrably outweigh the benefits, when assessed against the policies in this Framework taken as a whole.

---

32 NPPF, para.10. See *Barwood Strategic Land II LLP v East Staffordshire Borough Council and Secretary of State for Communities and Local Government* [2017] EWCA Civ 893, where Lindblom LJ held that the presumption is not a statutory presumption but only a presumption of planning policy which requires of a planning decision-maker an exercise of planning judgment within the balancing exercise mandated under Planning and Compulsory Purchase Act 2004, s.38(6) (which is a duty to have regard to the development plan unless material considerations indicate otherwise). Lindblom LJ also ruled that beyond para.11 there is no free-standing presumption in favour of sustainable development.

33 As established through statements of common ground (see NPPF, para.27). [This is fn 5 in the NPPF.]

34 The policies referred to are those in the NPPF (rather than those in development plans) relating to: habitats sites (and those sites listed in NPPF, para.176) and/or designated as Sites of Special Scientific Interest; land designated as Green Belt, Local Green Space, an AONB, a National Park (or within the Broads Authority) or defined as Heritage Coast; irreplaceable habitats; designated heritage assets (and other heritage assets of archaeological interest referred to in fn 63 of the NPPF); and areas at risk of flooding or coastal change. [This is fn 6 in the NPPF.]

For **decision-taking** this means:[35]

c) approving development proposals that accord with an up-to-date development plan without delay; or

d) where there are no relevant development plan policies, or the policies which are most important for determining the application are out-of-date,[36] granting permission unless:[37]

   i. the application of policies in this Framework that protect areas or assets of particular importance provides a clear reason for refusing the development proposed;[38] or

   ii. any adverse effects of doing so would significantly and demonstrably outweigh the benefits, when assessed against the policies in this Framework taken as a whole.

2.31 The presumption also impacts on neighbourhood planning:

> 13. The application of the presumption has implications for the way communities engage in neighbourhood planning. Neighbourhood plans should support the delivery of strategic policies contained in local plans or spatial development strategies; and should shape and direct development that is outside of these strategic policies.

PLAN-MAKING: KEY PRINCIPLES

2.32 The following paragraphs are taken from NPPF, Part 3 ('Plan-making'):

> 15. The planning system should be genuinely plan-led. Succinct and up-to-date plans should provide a positive vision for the future of each area; a framework for addressing housing needs and other economic, social and environmental priorities; and a platform for local people to shape their surroundings.

35 Unless material considerations indicate otherwise.

36 See NPPF, fn 6.

37 The so-called 'tilted balance'. This is the territory of planning judgment where the court will not go unless a case for intervention can be justified on established principles for judicial review. See *Secretary of State for Communities and Local Government v Hopkins Homes Ltd* [2017] UKSC 37, [2017] 1 WLR 1865.

38 See fn 36.

16. Plans should:

a) be prepared with the objective of contributing to the achievement of sustainable development;[39]

b) be prepared positively, in a way that is aspirational but deliverable;

c) be shaped by early, proportionate and effective engagement between plan-makers and communities, local organisations, businesses, infrastructure providers and operators and statutory consultees;

d) contain policies that are clearly written and unambiguous, so it is evident how a decision maker should react to development proposals;

e) be accessible through the use of digital tools to assist public involvement and policy presentation;

f) serve a clear purpose, avoiding unnecessary duplication of policies that apply to a particular area (including policies in this Framework, where relevant).

2.33 The NPPF does not contain policies for NSIPs which are determined in accordance with the decision-making framework set out in the PA 2008 and relevant National Policy Statements (NPSs) for major infrastructure, as well as any other matters that are considered both important and relevant (including policies within the NPPF).

DECISION-MAKING: KEY PRINCIPLES

2.34 The following paragraphs are taken from NPPF, Part 4 ('Decision-making').

38. Local planning authorities should approach decisions on proposed development in a positive and creative way. They should use the full range of planning tools available, including brownfield registers and permission in principle, and work proactively with applicants to secure developments that will improve the economic social and environmental conditions of the area. Decision-makers at every level should seek to approve applications for sustainable development where possible.

47. Planning law requires that applications for planning permission be determined in accordance with the development plan, unless material considerations indicate otherwise. Decisions on applications should be made as quickly as possible, and within statutory timescale unless a longer period has been agreed by the applicant in writing.

---

[39] This is a legal requirement of local planning authorities exercising their plan-making functions (section 39(2) of the Planning and Compulsory Purchase Act 2004). [This is fn 10 in the NPPF.]

PLANNING CONDITIONS AND OBLIGATIONS[40]

2.35 The following paragraphs are taken from NPPF, Part 4 ('Decision-making'):

> 54. Local planning authorities should consider whether otherwise unacceptable development could be made acceptable through the use of conditions or planning obligations. Planning obligations should only be used where it is not possible to address unacceptable impacts through a planning condition.
>
> 55. Planning conditions should be kept to a minimum and only imposed where they are necessary, relevant to planning and to the development to be permitted, enforceable, precise, and reasonable in all other respects. Agreeing conditions early is beneficial to all parties involved in the process and can speed up decision-making. Conditions that are required to be discharged before development commences should be avoided, unless there is clear justification.
>
> 56. Planning obligations must only be sought where they meet all of the following tests:[41]
>
> a) necessary to make the development acceptable in planning terms;
> b) directly related to the development; and
> c) fairly and reasonably related in scale and kind to the development.
>
> 57. Where up-to-date policies have set out the contributions expected from development, planning applications that comply with them should be assumed to be viable. It is up to the applicant to demonstrate whether particular circumstances justify the need for a viability assessment at the application stage. The weight to be given to a viability assessment is a matter for the decision maker, having regard to all the circumstances of the case, including whether the plan and the viability evidence underpinning it is up to date, and any change in site circumstances since the plan was brought into force. All viability assessments, including any undertaken at the plan-making stage, should reflect the recommended approach in national planning guidance, including standardised inputs, and should be made publicly available.

THE RURAL ECONOMY

2.36 The following paragraphs are taken from NPPF, Part 6 ('Building a strong, competitive economy'):

---

40 Made under TCPA 1990, s.106.

41 Also set out in Community Infrastructure Levy Regulations 2010 (SI 2010/948), reg.122(2).

83. Planning policies and decisions[42] should enable:

a) the sustainable growth and expansion of all types of business in rural areas, both through conversion of existing buildings and well-designed new buildings;
b) the development and diversification of agricultural and other land-based rural businesses;
c) ...
d) ...

84. Planning policies and decisions should recognise that sites to meet local business and community needs in rural areas may have to be found adjacent to or beyond existing settlements, and in locations that are not well served by public transport. In these circumstances it will be important to ensure that development is sensitive to its surroundings, does not have an unacceptable impact on local roads and exploits any opportunities to make a location more sustainable (for example by improving the scope for access on foot, by cycling or by public transport). The use of previously developed land, and sites that are physically well-related to existing settlements, should be encouraged where suitable opportunities exist.

GREEN BELT LAND

2.37 The following paragraphs are taken from NPPF, Part 13 ('Protecting Green Belt land').

133. The Government attaches great importance to Green Belts. The fundamental aim of Green Belt policy is to prevent urban sprawl by keeping land permanently open; the essential characteristics of Green Belts are their openness and permanence.

134. Green Belt serves five purposes:

a) to check the unrestricted sprawl of large built-up areas;
b) to prevent neighbouring towns merging into one another;
c) to assist in safeguarding the countryside from encroachment;
d) to assist in urban regeneration, by encouraging the recycling of derelict and other urban land.

135. The general extent of Green Belts across the country is already established. New Green Belts should only be established in exceptional circumstances ...

---

42 See *R (Sienkiewicz) v South Somerset District Council* [2013] EWHC 4090 (Admin), [2014] JPL 620.

> 136. Once established, Green Belt boundaries should only be altered where exceptional circumstances are fully evidenced and justified, through the preparation or updating of plans …
>
> …
>
> 141. Once Green Belts have been defined, local planning authorities should plan positively to enhance their beneficial use, such as looking for opportunities to provide access; to provide opportunities for outdoor sport and recreation; to retain and enhance landscapes, visual amenity and biodiversity; or to improve damaged and derelict land.

PROPOSALS AFFECTING GREEN BELT LAND

2.38 The following paragraphs are taken from NPPF, Part 13 ('Protecting Green Belt land'):

> 143. Inappropriate development is, by definition, harmful to the Green Belt and should not be approved except in very special circumstances.
>
> 144. When considering any planning application, local planning authorities should ensure that substantial weight is given to any harm to the Green Belt. 'Very special circumstances' will not exist unless the potential harm to the Green Belt by reason of inappropriateness, and any other harm resulting from the proposal, is clearly outweighed by other considerations.
>
> …
>
> 147. When located in the Green Belt, elements of many renewable energy projects will comprise inappropriate development. In such cases developers will need to demonstrate very special circumstances if projects are to proceed. Such very special circumstances may include the wider environmental benefits associated with increased production of energy from renewable sources.

CLIMATE CHANGE

2.39 The following sections are taken from NPPF, Part 14 ('Meeting the challenge of climate change, flooding and coastal change'):

> 148. The planning system should support the transition to a low carbon future in a changing climate, taking full account of flood risk and coastal change. It should help to: shape places in ways that contribute to radical reductions in greenhouse gas emissions, minimise vulnerability and improve resilience; encourage the reuse of existing resources, including the conversion of existing buildings; and support renewable and low carbon energy and associate infrastructure.

Planning for climate change

149. Plans should take a proactive approach to mitigating and adapting to climate change, taking into account the long-term implications for flood risk, coastal change, water supply, biodiversity and landscapes, and the risk of overheating from rising temperatures.[43] Policies should support appropriate measures to ensure the future resilience of communities and infrastructure to climate change impacts, such as providing space for physical protection measures, or making provision for the possible future relocation of vulnerable development and infrastructure.

150. New development should be planned for in ways that:

a) avoid increased vulnerability to the range of impacts arising from climate change. When new development is brought forward in areas which are vulnerable, care should be taken to ensure that risks can be managed through suitable adaptation measures, including through the planning of green infrastructure: and

b) can help to reduce greenhouse gas emissions, such as through its location, orientation and design. Any local requirements for the sustainability of buildings should reflect the Governments' policy for national technical standards.

151. To help increase the use and supply of renewable and low carbon energy and heat, plans should:

a) provide a positive strategy for energy from these sources, that maximises the potential for suitable development, while ensuring that adverse impacts are addressed satisfactorily (including cumulative landscape and visual impacts);

b) consider identifying suitable areas for renewable and low carbon energy sources, and supporting infrastructure, where this would help secure their development; and

c) identify opportunities for development to draw its energy supply from decentralised, renewable or low carbon energy supply systems and for co-locating potential heat customers and suppliers.

152. Local planning authorities should support community led initiatives for renewable and low carbon energy, including developments outside areas identified in local plans or other strategic policies that are being taken forward through neighbourhood planning.

...

154. When determining planning applications for renewable and low carbon development, local planning authorities should:

---

[43] In line with the objectives and provisions of the Climate Change Act 2008. [This is fn 48 in the NPPF.]

a) not require applicants to demonstrate the overall need for renewable or low carbon energy, and recognise that even small-scale projects provide a valuable contribution to cutting greenhouse gas emissions; and

b) approve the application if its impacts are (or can be made) acceptable.[44] Once suitable areas for renewable and low carbon energy have been identified in plans, local planning authorities should expect subsequent applications for commercial scale projects outside these areas to demonstrate that the proposed location meets the criteria used in identifying suitable areas.[45]

---

44 Except for applications for the repowering of existing wind turbines, a proposed wind energy development involving one or more turbines should not be considered acceptable *unless it is in an area identified as suitable for wind energy development in the development plan; and, following consultation, it can be demonstrated that the planning impacts identified by the affected local community have been fully addressed and the proposal has their backing* (emphasis added). [This is fn 49 in the NPPF.] This policy echoes the Written Ministerial Statement on localism and wind energy development made by Greg Clarke, the then SoS for Communities and Local Government, on 18 June 2015 (WMS of 18 June 2015). It is now plain that suitable areas for such development will need to be allocated clearly in a local or neighbourhood plan. Whether a proposal has the backing of the affected local community is a planning judgment for the LPA. See DCS reference 400-027-129 (reported in Compass Online on 11/08/2020) where an appeal involving a single turbine was dismissed: (a) on the basis of a mild to moderate impact on countryside character; and (b) as the inspector was unable to find support for the proposal from the community as a whole. It appeared that although a number of local residents objected to the proposal there was no evidence from the parish council or from local members which meant that the inspector could not be sure whether the proposal had community backing.

45 In *Bayliss v Secretary of State for Communities and Local Government* [2013] EWHC 1612 (Admin) Hickinbottom J stated that the NPPF, looked at as a whole, generally favoured renewable energy developments, whilst requiring the benefits of such developments to be balanced against possible harm to the environment. This was a case where the court held that a planning inspector had not erred in granting planning permission for the construction of four wind turbines near to an AONB. The benefits of the development were found to outweigh the potential harm to the view from the protected area. *See also Good Energy Generation Ltd v Secretary of State for Communities and Local Government* [2018] EWHC 1270 (Admin) where, in a case involving a wind farm development comprising 11 turbines, it was found that a developer's unilateral undertaking under TCPA 1990, s.106 proposing a community investment scheme and a reduced energy tariff for local residents, as part of its application for planning permission, was not capable of being a material consideration as it failed the requirements of Community Infrastructure Levy Regulations 2010 (SI 2010/948), reg.122. Although the inspector had concluded that whilst the public benefits of the scheme were extensive and very weighty, they were nevertheless insufficient to justify the serious harm that would be caused to the designated heritage assets (the site was close to an AONB and a heritage coast). The inspector dismissed the appeal and the challenge was dismissed by Lang J who found that the inducement making the proposal more attractive to local residents and to the LPA was not necessary to make the development acceptable in planning terms.

CONSERVING THE NATURAL ENVIRONMENT

2.40 The following national policies (which are of crucial importance to the grant of planning permission when it comes to wind and solar energy installations) are taken from NPPF, Part 15 ('Conserving and enhancing the natural environment'):

> 170. Planning policies and decisions should contribute to and enhance the natural and local environment by:
>
> a) protecting and enhancing valued landscapes,[46] sites of biodiversity or geological value and soils (in a manner commensurate with their statutory status or identified quality in the development plan);
> b) recognising the intrinsic character and beauty of the countryside, and the wider economic benefits from natural capital and ecosystem services – including the economic and other benefits of the best and most versatile agricultural land, and of trees and woodland;
> c) maintaining the character of the undeveloped coast, while improving public access to it where appropriate;
> d) minimising impacts on and providing gains for biodiversity, including by establishing coherent ecological networks that are more resilient to current and future pressures;
> e) preventing new and existing development from contributing to, being put at unacceptable risk from, or being adversely affected by, unacceptable levels of soil, air, water or noise pollution or land instability. Development should, wherever possible, help to improve local environmental conditions such as air and water quality, taking into account relevant information such as river basin management plans; and
> f) remediating and mitigating despoiled, degraded, derelict, contaminated and unstable land, where appropriate.

---

46 Although the term 'valued landscapes' is not defined in the NPPF, it has been held in in *Ceg Land Promotions II Ltd v Secretary of State for Housing and Communities* [2018] EWHC 1799 (Admin) that in determining whether a proposed development site was a 'valued landscape' within the meaning of what was then NPPF, para.109, it was necessary to consider the site as part of the wider landscape, rather than limit the consideration to the site's particular circumstances. Even though a site lacks a formal designation of landscape value (which is not the same as valued landscape) its visibility in the wider landscape might well mean that any development would appear as a significant incursion into open countryside. Such a site might well have local value and even well-used footpaths crossing the site which afford panoramic views. On the other hand, if it is a less sensitive site and is no more than general countryside it might not override a housing deficit. Such a site might well have limited landscape quality with no heritage, wildlife or ecological assets and no recreational or leisure function. There clearly has to be some demonstrable physical attribute to make the land valued and thus give it enhanced protection (see *Stroud DC v Secretary of State for Communities and Local Government* [2015] EWHC 488 (Admin) at [13]–[16], [18]).

171. Plans should: distinguish between the hierarchy of international, national and locally designated sites; allocate land with the least environmental or amenity value, where consistent with other policies in this Framework;[47] take a strategic approach to maintaining and enhancing networks of habitats and green infrastructure; and plan for the enhancement of natural capital at a catchment or landscape scale across local authority boundaries.

172. Great weight should be given to conserving and enhancing landscape and scenic beauty in National Parks, the Broads, and Areas of Outstanding Natural Beauty which have the highest status of protection in relation to these issues. The conservation and enhancement of wildlife and cultural heritage are also important considerations in these areas, and should be given great weight in National Parks and the Broads.[48] The scale and extent of development within these designated areas should be limited. Planning permission should be refused for major development[49] other than in exceptional circumstances,[50] and where it can be demonstrated that the development is in the public interest. Consideration of such applications should include an assessment of:

a) the need for the development, including in terms of any national considerations, and the impact of permitting it, or refusing it, upon the local economy;
b) the cost of, and scope for, developing outside the designated areas, or meeting the need for it in some other way;
c) any detrimental effect on the environment, the landscape and recreational opportunities, and the extent to which that could be moderated.

173. Within areas defined as Heritage Coast (and that do not already fall within one of the designated areas mentioned in paragraph 172), planning policies and decisions should be consistent with the special character of the area and the importance of its conservation. Major development within a Heritage Coast is unlikely to be appropriate, unless it is compatible with its special character.

---

47 Where significant development of agricultural land is demonstrated to be necessary, areas of poorer quality land should be preferred to those of a higher quality. [This is fn 53 in the NPPF.]

48 *English National Parks and the Broads: UK Government Vision and Circular 2010* provides further guidance and information about their statutory purposes, management and other matters. [This is fn 54 in the NPPF.]

49 For the purposes of paragraphs 172 and 173, whether a proposal is 'major development' is a matter for the decision maker, taking into account its nature, scale and setting, and whether it could have a significant adverse impact on the purposes for which the area has been designated or defined. [This is fn 55 in the NPPF.] This echoes the finding of Lindblom J in *R (The Field Forge Society) v Sevenoaks District Council* [2014] EWHC 1895 (Admin), [2015] JPL 22 that the meaning of the term 'major development' is a matter of planning judgment.

50 This is not to be equated with an exceptional need for affordable housing in an area *R (Mevagissey Parish Council) v Cornwall Council* [2013] EWHC 3684 (Admin).

Habitats and biodiversity

174. To protect and enhance biodiversity and geodiversity, plans should:

a) identify, map and safeguard components of local wildlife-rich habitats and wider ecological networks, including the hierarchy of international, national and locally designated sites of importance for biodiversity;[51] wildlife corridors and stepping stones that connect them; and areas identified by national and local partnerships for habitat management, enhancement, restoration or creation;[52] and

b) promote the conservation, restoration and enhancement of priority habitats, ecological networks and the protection and recovery of priority species; and identify and pursue opportunities for securing measurable net gains for biodiversity.

175. When determining planning applications, local planning authorities should apply the following principles:

a) if significant harm to biodiversity resulting from a development cannot be avoided (through locating on an alternative site with less harmful impacts), adequately mitigated, or, as a last resort, compensated for, then planning permission should be refused;

b) development on land within or outside a Site of a Site of Special Scientific Interest, and which is likely to have an adverse effect on it (either individually or in combination with other developments), should not normally be permitted. The only exception is where the benefits of the location proposed clearly outweigh both its likely impact on the features of the site that make it of special scientific interest, and any other broader impacts on the national network of Sites of Special Scientific Interest;

c) development resulting in the loss or deterioration of irreplaceable habitats (such as an ancient woodland and ancient or veteran trees) should be refused, unless there are wholly exceptional reasons[53] and a suitable corresponding strategy exists; and

d) development whose primary objective is to conserve or enhance biodiversity should be supported; while opportunities to incorporate biodiversity improvements in and around developments should be encouraged, especially where this can secure measurable net gains for biodiversity.

---

51 Circular 06/2005 provides further guidance in respect of statutory obligations for biodiversity and geological conservation and their impact within the planning system. [This is fn 56 in the NPPF.]

52 Where areas that are part of the Nature Recovery Network are identified in plans, it may be appropriate to specify the types of development that may be suitable within them. [This is fn 57 in the NPPF.]

53 For example, infrastructure projects (including nationally significant infrastructure projects, orders under the Transport Works Act and hybrid bills), where the public benefit would clearly outweigh the loss or deterioration of habitat. [This is fn 58 in the NPPF.]

176. The following should be given the same protection as habitats sites:

a) potential Special Protection Areas and possible Special Areas of Conservation;
b) listed or proposed Ramras sites;[54] and
c) sites identified, or required, as compensatory measures for adverse effects on habitats sites, potential Special Protection Areas, possible Special Areas of Conservation, and listed or proposed Ramras sites.

177. The presumption in favour of sustainable development does not apply where the plan or project is likely to have a significant effect on a habitats site (either alone or in combination with other plans or projects), unless an appropriate assessment has concluded that the plan or project will not adversely affect the integrity of the habitats site.

Ground conditions and pollution
178. Planning policies and decisions should ensure that:

a) a site is suitable for its proposed use taking account of ground conditions and any risks arising from land instability and contamination. This includes risks arising from natural hazards or former activities such as mining, and any proposals for mitigation including land remediation (as well as potential impacts on the natural environment arising from that remediation);
b) after remediation, as a minimum, land should not be capable of being determined as contaminated land under Part IIA of the Environmental Protection Act 1990; and
c) adequate site investigation information, prepared by a competent person, is available to inform these assessments.

179. Where a site is affected by contamination or land stability issues, responsibility for securing a safe development rests with the developer and/or landowner.

180. Planning policies and decisions should also ensure that new development is appropriate for its location taking into account the likely effects (including cumulative effects) of pollution on health, living conditions and the natural environment, as well as the potential sensitivity of the site or the wider area to impacts that could arise from the development. In doing so they should:

a) mitigate and reduce to a minimum potential adverse impacts resulting from noise from new development – and avoid noise giving rise to significant adverse impacts on health and the quality of life;[55]

---

54 Potential Special Protection Areas, possible Special Areas of Conservation and Proposed Ramsar sites are sites on which Government has initiated public consultation on the scientific case for designation as a Special Protection Area of Conservation or Ramsar site. [This is fn 59 in the NPPF.]

55 See Explanatory Note to the *Noise Policy Statement for England* (Department for Environment, Food & Rural Affairs, 2010). [This is fn 60 in the NPPF.]

b) identify and protect tranquil areas which have remained relatively undisturbed by noise and are prized for their recreational and amenity value for this reason;

c) limit the impact of light pollution from artificial light on local amenity, intrinsically dark landscapes and nature conservation.

...

CONSERVING THE HISTORIC ENVIRONMENT

2.41 The following national policies (which again are of importance to the grant of planning permission when it comes to proposed wind and solar energy installations located near to a heritage asset) are taken from NPPF, Part 16 ('Conserving and enhancing the historic environment'):

> 184. Heritage assets range from sites and buildings of local historic value to those of the highest significance, such as World Heritage Sites which are internationally recognised to be Outstanding Universal Value.[56] These assets are an irreplaceable resource, and should be conserved in a manner appropriate to their significance, so that they can be enjoyed for their contribution to the quality of life of existing and future generations.
>
> ...
>
> *Proposals affecting heritage assets*
> 189. In determining applications, local planning authorities should require an applicant to describe the significance of any heritage assets affected, including any contribution made by their setting.[57] The level of detail should be proportionate to the assets' importance and no more than is sufficient to understand the potential impact of the proposal on their significance. As a minimum the relevant historic

---

56 Some World Heritage Sites are inscribed by UNESCO to be of natural significance rather than cultural significance; and in some cases they are inscribed for both their natural and cultural significance. [This is fn 61 in the NPPF.]

57 By s.66(1) of the Planning (Listed Buildings and Conservation Areas) Act 1990 (better known as the Listed Buildings Act (LBA 1990)), when considering whether to grant planning permission for development which affects a listed building or its setting, the LPA (or the SoS) is to have 'special regard' to the desirability of preserving the building or its setting or any features of special architectural or historic interest which it possesses. See *Barnwell Manor Wind Energy Ltd v East Northamptonshire District Council* [2014] EWCA Civ 137, in which the Court of Appeal clarified the duty of LPAs under s.66(1). In *R (Lady Hart of Chilton) v Babergh* [2014] EWHC 3261 (Admin), [2015] JPL 491, it was held by Sales J that the effect of s.66(1) was that the desirability of preserving the setting of a listed building was a factor of considerable importance and weight, giving rise to a strong presumption against granting planning permission for development which would harm that setting. See also *Steer v Secretary of State for Communities and Local Government* [2017] EWHC 1456 (Admin) where it was held that the inspector had erred in focusing only upon the visual connection and ignoring historic, social and economic connections in considering whether there had been an impact on the setting of a listed building.

environment record should have been consulted and the heritage assets assessed using appropriate expertise where necessary. Where a site on which development is proposed includes, or has the potential to include, heritage assets with archaeological interest, local planning authorities should require developers to submit an appropriate desk-based assessment and, where necessary, a field evaluation.

190. Local planning authorities should identify and assess the particular significance of any heritage asset that may be affected by the proposal (including by development affecting the setting of a heritage asset) taking account of the available evidence and any necessary expertise. They should take this into account when considering the impact of a proposal on a heritage asset, to avoid or minimise any conflict between the heritage asset's conservation and any aspect of the proposal.

...

193. When considering the impact of a proposed development on the significance of a designated heritage asset, great weight should be given to the asset's conservation (and the more important the asset, the greater the weight should be). This is irrespective of whether any potential harm amounts to substantial harm, total loss or less than substantial harm to its significance.

194. Any harm to, or loss of, the significance of a designated heritage asset (from its alteration or destruction, or from development within its setting), should require clear and convincing justification. Substantial harm to or loss of:

a) grade II listed buildings, or grade II registered parks or gardens, should be exceptional;
b) assets of the highest significance, notably scheduled monuments, protected wreck sites, registered battlefields, grade I and II listed buildings, grade I and II registered parks and gardens, and World Heritage Sites, should be wholly exceptional.[58]

195. Where a proposed development will lead to substantial harm to (or total loss of significance of) a designated heritage asset, local planning authorities should refuse consent, unless it can be demonstrated that the substantial harm or total loss is necessary to achieve substantial public benefits that outweigh that harm or loss, or all of the following apply:

a) the nature of the heritage asset prevents all reasonable uses of the site; and
b) no viable use of the heritage asset itself can be found in the medium term through appropriate marketing that will enable its conservation; and

---

[58] Non-designated heritage assets of archaeological interest, which are demonstrably of equivalent significance to scheduled monuments, should be considered subject to the policies for designated heritage assets. [This is fn 63 in the NPPF.]

c) conservation by grant-funding or some form of not for profit, charitable or public ownership is demonstrably not possible; and

d) the harm or loss is outweighed by the benefit of bringing the site back into use.

196. Where a development proposal will lead to less than substantial harm to the significance of a designated heritage asset, this harm should be weighed against the public benefits of the proposal including, where appropriate, securing its optimum viable use.

197. The effect of an application on the significance of a non-designated heritage asset should be taken into account in determining the application. In weighing applications that directly or indirectly affect non-designated heritage assets, a balanced judgment will be required having regard to the scale of any harm or loss and the significance of the heritage asset.

...

UK SOLAR PV STRATEGY (PARTS 1 AND 2)

2.42 The Solar PV roadmap and strategy[59] set out the guiding principles for deployment of solar in the UK. It was originally published on 8 October 2013 and was last updated on 4 April 2014.

2.43 The roadmap sets out four guiding principles which form the basis of the government's strategy for solar PV. These principles are:

(a) Support for solar PV should allow cost-effective projects to proceed and to make a cost-effective contribution to UK carbon emission objectives in the context of overall energy goals – ensuring that solar PV has a role alongside other energy generation technologies in delivering carbon reductions, energy security and affordability for consumers.

(b) Support for solar PV should deliver genuine carbon reductions that help meet the UK's target of 15 per cent renewable energy from final consumption by 2020 and in supporting the decarbonisation of our economy in the longer term – ensuring that all the carbon impacts of solar PV deployment are fully understood.

(c) Support for solar PV should ensure proposals are appropriately sited, give proper weight to environmental considerations such as landscape and visual impact, heritage and local amenity, and provide opportunities for local communities to influence decisions that affect them.

(d) Support for solar PV should assess and respond to the impacts of deployment on: grid systems balancing; grid connectivity; and financial

---

59 www.gov.uk/government/publications/uk-solar-pv-strategy-part-1-roadmap-to-a-brighter-future.

> incentives – ensuring that we address the challenges of deploying high volumes of solar PV.

2.44 The second part of the strategy[60] focuses on the government's ambition for the key market segments, particularly opening up deployment on the roofs of commercial, industrial and larger public buildings, how this ambition will be realised through innovation and partnership, and the benefits for jobs and investment in the UK, in addition to delivering vitally important emissions reductions.

2.45 The national Strategy acknowledges that large-scale developments can have a negative effect on the rural environment and on local communities. However, this national Strategy is now several years old and in the planning balance is liable to have only moderate weight.

---

60 www.gov.uk/government/publications/uk-solar-pv-strategy-part-1-roadmap-to-a-brighter-future.

Chapter 3

Nationally Significant Infrastructure Projects

INTRODUCTION

3.1 As indicated in Chapter 2, renewable and low carbon development exceeding 50MW is considered under the PA 2008, which passes responsibility for dealing with development consent applications for what are termed NSIPs to PINS, which examines applications and makes recommendations to the SoS at the DBEIS for development consent on energy applications and associated development.

3.2 NSIPs are large-scale developments relating to energy, transport, water or waste. The PA 2008 introduced a new development consent process for NSIPs which was subsequently amended by the Localism Act 2011. A development consent order (DCO) removes the need to obtain several separate consents, including planning permission, and is designed to be a much quicker process than applying for these separately. The DCO process starts when an application is accepted by the National Infrastructure Planning Unit and takes approximately 12–15 months. The process is front-loaded with a number of pre-application consultation requirements which, depending on the complexity of the project, can take a number of years to carry out. The final decision on granting a DCO rests with the SoS in the relevant sector. Chapter 10, Case Study X deals at length with the DCO made by the SoS on 28 May 2020 in relation to Cleve Hill Solar Park on the north Kent coast, which will be the UK's largest solar farm (and largest battery energy storage system) when it comes online in 2023. The site has a predicted generating capacity of 350MW (enough to power over 91,000 homes and save 68,000 tonnes of CO_2 emissions per annum). It comprises 880,000 ground-mounted solar panels on a site said to be as large as 600 football pitches.

3.3 The Infrastructure Act 2015 amended the process for changing and revoking DCOs. These changes also involved the formation of a National Infrastructure Commission (NIC) to examine the country's long-term infrastructure needs.[1]

3.4 In March 2016 onshore wind farms with a capacity of over 50MW were removed from the NSIP regime. As previously indicated, onshore wind farms below the 50MW threshold fall within the TCPA 1990 which reflects the generating capacity threshold of the Electricity Act 1989 for section 36 consents for the construction, extension or operation of a generating station (which was disapplied by the PA 2008). Section 36 applies to proposals for onshore wind farms whose capacity exceeds 50MW. Section 36 also applies to proposals for offshore generating stations exceeding 50MW although the threshold is reduced to 1MW for a generating station within UK territorial waters.

POLICY STATEMENTS

3.5 Applications for DCOs are decided in accordance with NPSs which, after a process of public consultation and parliamentary scrutiny, are 'designated' or published by government. There are currently 12 designated or proposed NPSs coming under the categories of hazardous waste, water supply, energy, transport networks, aviation and ports. An emerging NPS will carry some weight for decision-takers in the development consent process. The amount of weight given will depend on how far along the process the NPS is and how much consultation has taken place.

3.6 NPSs give reasons for the policies set out in the statement, and include an explanation of how the policy takes account of government policy relating to the mitigation of, and adaptation to, climate change. They comprise the government's objectives for the development of nationally significant infrastructure in a particular sector and provide the framework within which an Examining Authority makes its recommendations to the SoS.

3.7 There are 12 designated NPSs setting out government policy on different types of national infrastructure development. There are five Energy NPSs,

---

1 The NIC reports on high-priority issues and produces an independent assessment of the UK's major infrastructure needs on a 30-year time horizon. These needs are brought forward into National Infrastructure Assessments (NIAs). The NIC became an Executive Agency of HM Treasury in January 2017. A framework document was published setting out the basis on which the NIC operates and outlines its roles and responsibilities. The framework also sets out how the government is required to respond to the NIC's reports and how its recommendations obtain endorsement by the government and are translated into planning policy. The NIC's reports are laid before Parliament for discussion and response on its recommendations by the government.

including an NPS specifically for renewable energy (NPS EN-3) which received designation on 19 July 2011.

3.8 A DCO application is normally determined in accordance with an NPS, subject to the exceptions listed in section 104 of the PA 2008. Under section 104, the SoS must decide any DCO application in accordance with any relevant NPS unless he or she is satisfied that to do so would: (a) lead to the UK being in breach of its international obligations; (b) be unlawful; (c) lead to the SoS being in breach of any duty imposed by or under any legislation; (d) result in adverse impacts of the development outweighing its benefits; or (e) be contrary to legislation about how the decisions are to be taken. Section 105 of the PA 2008 gives the SoS the power to take the decision on a DCO in the absence of an NPS which is required to be taken in accordance with the NPPF and any relevant local plan for the area where the development would be located.

THE STATUTORY PROCESS (I.E. THAT RELEVANT TO WIND AND SOLAR ENERGY)

3.9 Responsibility for decisions on these projects now rests with the SoS of the DBEIS. In practice planning inspectors (known as the 'Examining Authority' (ExA) in the legislation) from the National Infrastructure Directorate of PINS will make recommendations to help inform the SoS's decision. Section 14 to the PA 2008 sets out the projects which may be considered to be an NSIP and includes large-scale energy developments. Part 3 of the PA 2008 sets out the thresholds which these projects have to meet in order to be considered as nationally significant and require development consent. Information about all past and current projects decided under the NSIP regime are available on the National Infrastructure Planning Unit's Register of Applications webpage.[2]

3.10 The Examination procedure for NSIPs is set out in the Infrastructure Planning (Examination Procedure) Rules 2010 (SI 2010/103) and in the Infrastructure Planning (Interested Parties) Regulations 2010 (SI 2010/102). The application fees for DCOs are set out by the Infrastructure Planning (Fees) Regulations 2010 (SI 2010/106), as amended. The Infrastructure Act 2015 made provision for changes to the NSIP regime in respect of the timing of the appointment of the ExA, providing for two-person panels, and amending the process for changes to, and revocation of, DCOs. The Infrastructure Planning (Environmental Impact Assessment) Regulations 2017 (SI 2017/572) ('the 2017 Infrastructure Regulations') revoked and replaced the previous Infrastructure Planning (Environmental Impact Assessment) Regulations 2009 (SI 2009/2263)

---

[2] https://infrastructure.planninginspectorate.gov.uk.

to transpose changes made to Directive 2011/92/EU ('the EIA Directive') by EU Directive 2014/52/EU about EIA requirements and procedures into the infrastructure planning regime. For further information about the EIA Directive and the changes to it, see the Government's Explanatory Memorandum to the 2017 Infrastructure Regulations.

3.11 Any developer who wants their project to be dealt with under the DCO procedure will need first to ask the SoS for a direction. The SoS must be satisfied that the project falls within one of the prescribed types of project and is nationally significant. Typically this will mean the project must have a significant economic impact, is important for driving growth in the economy or has an impact across an area wider than a single local authority area. The NSIP regime under the PA 2008 is more limited in its extent in Wales.

3.12 The development consent process starts officially when an application is formally accepted by the National Infrastructure Planning Unit at PINS. This is when a formal timetable begins which lasts approximately 12–15 months until development consent is granted or refused. Before this starts, however, the developer must carry out extensive consultation on the proposed development which can take several years. For full information about this process see the National Infrastructure Planning website.[3] The website also has a dedicated page for each project that has been accepted or is close to being accepted. Each page provides links to all the documents associated with the project, the timetable and the latest developments. Prior to formally submitting an application for development consent, the developer is required to carry out extensive consultation on their proposals. The length of time taken to prepare and consult on the project will vary depending upon its scale and complexity. Applicants for a proposed NSIP must, amongst other documents, submit a draft of the proposed DCO with their application, together with an explanatory memorandum. The DCO should be written in the form of a statutory instrument. For further information see PA 2008: guidance on the pre-application process for major infrastructure projects.[4] When the developer submits a formal application for development consent PINS (on behalf of the SoS) then has a 28-day period in which to determine whether the application meets the requirements for formal Examination. Once a DCO application is submitted and accepted there is a process for members of the public (including MPs) to register as an 'interested party' to be able to take part in the Examination process, provide written evidence and speak at meetings. Before the formal Examination stage begins the public can register with PINS and submit a summary of their views about the application in writing. A preliminary meeting for these people will be run and chaired by an inspector. This stage of publicising

3 https://infrastructure.planninginspectorate.gov.uk.

4 www.gov.uk/government/publications/guidance-on-the-pre-application-process-for-major-infrastructure-projects.

the application and gathering representations takes approximately three months, but the timeframe is not set out in legislation.

3.13 In terms of Examination, PINS will invite interested parties to submit their views, hold hearings and will carefully consider all the evidence submitted. It is focused on written representations rather than a public inquiry, with hearings on issues only being held where necessary. The Examination is done by the ExA. The SoS decides whether the ExA should be either a single inspector or a panel of inspectors, depending on the complexity of the case and the likely public interest. Examination takes approximately six months.

3.14 In arriving at its decision PINS will prepare a report on the application to the SoS, including a recommendation on whether development consent should be granted, within three months of the end of the Examination period. The SoS then has a further three months to make the decision on whether to grant or refuse development consent. Section 107 of the PA 2008 and rule 23 of the Infrastructure Planning (Examination Procedure) Rules 2010 (SI 2010/103) allows for further time to be taken in the decision-making process. Under section 107 any extension to the statutory timetable would require the SoS to make a statement to Parliament and would not be a decision which is likely to be taken lightly. The SoS may reach a different decision on the DCO to that recommended by the ExA. Government guidance states that the SoS is required to notify all interested parties if he is inclined to disagree with the ExA's recommendation on any matter of fact mentioned in, or appearing to be material to, a conclusion reached by the ExA, or because the SoS proposes to take into consideration any new evidence or any new matter of fact. The SoS will set out the reasons for disagreement with the ExA and will give interested parties the opportunity to make representations in writing, in respect of any new evidence or new matter of fact, by an appropriate deadline. Once a decision has been issued by the SoS, there is a six-week period in which the decision may be challenged in the High Court by way of judicial review.

NATIONALLY SIGNIFICANT INFRASTRUCTURE PROJECT REGIME IN WALES

3.15 In Wales development consent is only required for certain energy generating projects, such as pipelines, overhead electricity line and harbour facility projects. The Planning (Wales) Act 2015 established a new category of development called Developments of National Significance (DNS). This enables planning applications for certain types of development above specified thresholds to be made directly to the Welsh Ministers. The provisions in the 2015 Act are supplemented by the Developments of National Significance (Specified Criteria and Prescribed Secondary Consents) (Wales) Regulations 2016 (SI 2016/53). Regulation 3 specifies the types of development which can be of national significance and extend to generating stations, underground gas storage facilities, facilities for liquid natural gas, gas reception facilities, airports, railways, rail freight interchanges, dams and reservoirs, transfer of water resources, waste water treatment plants and hazardous waste facilities. Further amendments to the Regulations have included those onshore wind projects above 50MW as a DNS. The current DNS threshold for energy generating stations in Wales is between 10MW and 50MW, except for onshore wind where there is now no upper limit. Further information about the DNS consenting process is available on the Welsh government's website[5] on Developments of National Significance and its Guidance on Developments of National Significance. The Wales Act 2017 devolves further responsibility for all energy generating development consents for projects up to 350MW onshore (other than wind) and offshore in Welsh territorial waters and for associated overhead lines to the Welsh Ministers. Energy generating projects between 50MW and 350MW have not yet been brought into the definition of a DNS. Energy generation development above 350MW continues to be determined by the UK SoS under the PA 2008 development consent regime.

---

5 https://gov.wales/planning-applications.

Chapter 4

Environmental Impact Assessment

INTRODUCTION

4.1 This chapter deals with the legislation covering Environmental Impact Assessment (EIA) which is liable to arise on applications involving wind and solar energy installations in view of the significant environmental effects of such development. The review of EIA development in this chapter will be confined to what is relevant to wind and solar energy development.

4.2 The process of EIA in the context of town and country planning is governed by the Town and Country Planning (Environmental Impact Assessment) Regulations 2017 (SI 2017/1012) ('the 2017 T&C Regulations').[1] These regulations apply to development which is given planning permission under Part III of the TCPA 1990.[2] The 2017 T&C Regulations consolidate with amendments the provisions of the 2011 Regulations. In Scotland the applicable regulations are the Town and Country Planning (Environmental Impact Assessment) (Scotland) Regulations 2017 (SI 2017/102). In Wales the applicable regulations are the Town and Country Planning (Environmental Impact Assessment) (Wales) Regulations 2017 (SI 2017/567). The revised EIA regulations in the three home countries came into force on the same date.

1 In force on 16/05/2017. The 2017 T&C Regulations revoke the Town and Country Planning (Environmental Impact Assessment) Regulations 2011 (SI 2011/1824) ('the 2011 Regulations'), subject to certain transitional arrangements contained in 2017 T&C Regulations, reg.76.

2 See NPPG at Paragraphs: 004 Reference ID: 4-004-20170728 to 016 Reference ID: 4-016-20170728, where the types of development covered by the 2017 T&C Regulations are set out in detail.

4.3 The 2017 T&C Regulations apply the amended EU directive[3] 'on the effects of certain public and private projects on the environment'. They apply only to certain types of development and can even apply to permitted development. The LPA, the SoS or a planning inspector must not grant consent for EIA development unless an EIA has been carried out.[4]

4.4 The screening thresholds for industrial estate development and urban development projects were raised in April 2015 as set out in the Annex to the guidance on the 2011 Regulations. Projects which are wholly outside sensitive areas and do not exceed the revised screening thresholds are not Schedule 2 development and should not be screened by the LPA. Where the LPA has, prior to 6 April 2015, screened a project which does not exceed the relevant revised threshold and has determined that it is EIA development, it will continue as such. It always remains open to the applicant to request that the SoS issues a screening direction to determine whether a development is likely to have significant effects on the environment such that an Environmental Statement (ES) would be required. Subsequent applications in relation to development which was determined to be EIA development prior to 6 April 2015, but which is below the thresholds introduced in 2015, should continue to be treated as EIA development.

PURPOSE OF ENVIRONMENTAL IMPACT ASSESSMENT

4.5 The aim of EIA is to protect the environment by ensuring that an LPA, when deciding whether to grant planning permission for a project which is likely to have significant effects on the environment, does so in the full knowledge of the likely significant effects and takes this into account in the decision-making

---

3 EU Directive 2014/52/EU usually referred to as the 'EIA Directive' to the planning system in England. The main changes from the 2011 Regulations are: (a) to the circumstances in which a project may be exempt from EIA regulation; (b) to the introduction of co-ordinated procedures for projects which are also subject to assessment under Directive 92/43/EEC on the conservation of natural habitats and of wild fauna and flora or Council Directive 2009/147/EC of 30 November 2009 of the European Parliament and of the Council on the conservation of Wild Birds; (c) to the list of environmental factors to be considered as part of the EIA process; (d) to the information to be provided to inform a screening decision and the criteria to be applied when making a screening decision; (e) to the way in which an environmental statement is to be prepared, including an amendment to the information to be included in it, the introduction of a requirement that it should be based upon a scoping opinion (where one has been obtained) and a requirement that it is to be prepared by a competent expert; (f) to the means by which the public is to be informed of projects which are subject to the EIA process; and (g) the introduction of a requirement for decision-makers to avoid conflicts of interest.

4 Reg.3.

process.[5] The 2017 T&C Regulations set out a procedure for identifying those projects which should be subject to an EIA and for assessing, consulting and coming to a decision on those projects which are likely to have significant effects on the environment.

4.6 In the non-energy sector EIA will usually only apply to a small proportion of projects. LPAs already have a well-established general responsibility to consider the environmental implications of developments which are subject to planning control. The 2017 T&C Regulations integrate EIA procedures into this framework and only apply to projects which are likely to have significant effects on the environment. Pre-application engagement is also clearly important in identifying when, and in what respects, a proposal should be subject to EIA.

OVERVIEW OF ENVIRONMENTAL IMPACT ASSESSMENT

4.7 The EIA process has five broad stages:

(a) *Screening*:[6] this is determining whether a project falls within the remit of the 2017 T&C Regulations, i.e. whether it is likely to have a significant effect on the environment and therefore requires an ES. A 'screening opinion' is a written statement of the opinion of the LPA as to whether development is EIA development. A 'screening direction' is a direction made by the SoS as to whether development is EIA development. Screening should normally take place at an early stage in the design of the project. However, it can occur after a planning application has been made or even after an appeal has been made.

(b) *Scoping*: this is determining the extent of the issues to be considered in the assessment and reported on in the ES. An applicant can ask the LPA for its opinion on what information needs to be included. This is called a 'scoping opinion'. Scoping directions may also be made by the SoS.[7]

(c) *Preparing an ES*: the ES must include at least the information reasonably required to assess the likely significant environmental effects of the

---

5 Reg.4, which sets out the EIA process, namely the preparation of an environmental statement and the carrying out of any consultation, publication and notification required by the 2017 T&C Regulations or any other enactment in respect of EIA development.

6 2017 T&C Regulations, Pt.2 (regs 5–7) which deals with screening.

7 Pt.4, regs 15–16.

development listed in regulation 18(3) and comply with regulation 18(4).[8] An applicant must ensure that the ES is prepared by competent experts. It must also be accompanied by a statement from the developer outlining the relevant expertise or qualifications of such experts.[9] The LPA must also make available any relevant environmental information in their possession.[10]

(d) *Making a planning application and consultation*: the ES must be publicised electronically and by public notice. The statutory consultation bodies and the public must be given an opportunity to give their views about the proposed development and the ES.

(e) *Decision-making*: the ES must be taken into account by the LPA and/or the SoS in deciding whether or not to grant consent for the development.

WHEN IS AN ENVIRONMENTAL IMPACT ASSESSMENT REQUIRED?

4.8 The LPA (or the SoS) should determine whether the project is of a type listed in Schedule 1 or Schedule 2 to the 2017 T&C Regulations. If, exceptionally, it is listed in Schedule 1 an ES is required in every case (Schedule 1 involves major development, whereas Schedule 2 development involves lesser development). Schedule 2 is broken down into types of development and the applicable thresholds and criteria. If a project is listed in Schedule 2 the LPA should consider whether it is likely to have significant effects on the environment. Reference

---

8 *Berkeley v Secretary of State for the Environment, Transport and Regions* [2001] 2 AC 603; the ES may consist of one or more documents, but it must constitute a single, accessible and easily comprehensible compilation of the relevant environmental information. It is also essential that the ES should be made available to the public and the public should be given an opportunity to comment on it. The case involved an appeal against a refusal to quash a planning permission relating to the redevelopment of a football stadium located on the bank of a river. The appellant argued that the permission had been granted without consideration of the need for an EIA. It was held that the court was not empowered to retrospectively dispense with the requirement to carry out an EIA on the ground that the outcome would have been the same or that the LPA or the SoS had all the information required to reach a decision on environmental issues. The SoS had granted planning permission for the redevelopment of the stadium. At first instance, an attempt to quash the decision failed (on the ground that the SoS had failed to consider the need to carry out an EIA in accordance with Council Directive 85/337/EEC). The decision at first instance was upheld by the CA but an appeal was allowed in the HL where it was held that in cases where the Directive applied, a planning permission would only be upheld if substantial compliance had been shown.

9 See NPPG at Paragraph: 043 Reference ID: 4-043-20170728 through to Paragraph: 045 Reference ID: 4-045-20170728 (dealing with submission of documents and publicity requirements).

10 See NPPG at Paragraph: 034 Reference ID: 4-034-20170728 through to Paragraph: 045 Reference ID: 4-045-20170728, under the main heading: 'Preparing an Environmental Statement'.

should be made to the thresholds and criteria for the identification of Schedule 2 development requiring an ES and indicative values for determining significant effects in the NPPG at Reference ID: 4-057-2070720 and 4-058-20150326.[11]

4.9 If a proposed project is listed in the first column in Schedule 2 and exceeds the relevant thresholds or criteria set out in the second column (sometimes referred to as 'exclusion thresholds and criteria') the proposal needs to be screened by the LPA to determine whether significant effects on the environment are likely and hence whether an ES is required. Projects listed in Schedule 2 which are located in, or partly in, a sensitive area also need to be screened, even if they are below the thresholds or do not meet the criteria.[12] Projects which are described in the first column of Schedule 2 but which do not exceed the relevant thresholds, or meet the criteria in the second column of the schedule, or are not at least partly in a sensitive area, are not Schedule 2 development.

PROCEDURE FOR DECIDING WHETHER A SCHEDULE 2 PROJECT IS LIKELY TO HAVE SIGNIFICANT EFFECTS ON THE ENVIRONMENT

4.10 When screening, the LPA must take account of the selection criteria in Schedule 3.[13] Every case should be considered on its own merits in a balanced way. When an LPA (or the SoS) issues its opinion, it must state the main reasons for its conclusion with reference to the relevant criteria in Schedule 3. Where it is determined that the proposed development is not EIA development, the LPA must state any features of the proposed development and any measures envisaged to avoid, or prevent what might otherwise have been, significant adverse effects on the environment.[14] LPAs will also need to consider carefully how such measures are secured. This will usually be through planning conditions or planning obligations.

---

11 Pt.3 to Sch.2 contains a section on the energy industry – see (a) and (i).

12 Sensitive areas are described in the 2017 T&C Regulations at reg.2 and include, as one might expect, Sites of Special Scientific Interest (SSSIs), National Parks, the Broads, properties appearing on the World Heritage List, scheduled monuments within the meaning of the Ancient Monuments and Archaeological Areas Act 1979, AONBs and European sites designated under the Birds or Habitats Directives (see further details at NPPG at Paragraph: 032 Reference ID: 4-032-20170728).

13 Which refer to the characteristics of the development, its location and the types and the characteristics of the potential impact although not all the criteria will be relevant in every case.

14 Reg.5.

4.11 Normally, only a very small proportion of Schedule 2 development will require an ES. To aid LPAs to determine whether a project is likely to have significant environmental effects, a set of indicative thresholds and criteria have been produced. The table gives an indication of the types of impact that are most likely to be significant for particular types of development. Where there is no requirement to use a screening checklist, LPAs can nonetheless ensure that the relevant issues are considered and to provide a clear audit trail.[15]

4.12 Having completed a screening exercise, the LPA must provide a screening opinion indicating either that an ES is required (a 'positive screening opinion') or is not required (a 'negative screening opinion'). The SoS can also direct that an ES is required in circumstances where, although the development of a type listed in Schedule 2 does not meet the relevant criteria or exceed the relevant thresholds, it is still likely to have significant environmental effects.[16]

---

15 For indicative screening thresholds see: www.government/uploads/system/uploads/attachmentdata/file/630689/eia-thresholds-table.pdf; which contains four columns: column 2 represents the 'exclusion thresholds' in Sch.2, below which EIA does not need to be considered (subject to the proposal not being in a sensitive area). The figures in column 3 are indicative only and are intended to determine whether significant effects are likely. However, when considering the thresholds, it is important to also consider the location of the proposed development. In general the more environmentally sensitive the location, the lower the threshold at which significant effects are likely. It follows, therefore, that the thresholds should only be used in conjunction with the general guidance in determining whether an ES is required and, in particular, the guidance on environmentally sensitive areas. Column 4 illustrates the issues that are most likely to need to be considered for different development types. However, there will be other issues which will be specific to the nature of the environment receptor. For example, ecological impacts are likely to be an issue for all development which is proposed to be located in a SSSI designated for its wildlife value. For EIA screening checklist see: www.gov.uk/government/publications/environmental-impact-assessment-screening-checklist; see also NPPG at Paragraph: 057 Reference ID: 4-057-2070720.

16 Reg.5(7).

OBTAINING A SCREENING OPINION FROM THE LOCAL PLANNING AUTHORITY

4.13 If anyone considering carrying out development of a kind listed in Schedule 2 is unsure whether their proposed development requires an ES, they may request the LPA to provide a screening opinion on the need for an ES.[17]

4.14 Generally, it will fall to LPAs in the first instance to consider whether a proposed development requires an ES. However, the SoS is empowered to make directions in relation to the need for an ES. Such screening directions can be made of the SoS's own volition, or following a request from any person. Directions of the SoS will normally be made in response to a request from a developer. Where the LPAs opinion is that an ES is required, or where an LPA fails to adopt a screening opinion within three weeks (or within an extended period agreed in writing with the person making the request), the person who requested the screening opinion of the LPA may request that the SoS make a screening direction. However, any person, where they consider a proposed development requires an ES, may write to the SoS requesting a screening direction, even though neither the relevant LPA nor the applicant takes that view.[18]

TREATMENT OF MULTIPLE APPLICATIONS

4.15 An application should not be considered if, in reality, it is an integral part of a more substantial development.[19] In such cases, the need for an ES must be considered in the context of the whole development. In other cases it is appropriate to establish whether each of the proposed developments could proceed independently.[20]

---

17 The request should include the information set out at reg.6(1). When compiling the information the developer must take into account the criteria of Sch.3 and where relevant the results of any relevant EIAs required under other EU legislation. In most cases, the EIA that is most likely to be relevant is the strategic environmental assessment undertaken during the preparation of the local plan for the area. Requirements for making any such submitted documents available to the public are set out in reg.28. Developers are encouraged to identify any features of their proposed development and any mitigation measures envisaged to avoid or prevent what might otherwise have been significant adverse effects on the environment and to include these within the information required to inform the screening decision. See also NPPG at Paragraph: 023 Reference ID: 4-023-20170728. LPAs should also have regard to the possible cumulative effects arising from any existing or approved development (Paragraph: 024 Reference ID: 4-024-20170728).

18 NPPG at Paragraph: 020 Reference ID: 4-020-20170728.

19 *R v Swale BC ex parte RSPB* [1991] 1 PLR 6.

20 *R (Candlish) v Hastings BC* [2005] EWHC 1539 (Admin), [2005] All ER (D) 178; *R (Baker) v Bath & NE Somerset Council* [2009] EWHC 3320 (Admin), [2009] All ER (D) 169 (Jul).

CAN AN ENVIRONMENTAL STATEMENT BE SUBMITTED WITHOUT A SCREENING OPINION?

4.16 This is acceptable but the applicant must make it clear that the information submitted is intended to constitute an ES. In cases of doubt the LPA should issue a screening opinion and should ask for further information if it needs it.[21] Clearly if an ES is not required the information, if material, will still be taken into account on the LPA's decision to grant planning permission.

WHAT IF A PLANNING APPLICATION FOR A SCHEDULE 2 DEVELOPMENT IS NOT ACCOMPANIED BY AN ENVIRONMENTAL STATEMENT?

4.17 When a LPA receives an application which appears to be an application for Schedule 2 development, and the application has not been the subject of a screening opinion or direction and there is no accompanying ES, the LPA must provide an opinion on the need for ES as if the applicant had requested such a screening opinion under regulation 6.[22] If the screening opinion is that an ES is required the LPA must notify the applicant in writing in accordance with regulation 11 that an ES is necessary. The developer has, within 21 days of receipt of such notification, to reply to the LPA stating their intention to provide an ES or to request a screening direction from the SoS. If the developer has not replied within 21 days the planning application will be deemed to have been refused. If the developer responds indicating that an ES will be provided the LPA should suspend consideration of the application unless it is already minded to refuse permission because of other material considerations, in which case it should so as quickly as possible and, in any event, before the end of the 21-day period when the application is deemed to have been refused.[23]

CALLED-IN APPLICATIONS WHERE THERE IS NO ENVIRONMENTAL STATEMENT

4.18 The SoS will consider whether the development is EIA development and will make a screening opinion and will, if necessary, seek further information from the applicant. If an ES is found to be required the LPA and the applicant will be informed. There is no right of appeal against such a notification. An applicant

---

[21] See further information requirements in regs 6(2) and (3).

[22] Reg.8.

[23] NPPG at Paragraph: 027 Reference ID: 4-027-20170728.

must reply within three weeks stating that an ES will be provided. Otherwise, at the end of such period, the SoS will inform the applicant that no further action will be taken on the application. Where the SoS decides that no screening opinion is required, and there has been no previous screening opinion to that effect, the SoS will make a screening direction to that effect which the LPA must ensure is placed on the planning register.

PROCEDURE FOR PLANNING APPEALS

4.19 The matter is dealt with in a similar way to a called-in application and the same procedures and time limits apply.[24] However, where an inspector dealing with an appeal considers that an ES might be required, that question will be referred to the SoS, in which case the inspector will be precluded from determining the appeal (except by refusing permission) until he receives a screening direction from the SoS. If the latter directs that an ES is required the inspector may not determine the appeal (except by refusing permission) until the applicant has submitted an ES. The SoS may direct that an ES is required at any time before the appeal is determined.[25]

DETERMINING PLANNING APPLICATIONS THAT HAVE BEEN SUBJECT TO AN ENVIRONMENTAL IMPACT ASSESSMENT

4.20 There are specific arrangements for considering and determining planning applications that have been subject to an EIA. These arrangements include consideration of the adequacy of the information provided, consultation, reaching a reasoned conclusion on the significant environmental effects of the proposed development, publicity, and informing consultation bodies and public of both the decision and the main reasons for it. The LPA must take into account the information in the ES, the responses to consultation and any other relevant information when determining a planning application.

---

[24] Reg.14.

[25] NPPG at Paragraph: 029 Reference ID: 4-029-20170728.

4.21 The LPA can always ask an applicant to provide further information.[26] Additional information of a substantive nature submitted voluntarily by an applicant must be treated in the same way as information required by the LPA. The 16-week time limit (albeit subject to extension by written agreement) for the determination of an EIA application continues to run while any correspondence about the adequacy of the information in an ES is taking place.[27] The SoS can also request additional information when determining a planning appeal.[28] Such further information will be regulated by the Inquiry Rules relating to the submission of evidence to local planning inquiries.[29]

4.22 If planning permission or subsequent consent is to be granted, the LPA must consider whether it is appropriate to require steps to be taken to monitor any mitigating measures identified through the EIA process. LPAs should also consider whether to include, where appropriate, provisions for any potential remedial action.[30]

4.23 Mitigation measures proposed in an ES are designed to limit or remove any significant adverse environmental effects of the development. LPAs will need to consider how these mitigation measures may be secured as, for instance, by way of planning conditions and planning obligations (either unilaterally or between the LPA and the developer). However, a condition requiring the development to be 'in accordance with the Environmental Statement' lacks clarity in the measures which need to be taken.

4.24 In cases where a consent procedure involves more than one stage (a multi-stage consent), for example, a first stage involving an outline planning permission

---

26 Does the ES contain all the information specified in regs 18(3) or (4) and any additional information specified in Sch.4? If further information is required the LPA must ask for it under regs 25/26. All information provided must be publicised and consulted on. All information provided should be limited to the 'main' or 'significant' environmental effects to which a development is likely to give rise and must be on relevant matters and directly relevant to reaching a reasoned conclusion on the significant effects of the proposed development on the environment; the LPA, the SoS or an inspector may also require an applicant or appellant to produce evidence to verify any information in the ES.

27 Where an ES has not been submitted with a planning application but the applicant indicates that they propose to provide one, consideration of the application should be suspended until the ES has been received (reg.20(8)).

28 NPPG at Paragraph: 048 Reference ID: 4-048-20170728.

29 Town and Country Planning (Inquiries Procedure) (England) Rules 2000 (SI 2000/1624); Town and Country Planning Appeals (Determination by Inspectors) (Inquiries Procedure) (England) Rules 2000 (SI 2000/1625).

30 Reg.26. Such measures must be proportionate.

and a second stage dealing with reserved matters, the effects of a project on the environment should normally be identified and assessed when determining the outline permission.[31]

---

[31] NPPG at Paragraph: 056 Reference ID: 4-056-20170728 re multi-stage consents.

Chapter 5

Habitats and Species Regulations 2017

INTRODUCTION

5.1 This chapter deals with the Conservation of Habitats and Species Regulations 2017 (SI 2017/1012) ('the Habitats Regulations 2017')[1] which incorporate into the law in England and Wales the requirements of the EU Directives on: (a) the conservation of natural habitats and of wild fauna and flora;[2] and (b) wild birds.[3] These Regulations are also liable to arise for consideration on applications involving wind and solar energy installations in view of the significant environmental effects of such development. The following is a brief overview of the provisions of the Habitats Regulations 2017 which came into force on 30 November 2017.[4] A more detailed analysis of these regulations is beyond the scope of this book.

---

1 Also have regard to the Conservation of Offshore Marine Habitats and Species Regulations 2017 (SI 2017/1013) in relation to offshore wind farms. See reg.28 and the need to address potential adverse effects on site integrity; see also Chapter 8, Case Study XXI at paras 111–115 under the sub-para. 'Offshore Ecology and Requirements of the Marine and Coastal Access Act 2009 and the Habitats Regulations 2017'.

2 Council Directive 92/43/EEC of 21 May 1992 on the conservation of natural habitats and of wild fauna and flora (Habitats Directive), as last amended by Council Directive 2013/17/EU of 13 May 2013.

3 Council Directive 79/409/EEC of 2 April 1979 on the conservation of wild birds, replaced by the Council Directive 2009/147/EC of 30 November 2009 of the European Parliament and of the Council on the conservation of wild birds (Birds Directive), as last amended by Council Directive 2013/17/EU of 13 May 2013.

4 In summary, the Habitats Regulations 2017 provide for the designation and protection of 'European sites', the protection of 'European protected species', and the adaptation of planning and other controls for the protection of European sites. By reg.42 those species identified in Sch.2 and their breeding sites/resting places are protected. It is in relation to these species that a European Protected Species Licence is required. The extent of the revocations affecting the 2010 Regulations is very limited (see Sch.7 and Explanatory Note).

OVERVIEW OF THE HABITATS REGULATIONS 2017

5.2 They impose duties on public bodies (including planning authorities) to exercise their nature conservation powers so as to comply with the Habitats Directive on the conservation of natural habitats and of wild fauna and flora and the new Birds Directive on the conservation of wild birds.[5]

5.3 They make provision for the selection, designation, registration and notification of sites to be protected under the Habitats Directive ('European sites').[6] Special Areas of Conservation (SACs) are strictly protected sites designated under the Habitats Directive. Special Protection Areas (SPAs) are similarly strictly protected sites classified in accordance with Article 4 of the Birds Directive. They are classified for rare and vulnerable birds and for regularly occurring migratory species.

5.4 They make provision for management agreements in relation to European sites.[7]

5.5 They make provision in respect of European sites for:

(a) the control of damaging operations;
(b) the control of potentially damaging operations including the power to make special nature conservation orders, stop notices and restoration orders;
(c) the provision of byelaws (including the creation of a criminal offence for breach of a stop notice); and
(d) compulsory purchase.[8]

---

5 Reg.9 requires public bodies to exercise their nature conservation functions so as to comply with the Habitats Directive and the new Wild Birds Directive; reg.10 imposes duties on public bodies in relation to wild bird habitats; and reg.11 requires nature conservation bodies to review and report on whether the obligations under reg.10 have been met.

6 Habitats Regulations 2017, regs 10–19 make provision for the selection, designation (or, in the case of special protection areas, classification), registration and notification of sites to be protected under the Habitats Directive ('European sites'). Regs 23–36 make provision in respect of European sites for: (a) control of damaging operations; (b) special nature conservation orders and restoration orders (see Sch.1 which has effect with respect to the making, confirmation and coming into operation of special nature conservation orders and amending and revoking orders); (c) byelaws; and (d) compulsory purchase. Regs 37–40 make provision for the protection of European marine sites.

7 Habitats Regulations 2017, regs 20–22.

8 Habitats Regulations 2017, regs 23–36.

5.6 They make provision for the protection of European marine sites and the making of management schemes in relation to such sites.[9]

5.7 They make provision for the protection of wild animals and plant species and habitats, including the surveillance of the conservation status of natural habitats and species protected under the Habitats Directive and the creation of a criminal offence to kill, capture or disturb those animals or to trade in them, along with the licensing of certain activities relating to animals and plants.[10]

5.8 They also require the effect on a European site to be considered before the granting of various consents or authorisations, including the grant of planning permission.[11] On 12 April 2018, the Court of Justice of the European Union (*People over Wind & Sweetman v Coillte Teoranta* Case C-323/17) ruled that Article 6(3) of the Habitats Directive must be interpreted as meaning that mitigation measures should be assessed within the framework of an appropriate assessment and that it was not permissible to take account of measures intended to avoid or reduce the harmful effects of the plan or project on a European site at the screening stage. The *People over Wind* case concerned the decision to allow the laying of cables across two European SACs (both in the Republic of Ireland). The cables were intended to connect a wind farm to the electricity grid and concerns had arisen that the proposal might have a significant impact on a protected species of freshwater pearl mussel. Therefore, many developments cannot now be screened out of requiring a full appropriate assessment under the Habitats Regulations 2017, reg.63, which requires more time and involves more consultation than would previously be spent on a 'screening request'. It also throws into question the legality of many strategic mitigation systems that have been put in place to protect sites such as the Dorset Heaths and Thames Basin Heaths. The ruling has major implications for

---

9 Habitats Regulations 2017, regs 37–40.

10 Habitats Regulations 2017, Pt.3, provides for the protection of certain wild animals and plants.

11 Pt.6 deals with the assessment of plans and projects. Regs 63–69 require the effect on a European site to be considered before the granting of consents or authorisations of a kind specified in regs 70–104; reg.70 is concerned with the grant of planning permission; reg.84 is concerned with the grant of development consent under the PA 2008; reg.87 is concerned with the construction or improvement of highways or roads; reg.89 is concerned with consents under the Electricity Act 1989; reg.101 is concerned with environmental permits under the Environmental Permitting (England and Wales) Regulations 2016 (SI 2016/1154); reg.103 is concerned with marine works.

developments where an assessment under the Habitats Regulations 2017 may be required.[12]

5.9 A competent authority (which includes the SoS, a government department, statutory undertaker, public body of any description or person holding a public office, the Welsh Ministers or any person exercising any of the functions of these parties)[13] may not give any consent or permission or other authorisation for a plan or project which is likely to have a significant effect on a European site and is not directly connected with or necessary to the management of that site, without making an *appropriate assessment* of the implications for that site in view of its conservation objectives.[14] However, if the competent authority is satisfied that, there being no alternative solutions, the plan or project must be carried out for imperative reasons of overriding public interest (which may be of a social or economic nature), it may agree to the plan or project notwithstanding a negative assessment of the implications for the European site or the European offshore marine site.[15]

5.10 Provision is also made for enforcement, including powers of entry, powers of search, powers in relation to specimens and samples and for offences.[16]

5.11 Provision is also made for the advisory role of the Joint Nature Conservation Committee, Natural England, the National Resources Body for Wales and Scottish Natural Heritage.[17]

---

12 *People over Wind* has been reviewed and confirmed by Dove J in *Canterbury City Council v Secretary of State for Housing, Communities and Local Government* [2019] EWHC 1211 (Admin). In *Gladman v SSHCLG & Medway Council* [2019] EWHC 2001 (Admin) Dove J said at [62]: 'The thrust of the CJEU's decision in *People over Wind* is to emphasise firstly, that a full and precise analysis of the effects of the proposal upon a Natura 200 site must inform the decision made under Article 6(3) of the Directive. The Appropriate Assessment must not have lacunae, and must remove all reasonable scientific doubt in relation to the effects of the proposal (paragraphs 36–38 of the judgment). Secondly, the CJEU in *People over Wind* emphasises that the provisions of Article 6(3) of the Habitats Directive are procedural as well as substantive, since Appropriate Assessment includes the requirement that the competent national authority will not agree to the plan or project until it has ascertained that it will not adversely affect the integrity of the site and, if appropriate, after having consulted with the general public (paragraph 39 of the judgment).'

13 Reg.7.

14 Reg.63. LPAs are required to carry out these assessments to make sure plans or projects affecting sites in and around EU designated SACs or SPAs have no harmful effects on them. An assessment has two stages: a screening stage and then a full 'appropriate assessment'.

15 Reg.64.

16 Habitats Regulations 2017, Pt.7, regs 123–125 set out the enforcement powers of wildlife inspectors and constables, including powers of entry, search and taking of samples.

17 Regs 134 and 135.

Chapter 6

Planning Guidance Relevant to Wind and Solar Energy Developments

INTRODUCTION

6.1 The object of this chapter is to pull together the relevant national guidance contained in the National Planning Practice Guidance (NPPG) for wind and solar energy developments and for consents for onshore and offshore electricity generation under the Electricity Act 1989 (section 36) and for overhead lines (section 37).

6.2 The NPPG provides advice on the planning issues associated with the development of renewable energy. It is kept under review and should be read alongside the NPPF. The NPPG can be a material consideration in planning decisions and should generally be followed unless there are clear reasons not to.

6.3 The chapter starts with a brief recap on the regulatory framework. It deals with guidance on plan-making in relation to the delivery of appropriately sited renewable energy developments. It then covers national guidance in its application to the relevant planning considerations which impact on decision-making and is considered to be essential reading for operators who are contemplating large-scale solar and onshore wind farm applications. The NPPG includes matters such as pre-application consultation, the assessment of landscape and visual impacts (and the information which will inform such assessments) and decommissioning. This chapter also deals with consents under the Electricity Act 1989 for onshore and offshore energy projects (including the position in Scotland), together with wayleaves and compulsory purchase orders sought by electricity companies when it comes to overhead lines on third party land.

REGULATORY FRAMEWORK UNDERLYING DECISION-MAKING

6.4 A brief recap on the decision-making regulatory framework is set out in the following list:

(a) Onshore energy projects with a generating capacity of 50MW or less are dealt with by LPAs under the TCPA 1990.
(b) In 2016 onshore wind farms with a capacity of over 50MW were removed from the NSIP regime under the PA 2008.
(c) Onshore and offshore energy projects with a generating capacity of more than 50MW still require consent under section 36 of the Electricity Act 1989. The body responsible for the grant of section 36 consents in the case of offshore installations below 100MW (but with a threshold of 1MW) rests with the MMO, whereas consents for offshore stations above 100MW rests with the SoS for the DBEIS as part of the NSIP regime under the PA 2008 and by Scottish Ministers for proposals in Scotland.
(d) A FEPA licence from the Marine and Fisheries Agency (an agency of DEFRA) is also required in the case of offshore consents.
(e) Above-ground electric lines in excess of 20kV or in cases less than 20kV where the supply is to more than one customer require consent under section 37 of the Electricity Act 1989.
(f) The threshold for NSIPs is for applications involving lines with a capacity greater than 132kV or which are greater than 2km in length. The DBEIS administers applications under section 37 below the NSIP threshold.
(g) Underground connections and overhead lines supplying less than a single customer with less than 20kV may be classed as permitted development.

NATIONAL PLANNING PRACTICE GUIDANCE – GUIDANCE ON CLIMATE CHANGE

Why is it important for planning to consider climate change?

6.5 The following paragraphs are taken from NPPG, Paragraph: 001 Reference ID: 6-001-20140306 (last updated 06/03/2017):

> In addition to supporting the delivery of appropriately sited green energy, effective spatial planning is an important part of a successful response to climate change as it can influence the emission of greenhouse gases. In doing so, local planning authorities should ensure that protecting the local environment is properly considered alongside the broader issues of protecting the global environment. Planning can also help increase resilience to climate change impact through the location, mix and design of development.

> Addressing climate change is one of the core land use planning principles which the [NPPF] expects to underpin both plan-making and decision-taking. To be found sound Local Plans will need to reflect this principle and enable the delivery of sustainable development in accordance with policies in the [NPPF]. These include the requirements for local authorities to adopt proactive strategies to mitigate and adapt to climate change in line with the provisions and objectives of the Climate Change Act 2008, and cooperate to deliver strategic priorities which include climate change.
>
> In addition to the statutory requirement to take the Framework into account in the preparation of Local Plans, there is a statutory duty on local planning authorities to include policies in their Local Plan designed to tackle climate change and its impacts. This compliments the sustainable duty on plan-makers and the expectation that neighbourhood plans will contribute to the achievement of sustainable development. The [NPPF] emphasises that responding to climate change is central to the economic, social and environmental dimensions of sustainable development.

How can challenges of climate be addressed through the local plan?

6.6 The following paragraph is taken from NPPG, Paragraph: 003 Reference ID: 6-003-20140612 (last updated 12/06/2014):

> There are many opportunities to integrate climate change mitigation and adaptation objectives into the Local Plan. Sustainability appraisal can be used to help shape appropriate strategies in line with the statutory duty on climate change and ambition in the Climate Change Act 2008.
>
> *Examples of mitigating climate change by reducing emissions:*
>
> ...
>
> - Providing opportunities for renewable and low carbon energy technologies

How can local planning authorities identify appropriate mitigation measures in plan-making?

6.7 The following paragraph is taken from NPPG, Paragraph: 007 Reference ID: 6-007-20140306 (last updated 06/03/2014):

> - ... In more energy intensive sectors, energy efficiency and generation of renewable energy can make a significant contribution to emissions reduction.

Can a local planning authority set higher energy performance standards than the building regulations in its local plan?

6.8 The following paragraph is taken from NPPG, Paragraph: 012 Reference ID: 6-012-20190315 (last updated 15/03/2019):

> Provisions in the Planning and Energy Act 2008 also allow development plan policies to impose reasonable requirements for a proportion of energy used in development in their area to be energy from renewable sources and/or to be low carbon energy from sources in the locality of the development.

NATIONAL PLANNING PRACTICE GUIDANCE – GUIDANCE ON RENEWABLE AND LOW CARBON ENERGY

Planning for renewable and low carbon energy

Why is planning for renewable and low carbon energy important?

6.9 The following paragraph is taken from NPPG, Paragraph: 001 Reference ID: 5-001-20140306 (last updated 06/03/2014):

> Increasing the amount of energy from renewable and low carbon technologies will help to make sure the UK has a secure energy supply, reduce greenhouse gas emissions to slow down climate change and stimulate investment in new jobs and businesses. Planning has an important role in the delivery of new renewable and low carbon energy infrastructure in locations where the local environmental impact is acceptable.

Are all energy developments handled by local planning authorities?

6.10 The following paragraph is taken from NPPG, Paragraph: 002 Reference ID: 5-002-20140306 (last updated 06/03/2014):

> Local planning authorities are responsible for renewable and low carbon energy development of 50 megawatts or less installed capacity (under the Town and Country Planning Act 1990). Renewable and low carbon development over 50 megawatts capacity are currently considered by the Secretary of State for Energy under the Planning Act 2008, and the local planning authority is a statutory consultee. It is the government's intention to amend legislation so that all applications for onshore wind energy development are handled by local planning authorities. Microgeneration is often permitted development and may not require an application for planning permission.

Developing a strategy for renewable and low carbon energy

How can local planning authorities develop a positive strategy to promote the delivery of renewable and low carbon energy?

6.11 The following paragraphs are taken from NPPG, Paragraph: 003 Reference ID: 5-003-20140306 (last updated 06/03/2014):

> The National Planning Policy Framework explains that all communities have a responsibility to help increase the use and supply of green energy, but this does not mean that the need for renewable energy automatically overrides environmental protections and the planning concerns of local communities. As with other types of development, it is important that the planning concerns of local communities are properly heard in matters that directly affect them.
>
> Local and neighbourhood plans are the key to delivering development that has the backing of local communities. When drawing up a Local Plan local planning authorities should first consider what the local potential is for renewable and low carbon energy generation. In considering that potential, the matters local planning authorities should think about include:
>
> - the range of technologies that could be accommodated and the policies needed to encourage their development in the right places;
> - the costs of many renewable energy technologies are falling, potentially increasing their attractiveness and the number of proposals;
> - different technologies have different impacts and impacts can vary by place;
> - the UK has legal commitments to cut greenhouse gases and meet increased energy demand from renewable sources. Whilst local authorities should design their policies to maximise renewable and low carbon energy development, there is no quota which the Local Plan has to deliver.

What is the role for community-led renewable energy initiatives?

6.12 The following paragraphs are taken from NPPG, Paragraph: 004 Reference ID: 5-004-20140306 (last updated 06/03/2014):

> Community initiatives are likely to play an increasingly important role and should be encouraged as a way of providing positive local benefit from renewable energy development. Further information for communities interested in developing their own initiatives is provided by the Department of Energy and Climate Change. Local planning authorities may wish to establish policies which give positive weight to renewable and low carbon energy initiatives which have clear evidence of local community involvement and leadership.
>
> Neighbourhood plans are an opportunity for communities to plan for community led renewable energy developments. Neighbourhood Development Orders and

> Community Right to Build Orders can be used to grant planning permission for renewable energy development. To support community based initiatives a local planning authority should set out clearly any strategic policies that those producing neighbourhood plans or Orders will need to consider when developing proposals that address renewable energy development. Local planning authorities should also share relevant evidence that may assist those producing a neighbourhood plan or Order, as part of their duty to advise or assist. As part of a neighbourhood plan, communities can also look at developing a community energy plan to underpin the neighbourhood plan.

How can local planning authorities identify suitable areas for renewable and low carbon energy?

6.13 The following paragraphs are taken from NPPG, Paragraph: 005 Reference ID: 5-005-20140306 (last updated 18/06/2015):

> There are no hard and fast rules about how suitable areas for renewable energy should be identified, but in considering locations, local planning authorities will need to ensure they take into account the requirements of the technology and, critically, the potential impacts on the local environment, including from cumulative impacts. The views of local communities likely to be affected should be listened to.
>
> When identifying suitable areas it is also important to set out the factors that will be taken into account when considering individual proposals in these areas. These factors may be dependent on the investigatory work underpinning the identified area.
>
> There is a methodology available from the Department of Energy and Climate Change's website on assessing the capacity for renewable energy development which can be used and there may be existing local assessments. However, the impact of some types of technologies may have changed since assessments were drawn up (e.g. the size of wind turbines has been increasing). In considering impacts, assessments can use tools to identify where impacts are likely to be acceptable. For example, landscape character areas could form the basis for considering which technologies at which scale may be appropriate in different types of location. Landscape Character Assessment is a process used to explain the type and characteristics of landscape in an area. Natural England has used Landscape Character Assessment to identify 159 National Character Areas in England which provide a national level database. Landscape Character Assessment carried out at a county or district level may provide a more appropriate scale for assessing the likely landscape and visual impacts of individual proposals. Some renewable energy schemes may have visual impacts on the marine and coastal environment and it may be appropriate to also to assess potential impacts on seascape character.

> Identifying areas suitable for renewable energy in plans gives greater certainty as to where such development will be permitted. For example, where councils have identified suitable areas for large scale solar farms, they should not have to give permission outside those areas for speculative applications involving the same type of development when they judge the impact to be unacceptable.
>
> In the case of wind turbines, a planning application should not be approved unless the proposed development site is an area identified as suitable for wind energy development in a Local or Neighbourhood Plan.

How are 'suitable areas' defined in relation to wind energy development?

6.14 The following paragraph is taken from NPPG, Paragraph: 032 Reference ID: 5-032-150618 (last updated 18/06/2015):

> Suitable areas for wind energy development will need to have been allocated clearly in a Local or Neighbourhood Plan. Maps showing the wind resource as favourable to wind turbines or similar will not be sufficient.

What technical considerations relating to renewable energy technologies affect their siting?

6.15 The following paragraphs are taken from NPPG, Paragraph: 006 Reference ID: 5-006-20140306 (last updated 06/03/2014):

> Examples of the considerations for particular renewable energy technologies that can affect their siting include proximity of grid connection infrastructure and site size, and:
>
> - for biomass, appropriate transport links,
> - for hydro-electric power, sources of water,
> - for wind turbines, predicted wind resource, considerations relating to air safeguarding, electromagnetic interference and access for large vehicles.
>
> Discussions with industry experts can help to identify the siting requirements and likely impacts of technologies. The National Policy Statements on the Department of Energy and Climate Change's website give generic and technology specific advice relevant to siting particular technologies. The Environment Agency has published advice showing which areas may be suitable for open loop ground source heat pumps as well as advice on the technologies it regulates.

Do criteria-based policies have a role in planning for renewable energy?

6.16 The following paragraphs are taken from NPPG, Paragraph: 007 Reference ID: 5-007-20140306 (last updated 06/03/2014):

> Policies based on clear criteria can be useful when they are expressed positively (i.e. that proposals will be accepted where the impact is or can be made acceptable). In thinking about criteria the National Policy Statements published by the Department of Energy and Climate Change provide a useful starting point. These set out the impacts particular technologies can give rise to and how these should be addressed.
>
> In shaping local criteria for inclusion in Local Plans and considering planning applications in the meantime, it is important to be clear that:
>
> - the need for renewable or low carbon energy does not automatically override environmental protections;
> - cumulative impacts require particular attention, especially the increasing impact that wind turbines and large scale solar farms can have on landscape and local amenity as the number of turbines and solar arrays in an area increases;
> - local topography is an important factor in assessing whether wind turbines and large scale solar farms could have a damaging effect on landscape and recognise that the impact can be as great in predominately flat landscapes as in hilly or mountainous areas;
> - great care should be taken to ensure heritage assets are conserved in a manner appropriate to their significance, including the impact of proposals on views important to their setting;
> - proposals in National Parks and Areas of Outstanding Natural Beauty, and in areas close to them where there could be an adverse impact on the protected area, will need careful consideration;
> - protecting local amenity is an important consideration which should be given proper weight in planning decisions.

Are buffer zones/separation distances appropriate between renewable energy development and other land uses?

6.17 The following paragraph is taken from NPPG, Paragraph: 008 Reference ID: 5-008-20140306 (last updated 06/03/2014):

> Local planning authorities should not rule out otherwise acceptable renewable energy developments through inflexible rules on buffer zones or separation distances. Other than when dealing with set back distances for safety, distance of itself does not necessarily determine whether the impact of a proposal is unacceptable. Distance plays a part, but so does the local context including factors

> such as topography, the local environment and near-by land uses. This is why it is important to think about in what circumstances proposals are likely to be acceptable and plan on this basis.

How can decentralised energy opportunities be identified?

6.18 The following paragraphs are taken from NPPG, Paragraph: 009 Reference ID: 5-009-20140306 (last updated 06/03/2014):

> There is an important contribution to be made by planning that is independent of the contribution from other regimes such as building regulations. For example, getting the right land uses in the right place can underpin the success of a district heating scheme. Similarly, planning can influence opportunities for recovering and using waste heat from industrial installations.
>
> Planning can provide opportunities for, and encourage energy development which will produce waste heat, to be located close to existing or potential users of the heat. Planning can also help provide the new customers for the heat by encouraging development which could make use of the heat.
>
> Information on local heat demand is published by the Department of Energy and Climate Change to assist planners and developers in identifying locations with opportunities for heat supply. See the national heat map and the UK combined heat and power (CHP) development map. This information will be supplemented in future by further work, including detailed mapping, on the potential for combined heat and power and district heating and cooling.

Particular planning considerations for active solar technology, solar farms and wind turbines

What are the planning considerations that relate to specific renewable energy technologies?

6.19 The following paragraph is taken from NPPG, Paragraph: 010 Reference ID: 5-010-20140306 (last updated 06/03/2014):

> Renewable energy developments should be acceptable for their proposed location. In addition to the factors that should be considered regarding the acceptability of a location for any form of renewable energy development there are particular considerations for the following technologies: … active solar technology (photovoltaics and solar water heating), solar farms and wind turbines. Also, local planning authorities may wish to consider how planning conditions or planning obligations can mitigate the impacts described.

What are the particular planning considerations that relate to active solar technology (photovoltaic and solar water heating)?

6.20 The following paragraphs are taken from NPPG, Paragraph: 012 Reference ID: 5-012-20140306 (last updated 06/03/2014):

> Active solar technology, (photovoltaic and solar water heating) on or related to a particular building is often permitted development (which does not require a planning application) provided the installation is not of an unusual design, or does not involve a listed building, and is not in a designated area. Where a planning application is required, factors to bear in mind include:
>
> - the importance of siting systems in situations where they can collect the most energy from the sun;
> - need for sufficient area of solar modules to produce the required energy output from the system;
> - the effect on a protected area such as an Area of Outstanding Natural Beauty or other designated areas;
> - the colour and appearance of the modules, particularly if not a standard design.

What are the particular planning considerations that relate to large-scale ground-mounted solar photovoltaic farms?

6.21 The following paragraphs are taken from NPPG, Paragraph: 013 Reference ID: 5-013-20150327 (last updated 27/03/2015):

> The deployment of large-scale solar farms can have a negative impact on the rural environment, particularly in undulating landscapes. However, the visual impact of a well-planned and well-screened solar farm can be properly addressed within the landscape if planned sensitively.
>
> Particular factors a local planning authority will need to consider include:
>
> - encouraging the effective use of land by focusing large scale solar farms on previously developed and non agricultural land, provided that it is not of high environmental value;
> - where a proposal involves greenfield land, whether (i) the proposed use of any agricultural land has been shown to be necessary and poorer quality land has been used in preference to higher quality land; and (ii) the proposal allows for continued agricultural use where applicable and/or encourages biodiversity improvements around arrays. See also a speech by the Minister for Energy and Climate Change, the Rt Hon Gregory Barker MP, to the solar PV industry on 25 April 2013 and Written Ministerial Statement on solar energy: protecting the local and global environment made on 25 March 2015;
> - that solar farms are normally temporary structures and planning conditions can be used to ensure that the installations are removed when no longer in use and the land is restored to its previous use;

- the proposal's visual impact, the effect on landscape of glint and glare (see guidance on landscape assessment) and on neighbouring uses and aircraft safety;
- the extent to which there may be additional impacts if solar arrays follow the daily movement of the sun;
- the need for, and impact of, security measures such as lights and fencing;
- great care should be taken to ensure heritage assets are conserved in a manner appropriate to their significance, including the impact of proposals on views important to their setting. As the significance of a heritage asset derives not only from its physical presence, but also from its setting, careful consideration should be given to the impact of large scale solar farms on such assets. Depending on their scale, design and prominence, a large scale solar farm within the setting of a heritage asset may cause substantial harm to the significance of the asset;
- the potential to mitigate landscape and visual impacts through, for example, screening with native hedges;
- the energy generating potential, which can vary for a number of reasons including, latitude and aspect.

The approach to assessing cumulative landscape and visual impact of large scale solar farms is likely to be the same as assessing the impact of wind turbines. However, in the case of ground-mounted solar panels it should be noted that with effective screening and appropriate land topography the area of a zone of visual influence could be zero.

What are the particular planning considerations that relate to wind turbines?

6.22 The following paragraphs are taken from NPPG, Paragraph: 014 Reference ID: 5-014-20150618 (last updated 18/06/2015):

The following questions should be considered when determining applications for wind turbines:

- Do local people have the final say on wind farm applications?
- How are noise impacts of wind turbines assessed?
- Is safety an issue when wind turbine applications are assessed?
- Is interference with electromagnetic transmissions an issue for wind turbine applications?
- How can the risk of wind turbines be assessed for ecology?
- How should heritage be taken into account in assessing wind turbine applications?
- Is shadow flicker and reflected light an issue for wind turbine applications?
- How to assess the likely energy output of a wind turbine?
- How should cumulative landscape and visual impacts from wind turbines be assessed?
- What information is needed to assess cumulative landscape and visual impacts of wind turbines?
- Decommissioning wind turbines.

Do local people have the final say on wind farm applications?

6.23 The following paragraphs are taken from NPPG, Paragraph: 033 Reference ID: 5-033-150618 (last updated 18/06/2015):

> The written ministerial statement made on 18 June 2015 is quite clear that when considering applications for wind energy development, local planning authorities should (subject to the transitional arrangement) only grant planning permission if:
>
> - the development site is in an area identified as suitable for wind energy development in a Local or Neighbourhood Plan; and
> - following consultation, it can be demonstrated that the planning impacts identified by affected local communities have been fully addressed and therefore the proposal has their backing.
>
> Whether the proposal has the backing of the affected local community is a planning judgement for the local planning authority.

How are noise impacts of wind turbines assessed?

6.24 The following paragraph is taken from NPPG, Paragraph: 015 Reference ID: 5-015-20140306 (last updated 06/03/2014):

> The report, ETSU-R-97: The assessment and rating of noise from wind farms should be used by local planning authorities when assessing and rating noise from wind energy developments. Good practice guidance on noise assessments of wind farms has been prepared by the Institute of Acoustics. The Department of Energy and Climate Change accept that it represents current industry good practice and endorses it as a supplement to ETSU-R-97. It is available on the Department of Energy and Climate Change's website.

Is safety an issue when wind turbine applications are assessed?

6.25 The following paragraphs are taken from NPPG, Paragraph: 016 Reference ID: 5-016-20140306 (last updated 06/03/2014):

> Safety may be an issue in certain circumstances, but risks can often be mitigated through appropriate siting and consultation with affected bodies:
>
> *Buildings*
> Fall over distance (i.e. the height of the turbine to the tip of the blade) plus 10% is often used as a safe separation distance. This is often less than the minimum desirable distance between wind turbines and occupied buildings calculated on the basis of expected noise levels and due to visual impact.

Power lines
National Grid, and/or the relevant Distribution Network Operators will be able to advise on the required standards for wind turbines being separated from existing overhead power lines.

Air traffic and safety
Wind turbines may have an adverse affect on air traffic movement and safety. Firstly, they may represent a risk of collision with low flying aircraft, and secondly, they may interfere with the proper operation of radar by limiting the capacity to handle air traffic, and aircraft instrument landing systems. There is a 15 kilometre (km) consultation zone and 30km or 32km advisory zone around every civilian air traffic radar, although objections can be raised to developments that lie beyond the 32km advisory zone. There is a c.15km statutory safeguarding consultation zone around Ministry of Defence aerodromes within which wind turbine proposals would be assessed for physical obstruction. See the Town and Country Planning (safeguarded aerodromes, technical sites and military explosives storage areas) direction 2002. Further advice on wind energy and aviation can be found on the Civil Aviation Authority and National Air Control Transport Services websites.

Defence
Wind turbines can adversely affect a number of Ministry of Defence operations including radars, seismological recording equipment, communications facilities, naval operations and low flying. Developers and local planning authorities should consult with the Ministry of Defence if a proposed turbine is 11 metres (m) to blade tip or taller, and/or has a rotor diameter of 2m or more.

Radar
In addition to air traffic radar, wind turbines may affect other radar installations such as weather radar operated by the Meteorological Office.

Strategic Road Network
The Highways Agency/Department for Transport have produced advice for siting wind turbines safely in relation to the strategic road network titled The strategic road network and the delivery of sustainable development (2013).

Is interference with electromagnetic transmissions an issue for wind turbine applications?

6.26 The following paragraph is taken from NPPG, Paragraph: 017 Reference ID: 5-017-20140306 (last updated 06/03/2014):

> Wind turbines can potentially affect electromagnetic transmissions (e.g. radio, television and phone signals). Specialist organisations responsible for the operation of electromagnetic links typically require 100m clearance either side of a line of sight link from the swept area of turbine blades. OFCOM acts as a central point of contact for identifying specific consultees relevant to a site.

How can the risk of wind turbines be assessed for ecology?

6.27 The following paragraph is taken from NPPG, Paragraph: 018 Reference ID: 5-018-20140306 (last updated 06/03/2014):

> Evidence suggests that there is a risk of collision between moving turbine blades and birds and/or bats. Other risks including disturbance and displacement of birds and bats and the drop in air pressure close to the blades which can cause barotrauma (lung expansion) in bats, which can be fatal. Whilst these are generally a relatively low risk, in some situations, such as in close proximity to important habitats used by birds or bats, the risk is greater and the impacts on birds and bats should therefore be assessed. Advice on assessing risks is available from Natural England's website.

How should heritage be taken into account in assessing wind turbine applications?

6.28 Thc following paragraph is taken from NPPG, Paragraph: 019 Reference ID: 5-019-20140306 (last updated 06/03/2014):

> As the significance of a heritage asset derives not only from its physical presence, but also from its setting, careful consideration should be given to the impact of wind turbines on such assets. Depending on their scale, design and prominence a wind turbine within the setting of a heritage asset may cause substantial harm to the significance of the asset.

Is shadow flicker and reflected light an issue for wind turbine applications?

6.29 The following paragraphs are taken from NPPG, Paragraph: 020 Reference ID: 5-020-20140306 (last updated 06/03/2014):

> Under certain combinations of geographical position and time of day, the sun may pass behind the rotors of a wind turbine and cast a shadow over neighbouring properties. When the blades rotate, the shadow flicks on and off; the impact is known as 'shadow flicker'. Only properties within 130 degrees either side of north, relative to the turbines can be affected at these latitudes in the UK – turbines do not cast long shadows on their southern side.
>
> Modern wind turbines can be controlled so as to avoid shadow flicker when it has the potential to occur. Individual turbines can be controlled to avoid shadow flicker at a specific property or group of properties on sunny days, for specific times of the day and on specific days of the year. Where the possibility of shadow flicker exists, mitigation can be secured through the use of conditions.

> Although problems caused by shadow flicker are rare, where proposals for wind turbines could give rise to shadow flicker, applicants should provide an analysis which quantifies the impact. Turbines can also cause flashes of reflected light, which can be visible for some distance. It is possible to ameliorate the flashing but it is not possible to eliminate it.

How to assess the likely energy output of a wind turbine?

6.30 The following paragraph is taken from NPPG, Paragraph: 021 Reference ID: 5-021-20140306 (last updated 06/03/2014):

> As with any form of energy generation this can vary and for a number of reasons. With wind turbines the mean wind speed at hub height (along with the statistical distribution of predicted wind speeds about this mean and the wind turbines used) will determine the energy captured at a site. The simplest way of expressing the energy capture at a site is by use of the 'capacity factor'. This though will vary with location and even by turbine in an individual wind farm. This can be useful information in considering the energy contribution to be made by a proposal, particularly when a decision is finely balanced.

How should cumulative landscape and visual impacts from wind turbines be assessed?

6.31 The following paragraphs are taken from NPPG, Paragraph: 022 Reference ID: 5-022-20140306 (last updated 06/03/2014):

> Cumulative landscape impacts and cumulative visual impacts are best considered separately. The cumulative landscape impacts are the effects of a proposed development on the fabric, character and quality of the landscape; it is concerned with the degree to which a proposed renewable energy development will become a significant or defining characteristic of the landscape.
>
> Cumulative visual impacts concern the degree to which proposed renewable energy development will become a feature in particular views (or sequences of views), and the impact this has upon the people experiencing those views. Cumulative visual impacts may arise where two or more of the same type of renewable energy development will be visible from the same point, or will be visible shortly after each other along the same journey. Hence, it should not be assumed that, just because no other sites will be visible from the proposed development site, the proposal will not create any cumulative impacts.

What information is needed to assess cumulative landscape and visual impacts of wind turbines?

6.32 The following paragraphs are taken from NPPG, Paragraph: 023 Reference ID: 5-023-20140306 (last updated 06/03/2014):

> In identifying impacts on landscape, considerations include: direct and indirect effects, cumulative impacts and temporary and permanent impacts. When assessing the significance of impacts a number of criteria should be considered including the sensitivity of the landscape and visual resource and the magnitude or size of the predicted change. Some landscapes may be more sensitive to certain types of change than others and it should not be assumed that a landscape character area deemed sensitive to one type of change cannot accommodate another type of change.
>
> In assessing the impact on visual amenity, factors to consider include: establishing the area in which a proposed development may be visible, identifying key viewpoints, the people who experience the views and the nature of the views.
>
> The Historic England website provides information on undertaking historic landscape characterisation and how this relates to landscape character assessment.
>
> The bullets below set out the type of information that can usefully inform assessments.
>
> *Information to inform landscape and visual impact assessments:*
>
> - a base plan of all existing windfarms, consented developments and applications received, showing all schemes within a defined radius of the centre of the proposal under consideration
> - for those existing or proposed windfarms within a defined radius of the proposal under consideration, a plan showing cumulative 'zones of visual influence'. (A zone of visual influence is the area from which a development or other structure is theoretically visible). The aim of the plan should be to clearly identify the zone of visual influence of each windfarm, and those areas from where one or more windfarms are likely to be seen
> - the base plan and plan of cumulative zones of visual influence will need to reflect local circumstances, for example, the areas covered should take into account the extent to which factors such as the topography and the likely visibility of proposals in prevailing meteorological conditions may vary
> - maps of cumulative zones of visual influence are used to identify appropriate locations for visual impact studies. These include locations for simultaneous visibility assessments (i.e. where two or more schemes are visible from a fixed viewpoint without the need for an observer to turn their head), and repetitive visibility assessments (i.e. where the observer is able to see two or more schemes but only if they turn around)

- sequential effects on visibility occur when an observer moves through a landscape and sees two or more schemes. Common routes through a landscape (e.g. major roads; long distance paths or cycle routes) can be identified as 'journey scenarios' and the proposal's impact on them can be assessed
- photomontages showing all existing and consented turbines, and those for which planning applications have been submitted, in addition to the proposal under consideration. The viewpoints used could be those identified using the maps of cumulative zones of visual influence. The photomontages could be annotated to include the dimensions of the existing turbines, the distance from the viewpoint to the different schemes, the arc of view and the format and focal length of the camera used
- at the most detailed level, description and assessment of cumulative impacts may include the following landscape issues: scale of development in relation to landscape character or designations, sense of distance, existing focal points in the landscape, skylining (where additional development along a skyline appears disproportionately dominant) and sense of remoteness or wildness

Decommissioning wind turbines

6.33 The following paragraph is taken from NPPG, Paragraph: 024 Reference ID: 5-024-20140306 (last updated 06/03/2014):

> Local planning authorities should consider using planning conditions to ensure that redundant turbines are removed when no longer in use and land is restored to an appropriate use.

When is pre-application consultation with the local community compulsory for wind turbine proposals?

6.34 The following paragraphs are taken from NPPG, Paragraph: 025 Reference ID: 5-025-20150415 (last updated 15/04/2015):

> There is a legal requirement to carry out pre-application consultation with the local community for planning applications for wind turbine development involving more than 2 turbines or where the hub height of any turbine exceeds 15 metres as identified in article 3 of the Town and Country Planning (Development Management Procedure) (England) (Order) 2015.
>
> The following questions should be considered when undertaking compulsory pre-application consultation with the local community for wind turbine proposals:
>
> - Who is responsible for conducting compulsory pre-application consultation with the local community for wind turbine proposals?
> - What must a prospective applicant for planning permission for a wind turbine do when undertaking compulsory pre-application consultation with the local community?

- How can a prospective applicant for planning permission for a wind turbine establish who needs to be consulted?
- Will compulsory pre-application consultation with the local community apply to planning applications for wind turbine(s) determined by the SoS?
- What role can the local planning authority play in compulsory pre-application consultation with the local community for wind turbine proposals?
- What happens if a prospective applicant for a wind turbine does not comply with the requirement to undertake compulsory pre-application consultation with the local community?

Who is responsible for conducting compulsory pre-application consultation with the local community for wind turbine proposals?

6.35 The following paragraph is taken from NPPG, Paragraph: 026 Reference ID: 5-026-20140410 (last updated 14/04/2015):

> The requirement to undertake compulsory pre-application consultation with the local community is the responsibility of the prospective applicant for planning permission.

What must a prospective applicant for planning permission for a wind turbine(s) do when undertaking compulsory pre-application consultation with the local community?

6.36 The following paragraphs are taken from NPPG, Paragraph: 027 Reference ID: 5-027-20150415 (last updated 15/04/2015):

> The requirements that must be fulfilled are set out in sections 61W and 61X of the Town and Country Planning Act 1990 and article 4 of the Town and Country Planning (Development Management Procedure) (England) (Order) 2015. In summary, a prospective applicant for planning permission must:
>
> - publicise the proposal in such a way as the applicant reasonably considers is likely to bring it to the attention of a majority of the people who live at, or otherwise occupy, premises in the vicinity of the land;
> - set out how persons may contact them regarding the proposal. The applicant must give sufficient information about the proposed timetable to ensure that people wishing to comment on the proposed development may do so in good time;
> - if they decide to go ahead with making an application for planning permission, have regard to any responses received when finalising the application to be submitted;
> - when submitting their application explain how the local community has been consulted, what comments have been received, and how account has been taken of those comments.

> These are minimum requirements, but it is in the prospective applicant's interest to conduct pre-application consultation to an appropriate standard to ensure that they fully understand the views of those within the vicinity of the land to which the application relates.

How can a prospective applicant for planning permission for a wind turbine(s) establish who needs to be consulted?

6.37 The following paragraphs are taken from NPPG, Paragraph: 028 Reference ID: 5-028-20140410 (last updated 10/04/2014):

> Where it is required, compulsory pre-application consultation must meet the legislative requirements set out in section 61W of the Town and Country Planning Act 1990. These require that applicants must publicise the proposal in such a way as the applicant reasonably considers is likely to bring it to the attention of a majority of persons who live at or otherwise occupy premises in the vicinity of the land.
>
> There is no one size fits all approach to pre-application consultation and, providing it meets the legislative requirements, decisions on the nature and extent of consultation will need to be made on a case by case basis and in light of the relevant circumstances. Pre-application consultation should be proportionate to the scale and nature of a proposed development, the local context and the people that might be materially affected by the planning impacts of the development.
>
> When deciding how and who to consult, prospective applicants will need to consider what is necessary in the specific circumstances of their proposal but a useful starting point is to consider the extent of engagement with the local community a local planning authority would normally undertake if a formal planning application were to be submitted. Prospective applicants are encouraged to discuss these matters with the local planning authority.

Will compulsory pre-application consultation with the local community apply to planning applications for wind turbine(s) determined by the Secretary of State?

6.38 The following paragraph is taken from NPPG, Paragraph: 029 Reference ID: 5-029-20140410 (last updated 10/04/2014):

> Compulsory pre-application consultation with the local community applies to applications under Part 3 of the Town and Country Planning Act which meet the criteria. Specific provision is made so that the duty applies to applications meeting the criteria made directly to the Secretary of State where a local planning authority has been designated as poorly performing under section 62A of the 1990 Act.

What role can the local planning authority play in compulsory pre-application consultation with the local community for wind turbine proposals?

6.39 The following paragraph is taken from NPPG, Paragraph: 030 Reference ID: 5-030-20140410 (last updated 10/04/2014):

> Local planning authorities are encouraged to work constructively with prospective applicants undertaking compulsory pre-application consultation with the local community. Under section 61W(7) of the Town and Country Planning Act 1990, an applicant must have regard to the advice (if any) given by the local planning authority about local good practice. See more general information on the role of the local planning authorities at the pre-application stage.

What happens if a prospective applicant for a wind turbine does not comply with the requirement to undertake compulsory pre-application consultation with the local community?

6.40 The following paragraph is taken from NPPG, Paragraph: 031 Reference ID: 5-031-20150415 (last updated 15/04/2015):

> If the requirements set out in sections 61W and 61X of the Town and Country Planning Act 1990 and article 4 of the Town and Country Planning (Development Management Procedure) (England) Order 2010 have not been met and a planning application is submitted, the local planning authority will not be able to validate it until the prospective applicant complies.

ELECTRICITY DEVELOPMENT CONSENTS

Consent process for onshore and offshore generating stations with a generating capacity above 50MW and 100MW in England and Wales

6.41 Onshore and offshore energy projects with a generating capacity of more than 50MW still require consent under section 36 of the Electricity Act 1989. The body responsible for the grant of section 36 consents in the case of offshore installations below 100MW (with a threshold of 1MW) rests with the MMO,[1] whereas consents for offshore stations above 100MW rest with the SoS for the DBEIS under the PA 2008 and by Scottish Ministers for proposals in Scotland.

---

1 See details on the MMO website at www.gov.uk/government/organisations/marine-management-organisation.

6.42 The PA 2008 passed responsibility for dealing with development consent applications for NSIP to PINS, which examines applications and makes recommendations to the SoS at the DBEIS for decisions on energy applications. Developers of proposed NSIPs should contact the PINS if considering submitting a development consent application. Details can be found on the national infrastructure planning portal. PINS has produced a guidance note for developers wishing to submit an application for a development consent for an NSIP.[2] Developers should also have due regard to the Energy NPSs.[3]

6.43 Except in certain circumstances, the PA 2008 disapplied the provisions of the Electricity Act 1989 in relation to consents for projects in England and Wales. The DBEIS continues to deal with consent applications made under the Electricity Act 1989 that were submitted to it prior to the provisions of the PA 2008 coming into force and which have not yet been determined. More can be found out about the consenting process under section 36 of the Electricity Act 1989 in the DBEIS guidance note.[4]

6.44 The DBEIS also administers the Electricity Act 1989 for overhead lines below 132kV and associated permissions (necessary wayleaves and compulsory purchase orders) in England and Wales. Section 37 (overhead lines) of the Electricity Act 1989 takes into account the views of the LPA, local people, statutory bodies (such as the Environment Agency), and other interested parties. All applications go through the LPA and appear on the local planning register. In some cases, there may be a public inquiry before the SoS makes a decision, usually as a consequence of an objection being received from the LPA. In July 2014 the DECC published revised guidance on the section 37 statutory consents regime for overhead lines in England and Wales.[5]

---

2 'Consents and planning applications for national energy infrastructure projects' published 22 January 2013; last updated on 06/11/2018.

3 'Overarching Energy NPS (EN-1)' (July 2011); 'Renewable Energy Infrastructure NPS (EN-3)' (July 2011); 'Electricity Networks Infrastructure NPS (EN-5)' (July 2011).

4 'The consenting process for onshore generating stations above 50MW in England and Wales' (October 2007). Consents in Scotland under the Electricity Act 1989 are issued by the Scottish Ministers.

5 'The statutory consents regime for overhead power lines in England and Wales under section 37 of the Electricity Act 1989'.

6.45 Guidance is also available in relation to variations of section 36 consents.[6] This guidance is about varying consents which have been granted under section 36 of the Electricity Act 1989 for the construction or extension, and operation, of electricity generating stations granted by the SoS for the DBEIS (or his predecessors) or the MMO. It explains how to lodge an application for variation under the Electricity Generating Stations (Variation of Consents) (England and Wales) Regulations 2013 (SI 2013/1570). By applying to vary a section 36 consent it may be possible to obtain authorisation for a generating station to be constructed, extended and/or operated in a way that would not be consistent with the existing consent.

Scotland

6.46 Marine Scotland, a directorate of the Scottish government, is responsible for dealing with applications for consent under section 36 of the Electricity Act 1989 for offshore generating stations in the Scottish waters (an application for variation of consent is made under the Electricity Generating Stations (Application for Variation of Consents) (Scotland) Regulations 2013 (SI 2013/304). The Scottish Executive is responsible for dealing with application for consent made under the same legislative regime for generating projects onshore.

Other consenting mechanisms

6.47 The DBEIS also administers applications made under the Transport and Works Act 1992 in respect of energy-related projects in those UK territorial waters adjoining England. For similar developments adjacent to Wales, the National Assembly for Wales is the determining body. The Transport and Works Act does not apply in Scotland.

---

6 'Varying consents granted under section 36 of the Electricity Act 1989 for generating stations in England and Wales – a guidance note on the new process' published by the DECC in July 2013. The guidance applies to England and Wales (and adjacent offshore areas) only. It does not apply to Scotland where applications to vary s.36 consents must be made to the Scottish Ministers. The guidance is likely to be of interest to developers and operators of generating stations (or proposed generating stations) which are the subject of s.36 consents as well as local authorities and other interested parties who are given an opportunity to comment upon applications from developers or operators to vary consents.

Environmental Impact Assessment Regulations (England & Wales)

6.48 When processing development applications, the DBEIS considers the environmental consequences of proposals, applying European requirements for EIAs.[7]

Offshore generating stations safety zones

6.49 See the Electricity (Offshore Generating Stations) (Safety Zones) (Application Procedures and Control of Access) Regulations 2007 (SI 2007/1948). See the guidance notes for applying for safety zones around offshore renewable energy installations.

DECOMMISSIONING OFFSHORE RENEWABLE ENERGY INSTALLATIONS

6.50 Sections 105–114 of the Energy Act 2004 introduce a decommissioning scheme for offshore wind and marine energy installations. Under the terms of the Act, the SoS may require a person who is responsible for one of these installations to submit (and eventually carry out) a decommissioning programme for the installation.

6.51 These provisions take into account the UK's international obligations under UNCLOS (United Nations Convention on the Law of the Sea) that anyone who constructs, extends, operates or uses an installation should be responsible for ensuring that it is decommissioned at the end of its useful life. They should also be responsible for meeting the costs of decommissioning.

6.52 The DBEIS considers that by imposing a legal obligation on operators to prepare and carry out a decommissioning programme (and by potentially requiring them to provide financial security) reduces the risk of them defaulting on their decommissioning liabilities.

6.53 The approach of the DBEIS is to seek decommissioning solutions which are consistent with the UK's international obligations as well as UK legislation, and

[7] Electricity Works (Environmental Impact Assessment) (England and Wales) Regulations 2000 (SI 2000/1927). These regulations were updated in 2007 to reflect the EU's Public Participation Directive (Directive 2003/35/EC of the European Parliament and of the Council of 26 May 2003).

which have a proper regard for safety, the environment and other legitimate uses of the sea and economic considerations.[8]

WAYLEAVES AND COMPULSORY PURCHASE ORDERS

6.54 The DBEIS also administers the process for necessary (compulsory) wayleaves and compulsory purchase orders sought by electricity companies for rights over third party land. Guidance is available online on wayleave procedures for applicants, landowners and occupiers. Public inquiries relating to electric lines are held in accordance with the Acquisition of Land Act 1981 and the Compulsory Purchase (Inquiries Procedure) Rules 2007 (SI 2007/3617).

---

8 'Decommissioning of offshore renewable energy installations under Energy Act 2004 – Guidance note for industry' (January 2011 (revised)).

Chapter 7

Wind Farms

INTRODUCTION

7.1 Wind farms consist of many individual wind turbines which are connected to the grid. A large wind farm may consist of a large number of individual wind turbines distributed over an extended area, although the land in between may still be used for agricultural or other purposes. They do, however, have a significant impact on the landscape and habitats as typically they need to be spread over more land than power stations and need to be built in rural areas. Offshore wind is steadier and stronger than on land and offshore farms have less visual impact, but construction and maintenance costs are very much higher. Small onshore wind farms can feed some energy into the grid or provide electric power to isolated off-grid locations.

7.2 The UK's investment in offshore wind power has resulted in a rapid decrease in the usage of coal as an energy source over the past decade (now down to 1% from around 40% in 2010) as well as a drop in the usage of natural gas as an energy source in 2017.

7.3 The scope of this chapter is to take a general look at onshore and offshore wind farms. There is currently 6–7GW of offshore wind power generation in the UK with a further 4–5GW having secured development contracts (Europe remains the technology leader in installed offshore wind capacity although China, the top wind power producing country, is closing the gap). The picture is one of rapid growth. It said that by 2030, between one-fifth and one-third of the UK's electricity could come from offshore wind power (Denmark is the country with the highest penetration of wind power, with 43% of its consumed electricity coming from wind in 2017). Thanks to plummeting costs, offshore wind has become an increasingly affordable source of clean energy. The position for the time being is, however, uncertain when it comes to onshore wind farm development in the UK.

WRITTEN MINISTERIAL STATEMENT APPLYING TO PROPOSED ONSHORE WIND ENERGY DEVELOPMENT

7.4 The position is less clear in the case of onshore development as planning permission for onshore wind farms has been made more difficult to obtain since 2015. This is a direct consequence of the Written Ministerial Statement on localism and wind energy made by Greg Clarke, the then SoS for Communities and Local Government, on 18 June 2015 (WMS of 18 June 2015), in which he set out considerations to be applied to proposed onshore wind energy development so that local people have the final say on wind farm applications, fulfilling the commitment made in the Conservative election manifesto.

7.5 From this time it has become government policy that when determining planning applications for wind energy development involving one or more wind turbines, LPAs should only grant planning permission if the development site is in an area identified as suitable for wind energy development in a local or neighbourhood plan, and it can be demonstrated that the planning impacts identified by affected local communities have been fully addressed and therefore the proposal has their backing. In applying these new considerations, suitable areas for wind energy development will need to have been allocated clearly in a local or neighbourhood plan. Maps showing the wind resource as favourable to wind turbines, or similar, will not be sufficient. Whether a proposal has the backing of the affected local community is a planning judgment for the LPA.

REPORT OF THE HOUSE OF COMMONS SCIENCE AND TECHNOLOGY COMMITTEE PUBLISHED ON 22 AUGUST 2019

7.6 The rationale for the 2015 statement was undoubtedly political, but the government is being strongly urged to support onshore wind installations consistently with its target to eliminate all emissions by 2050. The report of the Science and Technology Committee published on 22 August 2019 (*Technologies for meeting the Clean Growth emissions reduction targets*) identified ten areas where government policy that supports the implementation of low carbon technology has been delayed, cut back or undermined carbon reductions, including: (a) the closure of the FiT for low carbon power generation in 2019; (b) the exclusion of onshore wind and large-scale solar power from the financial support mechanism available to other renewable power technologies since 2017 (which is soon to be lifted); and (c) the difficulty in obtaining planning permission for onshore wind farms since 2015.

REPOWERING EXISTING ONSHORE WIND TURBINES

7.7 The Committee also noted that planning consent and technological lifetimes meant that most existing onshore wind farms were expected to last 25 years before needing to be decommissioned, or 're-powered' with upgraded equipment. The government, it suggests, should ensure that national policy facilitates the repowering of existing sites and that there needed to be a 'clear' permission framework for repowering existing onshore wind farms in place by the end of 2020.

HOW DO OFFSHORE AND ONSHORE WIND FARMS WORK?

7.8 Wind turbine blades rotate when hit by the wind. The blades of most turbines will start turning at wind speeds of 3–5m per second, which is a gentle breeze with a wind speed of 36–54kph or 10–15m per second producing maximum generation power (with typical fluctuations of up to 20% from hour to hour depending on the strength of the wind). The spinning motion turns a shaft in the nacelle which is the box-like structure at the top of a wind turbine. A generator built into the nacelle then converts the kinetic energy of the turning shaft into electricity. This energy is transferred to the gearbox which converts the slow speed of the spinning blades into higher-speed rotary motion turning the drive shaft quickly enough to power the electricity generator. Sensors in the wind turbine also allow it to turn and adjust its angle for optimum wind capture. All wind turbines, large or small, use the same mechanics to generate electricity. Almost all currently operating offshore wind farms have fixed foundations underwater and are installed in relatively shallow waters of up to 50–60m.

7.9 Most onshore wind turbines have a capacity of 2–3MW which can produce over 6 million kWh of electricity every year, which is enough to meet the electricity demand of around 1,500 average households. Up to a certain level the faster the wind blows, the more electricity is generated. When the wind speed doubles, up to eight times more electricity is generated. If the wind is too strong, turbines will shut themselves down to prevent being damaged. Wind farms are carefully planned to make sure they are in locations with a reliable amount of wind all year round, not least in coastal locations. The UK's exposed position on the north-west corner of Europe makes it particularly windy, particularly in Scotland. As the wind blows all year round wind power is a generally reliable, if intermittent, renewable power source. It also tends to be windiest in winter which means that wind turbines can produce more power at a time of the year when demand for electricity is at its peak.

7.10 Offshore wind turbines are connected through an internal grid to an offshore substation where the voltage is increased to improve transmission over long distances. From the offshore substation electricity is transmitted onshore through a control centre and then to the grid.

HOW EFFICIENT IS WIND POWER?

7.11 A wind turbine is typically 30–45% efficient, rising to 50% efficient at times of peak wind. Wind turbines in the UK are generally producing electricity 70–80% of the time, making them a reliable source of power throughout the year. It is plain that wind is an intermittent energy source which cannot make electricity nor be dispatched on demand. It also gives variable power which, though consistent from year to year, is nonetheless variable over shorter time scales. It therefore has to be used in conjunction with other electric power sources to give a reliable supply. Where there is significant reliance on wind power in a particular region more conventional power sources will be needed to back it up and the grid may need to be upgraded.

HOW MUCH OF THE UK'S ELECTRICITY COMES FROM WIND POWER?

7.12 In 2018, around 15% of the UK's electricity was generated from wind power. Just five years before, the percentage was just over 7%. By the third quarter of 2019, 19% of the UK's electricity came from wind, demonstrating just how fast wind power capacity in the UK is growing. In April 2019 there were 7,779 onshore wind turbines and 1,932 offshore turbines in the UK producing over 56 million MWh of energy a year which is sufficient to power over 14.9 million homes.

ADVANTAGES OF OFFSHORE WIND

7.13 Wind turbines can be built that are larger and taller than their onshore counterparts, allowing for greater energy collection offshore where there is much higher wind speed/force than onshore. The widely used GE 1.5MW model, for example, consists of 35m blades atop a 65m tower for a total height of 100m. The blades sweep a vertical airspace of just under an acre. By contrast, in 1985, wind turbines were less than 1MW with rotor diameters of around 15m.

7.14 Wind farms tend to be far out at sea, which means that they are much less intrusive (and much less susceptible to objection than onshore sites) allowing for much larger farms to be created per square mile.

7.15 Wind farms have relatively little effect on the environment. They are not built in shipping lanes or in fishing areas or within a sensitive environment.

7.16 There are no physical restrictions such as hills or buildings that can block the wind flow.

7.17 The cost of offshore wind power has historically been higher than that of onshore wind generation, but costs have been decreasing rapidly in recent years. Offshore wind costs have fallen by 32% from just a year ago (2018) and by 12% compared with the first half of 2019, according to new research from Bloomberg New Energy Finance.

DISADVANTAGES OF OFFSHORE WIND (SEE ALSO ONSHORE WIND FARMS WHERE THERE IS SOME OVERLAP)

7.18 The biggest disadvantage of an offshore wind farm is its cost. However, because a wind farm has no fuel costs it is much more stable than the volatile prices of fossil fuel sources. Onshore wind farms can be expensive to build and maintain and because of their hard-to-reach locations, they are susceptible to damage from very high-speed winds during storms and are expensive to repair and decommission.

7.19 The effect of offshore wind farms on marine life and birds is not yet fully understood.

7.20 Offshore wind farms that are built closer to coastlines (generally within 26 miles) can be unpopular with residents as it can affect property values and tourism.

SEVEN OF THE TEN LARGEST OFFSHORE WIND FARMS IN THE WORLD ARE IN UK WATERS

7.21 The following list sets out the top ten offshore wind farms:

(1) *Walney Extension* (14km west of Walney Island off the coast of Cumbria) having a capacity of 659MW. Commissioning date 2018.
(2) *London Array* (the 175 turbines are located off the Kent coast in the outer Thames estuary) having a capacity of 630MW. Commissioning date 2013.
(3) *Gemini Wind Farm* (located off the coast of the Netherlands) having a capacity of 600MW. Commissioning date 2017.

(4) *Beatrice* (located 13km off the NE coast of Scotland) having a capacity of 588MW. Commissioning date 2019.

(5) *Gode Wind* (located in the German sector of the North Sea) having a capacity of 582MW. Commissioning date 2017.

(6) *Gwynt y Môr* (the 160 turbines are located off the coast of North Wales) having a capacity of 576MW. Commissioning date 2015.

(7) *Greater Gabbard* (the 107 turbines are located 23km off the Suffolk coast) having a capacity of 504MW. Commissioning date 2012.

(8) *Borkum Riffgrund 2* (in German waters) having a capacity of 450MW. Commissioning date 2019.

(9) *Horns Rev 3* (in Danish waters in the North Sea) having a capacity of 407MW. Commissioning date 2019.

(10) *Dudgeon* (32km north of Cromer off the Norfolk coast) having a capacity of 402MW. Commissioning date 2017.

7.22 The Hornsea Offshore Wind Farm under construction in the North Sea will become the world's largest wind farm when completed. The development has been split into a number of subzones. The 1.2GW Project One gained planning consent in 2014. A second 1.4GW Project Two was given planning consent in 2016. In 2016 a third subzone was split into two projects Project Three and Project Four, with approximate capacities of 1–2GW and 1GW, increasing the capacity of the developed project to a maximum of 6GW (or 6,000MW). Construction of the first phase started in January 2018 and the first turbines began supplying power to the UK National Grid in February 2019.

ADVANTAGES OF ONSHORE WIND

7.23 The cost of onshore wind farms is relatively cheap, allowing for mass farms of wind turbines. According to a recent report prepared for the European Commission, the world's cheapest source of energy is now onshore wind power, even after other factors such as air quality, health impacts and overheads, and the costs of climate change are taken into account. Full Fact (the UK's leading independent fact checking charity) predicts that the electricity generated by onshore wind farms in the next few years is expected to cost less to produce, or similar, than electricity from other main renewable sources. However, it is still expected to cost more than power from gas-fired plants.

7.24 Wind is one of the most useful sources of renewable energy. It has fewer effects on the environment compared to any other source of energy. Wind turbines do not require fuel or water for cooling and they do not emit toxic gases.

7.25 Onshore wind farms are generally located in areas where there is low conservation or habitat value.

7.26 The shorter distance between the wind turbine and the consumer allows for less voltage drop off on the cabling.

7.27 Wind turbines are very quick to install (in contrast it can take 20 years to build a nuclear power station).

DISADVANTAGES OF ONSHORE WIND

7.28 One of the biggest issues of onshore wind farms is that many deem them to be an eyesore on the landscape. They are undoubtedly intrusive features in the countryside. Wind turbines are really big structures. The tower itself is typically between 61m and 91m tall. When you add in the height of the blades, some turbines can be as much as 122m high. The blades are also large. There are typically three wind blades on a wind turbine with each blade being between 35m and 45m in length. The bases of the turbines are normally 3–5m in diameter and the foundations, which run to 9m into the ground, are 5m across. A 2MW onshore wind turbine can be in the region of 260 tons.

7.29 Additional environmental impacts arising from site clearance, access roads, transmission lines and substations can result in what has been termed 'energy sprawl' and can also have a negative impact on tourism in areas known for natural landscape and panoramic views.

7.30 They do not produce consistent energy all year round due to often poor wind speed or physical blockages such as buildings or hills.

7.31 Wind turbines do generate some noise. At a residential distance of 300m this may be around 45dB, which is slightly louder than a refrigerator. At a distance of 1.5km (1 mile) they become inaudible. There are anecdotal reports of negative health effects from noise on people who live very close to wind turbines (headaches from infrasonic sounds). Peer-reviewed research has generally not supported these claims. Some people living near the turbines also complain about shadow flicker in bright sunlight. Local opposition often exists and has delayed or aborted a number of projects. For example, there are concerns that some installations can negatively affect TV and radio reception and weather radar, as well as produce excessive sound and vibration levels leading to (so it is claimed) a decrease in property values.

7.32 Habitat loss and habitat fragmentation are the greatest impact of wind farms on wildlife. There are also reports of higher bird and bat mortality at wind turbines than there are around other artificial structures. Prevention and mitigation of wildlife fatalities (typically birds of prey) affect the siting and operation of wind turbines. From a distance, the blades seem to move slowly, but the tip speed on turbines can approach 200mph creating deadly obstacles for birds.

7.33 Wind turbines can potentially impact upon the radar the aviation industry needs to operate safely and effectively. Impacts could include physical obstructions, the generation of unwanted returns on Primary Surveillance Radar (PSR), and effects on the overall performance of communication, navigation and surveillance equipment and turbulence. Planning objections and conditions can be raised by the Ministry of Defence or civilian bodies (National Air Traffic Services (NATS), UK Civil Aviation Authority and airport operators) and the issue is a significant barrier to the deployment of both onshore and offshore wind power. A survey reported that approximately 3GW of wind farm applications that were submitted for planning approval in 2013 were subject to objections or conditions from the aviation sector. The industry estimates that radar issues account for approximately 12GW of objections in the planning system as a whole. Many civil licensed aerodromes are safeguarded, either through statute or through arrangements with the LPA. Safeguarding is a process of consultation between an LPA and consultees to ensure that the operation and development of the aerodrome are not inhibited by buildings, structures, erections or works which infringe protected surfaces, obscure runway approach lights or have the potential to impair the performance of aerodrome communication, navigation and surveillance systems. The distance from the aerodrome that consultation may be required for a proposed wind turbine development will depend on the facilities and type of operation at the aerodrome concerned. A number of mitigation techniques are available to help counter the effects of wind turbines on radars. These can vary from interim work-rounds (e.g. moving the locations of the wind turbines) to the use of infill radars. Further information is available in the Civil Aviation Authority's *CAP 764, CAA Policy and Guidelines on Wind Turbines* document.[1]

7.34 The high cost of decommissioning wind turbines.

1 Available on the Civil Aviation Authority website at http://publicapps.caa.co.uk/docs/33/Cap764.pdf.

CHECKLIST OF REQUIREMENTS FOR WIND ENERGY PROJECTS

7.35 The Local Government Association has issued a helpful checklist when it comes to: (a) the identification of suitable sites for wind energy development; and (b) planning and regulatory requirements:[2]

> **WIND ENERGY PROJECT CHECKLIST**
> Wind energy projects can take from a few months up to several years to deliver. This will depend on the scale and complexity of the planning and installation process. Some of the practical issues in identifying suitable sites for a wind energy project are set out in this section. You'll also find information on the planning and delivery process.
>
> ***Planning and regulatory requirements***
> Wind turbines currently require planning permission at all scales. The Government has consulted on proposals to grant permitted development rights for micro-wind turbines on domestic and non-domestic properties, within certain limits.
>
> Where the installation of micro or small wind turbines is proposed as part of a new property development, details of the installation need to be submitted as part of the overall planning application.
>
> Planning permission can be one of the biggest barriers to project development for larger wind turbines and commercial wind farms, with the potential to introduce significant delays. Extensive consultation with institutional stakeholders and community engagement is required for wind turbine projects.[3] Projects [and the larger wind farms will normally be EIA development and will require an Environmental Statement] will require environmental and other impact assessments [along with proposed mitigation] which should cover:

---

2 Adjustments have been made to this section (to be found in square brackets) to widen the range of helpful impact and other assessments and to include assessments covering energy and climate change.

3 See Chapter 8, Case Study VII at 'Comment' section in relation to the *Resilient Energy Severndale Ltd* case and its reference to: (a) the general guidance published by the DECC in October 2014: 'Community Benefits from Onshore Wind Developments: Best Practice Guidance for England'; (b) 'Best Practice Guidance on Community Engagement' (which was published alongside (a)); and (c) the speech of Lord Sales JSC in *Resilient Energy Severndale Ltd* at [12]–[16] in which he restates the law in this field and also mentions these publications. Contributions towards a community fund are now a common practice for wind farm proposals although not, of course, a material consideration in its own right.

- landscape [and visual impacts including cumulative impacts][4]
- ecological [and ornithological impacts], with surveys at key times of year for the species concerned
- archaeology, hydrology and geology impacts (in relation to foundations required for the turbines)
- [impact on the setting of heritage assets]
- [impacts on residential amenity including visual] noise and shadow flicker
- aviation safety and radar
- [traffic impacts during construction and when operational: also consider the need for a Construction Management Plan dealing with good practice and mitigation measures such as those involving risks of pollution to watercourses and groundwater sources during construction stage]
- [socio-economic impacts such as tourism, recreational and benefits to rural economy]

[It will obviously be desirable for an applicant to assess these adverse effects against the likely community and environmental benefits arising from the wind farm development, including climate change considerations, such as what the wind farm capacity will be in terms of electricity generation and its displacement of carbon dioxide and the resulting contribution it would make towards meeting targets for renewable energy generation. Energy and related planning policy considerations are important material considerations and will be relevant to the assessment of the planning balance.]

Applications for the largest wind farms with capacities greater than 50MW are not determined by the local planning process. They need to obtain development consent from the Secretary of State under the Planning Act 2008. The application needs to be submitted to the Infrastructure Planning Commission (at a future date this will be replaced by the Major Infrastructure Planning Unit).

---

4 When it comes to the selection of a suitable site for a wind farm it is as well to avoid designated landscapes and sites that include listed buildings from which the wind turbines can be seen.

Identifying suitable sites
Designated areas and approximate setback distances

Designated nature conservation areas	Designated nature conservation areas should be avoided, and a setback distance from the boundary of the designated area may be recommended by ecologists, for example, where sites are used by birds.
Designated landscape	Designated landscapes may or may not be suitable for wind turbines, depending on the reason for their designation and the impact that wind turbines may have on this. Views from designated landscapes to wind turbine sites in the vicinity may also need to be taken into account.
Bats	Hedgerows and woodland areas need to be avoided to reduce the potential impact on bats. Separation distances of around 50m for hedgerows and 100m for woodland may be required for large turbines.
Greenbelt	Greenbelt should be taken into account when deciding if a location is suitable, but is not an absolute constraint on wind energy development.
Residential properties	A setback distance of at least 600–800 metres from residential properties for large wind turbines. This may be reduced for smaller projects. Other land uses, including non-residential buildings and agriculture, can still be accommodated in this zone.
Infrastructure	Minimum distances from roads, power lines, gas pipelines and other infrastructure, which are required by the Highways Agency and other infrastructure operators including National Grid.
Exclusion area	Exclusion areas around airports, airfields and MOD [Ministry of Defence] land, which should be determined in consultation with the relevant bodies depending on the nature of the project.
Communication links	Communications links need to be taken into account in consultation with the relevant telecoms operators.

COST AND OVERHEADS OF WIND TURBINES

7.36 Useful information has been obtained about this online from Renewables UK,[5] a firm of engineering consultants and project delivery experts:

5 www.renewableuk.com.

How much does a wind turbine cost?

How much does a wind turbine cost? The total project cost will depend on many factors, including the cost of the turbine itself, the extent and scope of supporting environmental work for the planning application, the cost of any electrical distribution network ('grid') upgrades and the cost of site works including access roads, foundation and cabling costs.

There are economies of scale so larger turbines cost less per kW-installed than smaller ones, and single turbine sites costing more per kW than multiple turbine sites. Having said all of that, a reasonable conservative budget price for the 'example' turbines used throughout this webpage would be:

Maximum power output	*Typical turbine type*	*Project cost*
100kW	Norvento nED100	£345k
800kW	Enercon E53	£1.03m
1MW	EWT DW61	£1.25m
3MW	Enercon E82	£2.33m
3.5MW	Enercon E126 EP3	£3.13m

For reference, typically the actual wind turbine costs around 69% of the total project cost.

What is the cost to operate wind turbines?

All of the major wind turbine manufacturers offer long-term warranty and maintenance packages for 5 to 15 years (depends on turbine size and manufacturer) which we would always recommend using. The other significant cost to operate wind turbines to consider are business rates and insurance.

There are all sorts of subtleties to how these costs are calculated, but at a very basic level the table below will give a good indication of the Operation and Maintenance (O&M) costs for a single wind turbine. For multiple-turbines just scale-up the figures below.

Maximum power output	*Typical turbine type*	*Annual O&M cost*
100kW	Norvento nED100	£9k
900kW	EWT DW52/54	£36k
1MW	EWT DW61	£45k
3MW	Enercon E82	£86k
3.5MW	Enercon E126 EP3	£174k

O&M = Operating & Maintenance

REPOWERING/DECOMMISSIONING WIND FARMS

7.37 The older wind farms are coming to the end of their initial leases and 20–25 year operational lives and the older technology is bound to require updating if the wind farm is to continue in operation (it seems evident that wind turbines have a shorter life span than most other technologies). Inevitably, developers have to look at their repowering options which will usually necessitate changes in on-site operations and perhaps even a need for additional land. Quite apart from the planning considerations arising from a departure from an existing planning permission, the repowering process also engages landlords whose consent will be needed to make alterations on site and to extend leases which normally include an option for the developer to extend the term for another 25 or 30 years on terms to be agreed. Inevitably there will be rental issues to overcome if the developer is looking to upgrade the pre-existing use or to install more than one form of renewable energy technology and/or battery storage facilities.

7.38 In some instances, where the wind farm has reached the end of its useful life developers may decide to completely remove the wind farm and, pursuant to planning conditions, undertake a complete reinstatement of the site to its former condition. The cost of decommissioning is huge. By way of example, the concrete foundations used to anchor the wind turbines can be as deep as 5m and can be hard to fully remove. In addition, the rotor blades contain glass and carbon fibres that give off dust and toxic gases. Decommissioned blades are difficult and expensive to transport. They can be anywhere from 30m to 91m long and must be cut up on site before being moved off site on specialist equipment to a landfill site that may not even have the capacity for the blades.

7.39 New projects commit to set aside 2–3% of the capital cost each year for decommissioning, but it is unclear whether this amount will be sufficient to cover the costs when the wind turbines are dismantled 20 or so years later. The costs of decommissioning depends on location (offshore or onshore) and the age of the technology as newer turbines are larger than the older models. For instance, in Minnesota, Xcel Energy estimated that it will cost the company $532,000 (in 2019 dollars) to decommission *each* of its wind turbines at its Noble facility, a total cost of $71 million to decommission the 134 turbines. Decommissioning at the Palmer's Creek Wind facility in Chippewa County, Minnesota, is also estimated to cost $7,385,822 for decommissioning the 18 wind turbines operating at that site at a cost of $410,000 per turbine (roughly equivalent to £316,000 per turbine).

7.40 An offshore wind farm in the UK was decommissioned by the German energy group E.ON earlier this year. The Blyth offshore wind farm was a two-wind-turbine farm. One of the two wind turbines was recycled and reused for spare parts within the company's onshore fleet and the other was used for training purposes by the Port of Blyth. The plant had a shorter life span than most commercial wind projects, operating for just 19 years (the 4MW facility off the Northumberland coast powered 2,000 homes). The company did not release the cost for dismantling the Blyth wind farm, but indicated that it was similar to building the project. Repowering of offshore wind farms is deemed unlikely because of the rapid evolution of the offshore turbine technology. The decommissioning of offshore wind turbines is therefore problematic once their useful life is over. In Europe, where land prices are high and where the disposal of waste is subject to intense regulation, repowering makes commercial sense if this is feasible, and especially in the UK where obtaining planning permission for new onshore sites is known to be difficult and prolonged. It is also understood that some redundant turbines are even being resold to developing nations.

Chapter 8

Case Studies Involving Wind Power Projects

CASE STUDY I

Permission Granted for Four Wind Turbines near to an Area of Outstanding Natural Beauty

Bayliss v Secretary of State for Communities and Local Government [2013] EWHC 1612 (Admin) (13 June 2013)

1. The applicant (B) applied to quash a decision of the SoS, by his planning inspector, to grant planning permission to the third respondent (P) for the construction of wind turbines. P had sought planning permission to construct four wind turbines next to an AONB. The LPA refused P's application. The inspector concluded that the development would be visible from the AONB and would cause some limited harm to it but overall the benefits of the development outweighed the harm. B submitted that: (a) the inspector should have given greater weight to the harm caused to the AONB; and (b) the benefits of the turbines were not as great as P had suggested and the inspector's comment that the area had 'the best wind resource in Dorset' was inaccurate.

2. The application to quash was refused.

3. Planning decision-makers had to have regard to the provisions of the development plan and proposed developments had to be in accordance with the plan looked at as a whole, rather than with every policy in the plan. That presumption was rebuttable by 'other material considerations' under section 70(2) of the TCPA 1990. 'Material considerations' included statements of central government policy and local guidance but the weight to be given to such considerations was a matter of planning judgment for the decision-maker. In exercising any function affecting an AONB, the SoS, and any inspector acting on

his behalf, was required by section 85 of the Countryside and Rights of Way Act 2000 to have regard to the purpose of conserving and enhancing the AONB. The policy guidance documents made it clear that great weight was to be given to conserving the landscape. However, the inspector's consideration of the harm to the AONB had to be seen in its proper context. It was common ground that onshore wind was an important element in meeting the government's target for generating electricity from renewable sources. The NPPF, looked at as a whole, generally favoured renewable energy developments, whilst requiring the benefits of such developments to be balanced against possible harm to the environment. It was clear that the inspector had well in mind the special nature of the AONB and harm the development might have upon it, as required by the policy guidance. His consideration of that harm was particular: he considered that the development would cause limited harm to a limited part of the AONB. He dealt with the issue adequately and properly and did not consider the harm to the AONB to be a powerful factor in all the circumstances of the case.

4. The inspector had to balance the benefits of the development against the factors that weighed against the proposal. On any view the development would make a meaningful contribution to renewable electricity and if there were other areas of Dorset where the wind was such that developments there might make bigger contributions that was irrelevant to the inspector's planning determination. He was not making a relative assessment. Further, whether the capacity of the development was 25%, as put forward by P, or 19%, as put forward by the local authority, the inspector clearly considered that benefits outweighed the harm. Even at a rounded-up figure of 20% the benefits were substantial, in the light of the general policy encouraging renewable energy.

Comment

5. This was a small wind farm development comprising only four turbines which were going to be visible from an AONB. In the exercise of his planning judgment the inspector took the view that although there would be some limited harm to the local landscape, overall the benefits arising from the contribution to renewable energy outweighed that harm. This was a material consideration. The case makes it plain: (a) that the planning balance is the preserve of the inspector with which the court is unlikely to interfere; and (b) that a consideration of suitable alternative locations for a proposed renewable energy development will usually be an irrelevant factor in the planning balance.

CASE STUDY II

Wind Farm Close to Listed Buildings

Barnwell Manor Wind Energy Ltd v East Northamptonshire District Council [2014] EWCA Civ 137 ('*Barnwell Manor*') (18 February 2014)

1. The LPA refused the developer's application for planning permission to build a four-turbine wind farm on land in a conservation area which contained a number of listed buildings including a collection of Grade I listed buildings and gardens. The developer appealed to the SoS for Communities and Local Government, who appointed a planning inspector to determine the appeal. By section 66(1) of the Planning (Listed Buildings and Conservation Areas) Act 1990 the inspector was under a duty when considering whether to grant planning permission to 'have special regard to the desirability of preserving' a listed building or its setting. Listed buildings came within the definition of 'designated heritage assets' in the government's Planning Policy Statement 5 and practice guide. The inspector concluded that while the wind farm would fall within and affect the settings of a wide range of heritage assets, on balance the significant benefits of the proposed development in terms of the renewable energy which it would produce outweighed the less than substantial harm which it would cause to the setting of such designated heritage assets and the wider landscape, and accordingly granted planning permission. One of the reasons given for the inspector's conclusion that the harm would be less than substantial was that 'any reasonable observer' would know that the development was a modern addition to the landscape, separate from the planned historic landscape or building he was within or considering or interpreting. The judge granted an application by, among others, the LPA under section 288 of the TCPA 1990 to quash the inspector's decision on the ground that it was flawed because, among other things, he had failed to give effect to the duty under section 66(1) by not giving sufficient weight to the desirability of preserving the setting of the listed buildings. The developer appealed.

2. In dismissing the appeal the Court of Appeal found that section 66(1) required the decision-maker to give 'the desirability of preserving the building or its setting' not merely careful consideration for the purpose of deciding whether there would be some harm, but considerable importance and weight when balancing the advantages of the proposed development against any such harm. The general duty applied with particular force if harm would be caused to the setting of a Grade I listed building, which was a designated heritage asset of the highest significance. If the harm to the setting of the Grade I listed building would

be less than substantial, the strength of the presumption against the grant of planning permission would be lessened but it would not be entirely removed. Since the inspector had not given considerable importance and weight to the desirability of preserving the setting of the listed buildings when carrying out the balancing exercise, he had not given proper effect to the section 66(1) duty with the result, as the court found, that the judge had been right to conclude that the inspector's decision was flawed on that basis.

Comment

3. Assistance is derived from the helpful article 'How to Avoid Significant Pitfalls in Heritage' by Richard Ground QC and Emma Dring at [2019] JPL (Issue 1), pages 3–9. The article notes that it was held in *Barnwell Manor* that if a decision-maker concluded that a proposal will cause harm to a listed building or conservation area, that harm must be given 'considerable importance and weight'. It gives rise to a 'strong presumption' that planning permission should not be granted ([22]–[23] of the judgment). Since *Barnwell Manor* several decisions were quashed on the basis that decision-makers had failed to demonstrate that they had given such considerable importance and weight to the effect of the development on the settings of heritage assets.

4. The decision in *Barnwell Manor* involved an appeal against a decision quashing an inspector's grant of planning permission to build a four-turbine wind farm on land in a conservation area which contained a number of listed buildings, including a collection of Grade I listed buildings and gardens. It was common ground between the parties at the inquiry that the group of designated heritage assets at Lyveden New Bield was probably the finest surviving example of an Elizabethan garden, and that as a group the heritage asset at Lyveden New Bield had a cultural value of national, if not international significance. The inspector had found that:

> this group of designated heritage assets has archaeological, architectural, artistic and historic significance of the highest magnitude.

5. The inspector also found that the wind turbines:

> would be visible from all around the site, to varying degrees, because of the presence of trees. Their visible presence would have a clear influence on their surroundings in which the heritage assets are experienced and as such they would fall within, and affect, the setting of the group.

6. Despite these findings it was the planning judgment of the inspector, in allowing the developers' appeal, that although the proposal would not accord with the development plan, its benefits outweighed its harm to the setting of the

heritage assets. The High Court quashed the decision of the inspector in finding that the inspector had not complied with his duty under section 66(1), and the developers' appeal was duly dismissed by the Court of Appeal, which ruled that the inspector had not given considerable importance and weight to the desirability of preserving the setting of the affected listed buildings when carrying out the section 66(1) balancing exercise, which meant that his decision had been flawed on that basis.

7. This decision makes it plain that when it comes to the selection of a suitable site for a wind farm it is as well to avoid designated landscapes and sites that include listed buildings from which the wind turbines could be seen. In *Barnwell Manor* the closest turbine was around 1.3km from the boundary of the registered park and only 1.7km from Lyveden New Bield itself. It was hardly surprising in the circumstances that Sullivan LJ (at [42]) had difficulty in understanding how the turbine array would not substantially harm the setting of heritage assets of national significance contrary to the policy approach then found within the government's Planning Policy Statement 5 and practice guide when the permission was granted.

CASE STUDY III

Wind Turbine in Green Belt

Holder v Gedling Borough Council [2016] EWHC 3095 (Admin) (2 December 2016)

1. The claimant (C) sought judicial review of the LPA's decision to permit the erection of a wind turbine on farmland in the Green Belt. The proposal was to erect a 50m wind turbine within 120m of a bridleway. In granting permission, the planning committee accepted the planning officer's conclusion that there were very special circumstances justifying the erection of the turbine within the Green Belt. C's challenge focused on the contents of the planning officer's report.

2. C submitted that the LPA had erred in: (a) taking into account the generic benefits of generating renewable energy; (b) disregarding the fact that there were already a number of solar panels on the land; (c) concluding that revenue from the turbine would help secure the future of the farm and support the rural economy; (d) treating mitigation measures, such as tree planting, as free-standing benefits; (e) considering that any alternative renewable energy sources had to generate the same amount of energy as the turbine; (f) failing to consider impact of the turbine on the safety and amenity of bridleway users; (g) failing to recognise that the WMS of 18 June 2015 required that an application be refused if the concerns of local residents had not been addressed. Each of these complaints is dealt with below.

3. The application to quash the LPA's decision to permit the erection of a wind turbine on farmland in the Green Belt failed.

The generic benefits of generating renewable energy

4. There was no error of logic or evaluation in the planning officer's reasoning. He indicated that the general need to generate renewable energy should be given moderate weight in determining whether there were very special circumstances justifying development in the Green Belt. He considered that the turbine would make a valuable contribution to national climate change targets and that contribution was capable of being taken into account. However, he indicated that that contribution was insufficient of itself to overcome the presumption that development in the Green Belt was inappropriate. It had to be considered alongside any other benefits. Lastly, he considered it relevant that the turbine was technologically efficient, would generate a relatively significant volume of

renewable energy for 24 years and that its contribution to climate change mitigation was consistent with the NPPF (see [21]–[25] of judgment).

Existing solar panels

5. It was hard to see why the existence of the solar panels should be of great significance. The local authority had no control over their installation, and had the farmers decided to install them after erecting the turbine, it could not have objected on the basis that the turbine provided ample renewable energy capacity. It was therefore hard to see why it should be able to object to the turbine on the basis that the solar panels were providing renewable energy ([26]–[28]).

The nexus between turbine revenues and the farm business

6. The farmers claimed that the turbine would provide a regular income to hedge against volatility in agricultural market prices. However, the claimant questioned whether all the revenue from the turbine would be used to support the farm. The planning officer accepted that the revenue would be available for farm purposes and concluded that the turbine was consistent with the NPPF's policy of supporting a prosperous rural economy and promoting diversification. That was a proper and rational conclusion: the evidence showed that the farm was a closely held family concern with a strong business link to the turbine ([29]–[31], [36]–[38]).

Mitigation measures

7. A mitigation measure could amount to a discrete benefit, even if it did not entirely mitigate the harm to which it was addressed. The planting proposed by the farmers would only partially mask the turbine, but it would enhance the area's landscape character and ecology and could therefore be treated as a discrete benefit. Once it was recognised that the planting served different functions that were not mutually exclusive, balancing the pros and cons was a matter of planning judgment. The planning officer had conducted a proper analysis and the committee had not erred by relying on it ([42]–[43]).

Alternative sources of renewable energy

8. The committee had before it competing contentions as to alternative technologies. It was aware of the revenue likely to be generated by the turbine, the range of alternative technologies, and the pros and cons of each. The matter was one of planning judgment and the committee's conclusion was not irrational ([46], [49]).

Impact on safety and amenity

9. The committee was aware that a number of riders had complained that their horses had been spooked by the turbine. It reached its conclusion having properly evaluated all the issues relating to safety and amenity ([50], [57]–[59]).

Written Ministerial Statement of 18 June 2015

10. The planning officer had acted properly by telling the committee that the statement had to be given substantial weight, opining that permission could properly be granted and leaving the committee to form its own view. That was a pragmatic approach: the statement was not easy to interpret. However, it did not endorse the principle that a vocal minority could exert decisive influence in a way that it could not previously have done, *R (West Berkshire DC) v Secretary of State for Communities and Local Government* [2016] EWCA Civ 441, [2016] 1 WLR 3923, [2016] 5 WLUK 220 applied. It was for the committee to take account of the objections and balance the competing arguments ([60], [66]–[72]).

Comment

11. This case is of interest in that it looks at the role of the WMS of 18 June 2015 in decision-making which, on its face, would arguably make it virtually impossible for consent to be granted for onshore wind development. The WMS is clearly a material consideration and compliance with it is a matter of planning judgment. Clearly, the WMS will weigh heavily with LPAs and inspectors, and promoters will be loath to invest heavily in such development.

12. In *Holder* Green J criticised the wording of the WMS, which states in its introduction that 'local people have the final say on wind farm applications'. His view was that this was not a justification for attributing decisive weight to the particular views of particular local people. To do so would fetter the discretion of the decision-making body. In the result, the fact that the WMS purports to give local people the final say is not strictly true. It means that the objections of a local action group cannot be the sole reason for refusing to grant planning permission for an onshore development.

13. There is, however, a serious risk that the way in which the WMS is worded will create in the minds of local people a belief that they can in fact block onshore wind farm development. What is crucial, of course, is whether or not: (a) the development site is one that is identified in the relevant development plan as being suitable for wind energy development (how many plans actually contain spatially specific strategies allocating sites for wind energy – to do so would be politically contentious and is no doubt a debate which an LPA would choose to avoid, dealing instead with applications as they arrive for consideration); and (b) the planning impacts identified by affected communities have been fully addressed.

On any reckoning, the WMS creates a tougher climate for onshore wind projects even though the NPPF still contains helpful provisions when it comes to renewable energy development. Clearly, promoters of wind farm development will have to work much more closely with LPAs to find appropriate sites to be allocated in the development plan before making an application for planning permission. The fact that the WMS came alongside a government announcement that a key subsidy for onshore wind developers would end a year early was, at the time, something of a blow to developers in the sector.

14. Is it not high time for a reappraisal of the WMS of 18 June 2015?

CASE STUDY IV

Wind Turbines and Community Benefits as Material Considerations

Good Energy Generation Ltd v Secretary of State for Communities and Local Government, Cornwall Council and Communities Against Rural Exploitation (Care) [2018] EWHC 1270 (Admin) (25 May 2018)

1. Good Energy Generation Ltd (C) sought planning permission to construct a wind farm development including up to 11 wind turbines on a site in Cornwall. The LPA refused permission and C appealed to the SoS. The inspector held an inquiry in 2016 before recommending that the appeal be dismissed. The SoS agreed with the recommendation and dismissed the appeal on the basis of harm to heritage assets and harm to a nearby AONB. The SoS did not consider that the benefits of the scheme outweighed these harms, nor did he consider that the planning obligations would overcome the reasons for dismissing the appeal and refusing planning permission. C had proposed a number of community benefits within a unilateral undertaking, including a contribution to be paid into a community benefit fund, a community investment scheme open to local residents and a reduced electricity tariff that would be available to local residents. Before the section 288 challenge to that decision was determined, the Court of Appeal had held in *R (Peter Wright) v Forest of Dean DC and Resilient Energy Severndale Ltd* [2017] EWCA Civ 2102, [2018] JPL 672, that a community fund did not serve a planning purpose or fairly and reasonably relate to the development proposed. The challenge therefore proceeded in relation to the investment scheme and reduced tariffs only.

2. C sought to challenge the SoS's decision on the basis of two grounds: (a) that the SoS and the inspector erred in law in disregarding the benefits offered by C in a unilateral undertaking as these were material considerations which were not excluded by regulation 122 of the Community Infrastructure Levy Regulations 2010 (SI 2010/948) ('CIL Regulations'); and (b) that the SoS failed to have proper regard to the newly adopted Cornwall Local Plan, and he failed to determine the extent of any conflict with it. Neither the SoS, nor the inspector, had proper regard to the Council's Supplementary Planning Document (SPD) 'Cornwall Renewable Energy Planning Advice March 2016', nor did they determine the extent of any conflict with it.

3. Lang J dismissed the claim and held as follows:

(a) The inspector considered that the community benefit fund and local tariff scheme would not be compliant with regulation 122 of the CIL Regulations and the SoS agreed. The CIL Regulations post-date much of the case law in this area and now, where there is a section 106 agreement, the tests in regulation 122 have to be applied by the decision-maker. Lang J agreed with Gilbart J in *R (Working Titles Films Ltd) v Westminster CC* [2016] EWHC 1855 (Admin), [2017] JPL 173, that the question of what is 'necessary' for the purposes of the CIL Regulations is now a test in law which it was not prior to the commencement of the CIL Regulations. The inspector and the SoS were entitled to conclude, in the exercise of their judgment, that no weight could be attached to the local tariff and the community investment scheme in determining the appeal as they were not material considerations which complied with regulation 122. The local tariff was essentially an inducement to make the proposal more attractive to local residents and to the LPA. The scheme was not necessary to make the development acceptable in planning terms under regulation 122. Additionally, the investment scheme was not a community-led initiative, it was merely a potential investment opportunity and was not necessary to make the development acceptable.

(b) It could not be assumed that the SoS overlooked any aspect of the local planning policies merely because they were not specifically referred to in the decision letter. Nor was the SoS required to make separate reference to an SPD which was to be read alongside the adopted local plan and express reference was made to the plan. There was no basis for concluding that the SoS overlooked or ignored the SPD.

Comment

4. It is now plain that a unilateral undertaking that includes a community investment scheme open to local residents along with a reduced electricity tariff to local residents are not material considerations as they fail to comply with the tests laid down in regulation 122 of the CIL Regulations, and the requirement that a planning obligation can only 'constitute a reason for granting planning permission' if it was: (a) necessary to make the development acceptable in planning terms; (b) directly related to the development; and (c) fairly and reasonably related in scale and kind to the development. It means that officer's reports must make it clear that these are benefits which do not enable permission to be granted, although there is no reason why members should not be informed that such community benefits are on offer, merely that they are not recognisable planning benefits. Such benefits should be kept separate from other benefits that are compliant with regulation 122.

CASE STUDY V

Policies Requiring Exceptional Circumstances in the Context of a Wind Farm Development involving Seven Wind Turbines on Land in Powys

Campaign for the Protection of Rural Wales (Brecon & Radnor Branch) v The Welsh Ministers, Powys County Council and Hendy Wind Farm Ltd [2019] EWHC 621 (Admin) (18 March 2019)

1. The short judgment of Sir Wyn Williams on a renewed application for permission to apply for a statutory review of a decision by the Welsh Ministers to allow an appeal against the refusal of Powys County Council to grant planning permission is set out in full below. The issue of costs is retained as it is not without interest to practitioners in the context of failed permission cases.

> 1. The Claimant renews an application for permission to apply for a statutory review, pursuant to section 288 of the Town and Country Planning Act 1990, of a decision by the Defendant to allow an appeal against the refusal of the First Interested Party to grant planning permission for development encompassing the construction and operation of seven wind turbines with a maximum tip height of 110m (hub height 69m) together with associated consequential development situated upon land near the A44 trunk road near Llandegley, Powys. Permission to apply was refused on the papers by Lewis J. Prior to the oral renewal hearing I was provided with detailed skeleton arguments on behalf of the Claimant and Second Interested Party. At the hearing itself I heard reasonably detailed oral submissions on behalf of the Claimant, oral submissions on behalf of the Defendant which were, understandably, shorter and, orally, Mr Elvin QC contented himself with supporting the submissions of Mr Lewis for the Defendant and adding a few supplementary points of his own.
>
> 2. Unusually, following a renewed permission hearing, I decided that I needed time to consider the issues raised before me – hence this written judgment.
>
> 3. The Defendant's decision to allow the appeal and grant planning permission for the development proposal made by the Second Interested Party (hereinafter referred to as 'Hendy') followed a lengthy public inquiry before an Inspector who was appointed to recommend to the Defendant how the appeal should be determined. In the instant case the Inspector recommended that the appeal should be dismissed. The Defendant took a different view.
>
> 4. At the inquiry a wide range of issues were considered. At paragraph 322 of his Report to the Defendant, the Inspector summarised the main issues to be considered as follows:-

The main considerations are the effect of the proposed development on

(i) the landscape character and visual amenity of the area;
(ii) the setting of heritage assets in the locality; and
(iii) whether any harm identified in relation to the foregoing considerations is outweighed by the benefits of the scheme, particularly its contribution to renewable energy generation and combating the effects of climate change.

It is clear from the paragraphs which followed that the Inspector considered each of those issues in detail and, did so against the relevant planning policy background. No one has suggested to the contrary.

5. It is common ground that both the Inspector, in making his recommendation, and the Defendant, in determining the appeal, had to grapple with and, if appropriate, apply paragraph 6.5.5 of Planning Policy Wales (Edition 9) ('PPW') which reads as follows:-

> 6.5.5 The conservation of archaeological remains is a material consideration in determining a planning application, whether those remains are a scheduled monument or not. Where nationally important archaeological remains, whether scheduled or not, and their settings are likely to be affected by proposed development, there should be a presumption in favour of their physical protection in situ. It will only be in exceptional circumstances that planning permission will be granted if development would result in an adverse impact on a scheduled monument (or an archaeological site shown to be of national importance), or have a significantly damaging effect upon its setting. In cases involving less significant archaeological remains, local planning authorities will need to weigh the relevant importance of the archaeological remains and their settings against other factors, including the need for the proposed development.

At the inquiry it was very much the case for the Claimant and the First Interested Party that the proposed development would have a significantly damaging effect upon the setting of four scheduled ancient monuments ('SAMs'). I understand that those parties argued, too, that as a consequence it could only be 'in exceptional circumstances' that planning permission should be granted.

6. It is at least possible that Hendy took a somewhat different approach at the inquiry to the interpretation and effect of paragraph 6.5.5. The case for Hendy is set out at paragraphs 115 to 159 of the Inspector's report. At paragraph 136 he records the following as being part of Hendy's submissions:

> 136. In the circumstances it is clear that the reference in the policy to exceptional circumstances does not require anything more than a balancing exercise and if the conclusion is reached that the need for

> and benefits for the proposal outweigh any harm to the heritage interest this will amount to exceptional circumstance, albeit it will be prudent to address the issue and make it clear that one had found there to be exceptional circumstances, as Mr Croft acknowledged.

7. It may be (my emphasis) that the Inspector did not reach a clear view about whether Hendy's approach to the interpretation of paragraph 6.5.5 was correct. That is not necessarily surprising since his judgment was that the adverse impact upon the setting of the SAMs taken together with the adverse impacts of the development proposal upon the landscape more generally outweighed the benefits to be derived from the proposed development – see paragraph 409 of the Inspector's Report. That said, the Inspector did record that 'the benefit associated with renewable energy production is capable of providing circumstances that are exceptional given the generally supportive thrust of national policy' – see paragraph 408. As I read that sentence in the context of the paragraph as a whole, the Inspector was saying no more and no less than the benefit of a renewable energy production scheme was capable of providing circumstances that were exceptional. It is worth noting that the Claimant, through Mrs Townsend, does not suggest the contrary.

8. Before turning to the approach adopted by the Defendant as set out in her decision letter it is as well to have in mind the benefit of the proposed development as identified by the Inspector. At paragraph 406 of his report, he concluded that the 'main benefit' arising from the scheme was its contribution to the production of renewable energy and consequential reduction in CO_2 emissions. He described the contribution as significant in that it was capable of meeting the power needs of up to 12,578 homes and it would displace approximately 26,980 tonnes of CO_2 a year. He went on:-

> In the context of the supportive stance of national planning policy and the need to meet increasingly ambitious national and international targets this is a benefit that attracts significant weight.

9. In her decision letter the Defendant accepted, expressly, that the Inspector had identified, correctly, the main issues which were determinative of the appeal – see paragraph 11. At paragraph 41 and following the Defendant set out the benefits of the scheme as they had been described by the Inspector. At paragraph 54 she highlighted the main benefit of the scheme as identified by the Inspector and set out above in paragraph 8.

10. Between paragraphs 60 and 68 the Defendant set out the reasoning which underpinned her decision to reject the Inspector's recommendation and allow Hendy's appeal. It is necessary to set out paragraphs 60 to 66 in full:-

> 60. The Welsh Government is committed to renewable and low carbon energy generation and Planning Policy Wales sets out the need to take into account the wider environmental, social and economic benefits

and opportunities from renewable and low carbon energy development as part of the Government's overall commitment to tackle climate change. In this case I am satisfied the Inspector has considered the relevant issues in full, however, I do not agree with the conclusions of his balancing exercise and his resulting conclusion.

61. PPW notes in the short to medium term, wind energy continues to offer the greatest potential for delivering renewable energy and the need for wind energy is a key part of the Welsh Government's vision for future renewable electricity production. This should be taken into account by decision makers when determining such applications.

62. The Inspector notes the contribution the proposal would make towards meeting the need for national energy targets is considered to weigh in favour of the development. The proposal will generate up to 17.5MW and would provide a valuable source of renewable energy which should be afforded significant weight. As the Inspector recognises, whether planning permission should be granted for the proposal rests on the balance between the benefits of generating electricity from renewable onshore wind and the identified impacts of the scheme on landscape and visual amenity, the setting of the SAMs and other matters raised in evidence.

63. In terms of landscape and visual amenity, the Inspector states the scheme would have a substantially detrimental effect on the visual character of the landscape. I note the proposed wind turbines would be located outside the Strategic Search Areas and Technical Advice Note (TAN): 8 states outside SSAs there is a balance to be struck between the desirability of renewable energy and landscape protection. Whilst I acknowledge the Inspector's conclusions on this issue, I note the site is not located within a nationally designated landscape and the proposal would not impact on any national landscape designation.

64. In this context, I consider the benefits of the proposal in terms of delivering renewable energy are material considerations which are sufficient to outweigh the identified impacts of the scheme on landscape and visual amenity and the balance, therefore, weighs in favour of the appeal.

65. With regard to historic assets, the Inspector concludes the extent to which the setting of the scheduled monuments would be altered by the large and moving structures would represent a significantly damaging effect, in terms of paragraph 6.5.5 of PPW. Paragraph 6.5.5 of Planning Policy Wales (PPW) states 'It will only be in exceptional circumstances that planning permission will be granted if development would result in an adverse impact on a scheduled monument (or an

> archaeological site shown to be of national importance) or has a significantly damaging effect upon its setting.'
>
> 66. Whilst I do not disagree with the Inspector's conclusion the proposal will have a significant impact on the setting of historic assets, however, I consider in this case, the need for development which produces renewable energy outweighs the presumption against grant of permission in relation to the impact on the setting of SAMs. Paragraph 62.3 of PPW states 'the public benefit of taking action to reduce carbon emissions, or to adapt to the impact of climate change, should be weighed against any harm to the significance of historic assets.' I am of the view, in this case, the proposal's contribution to renewable energy targets constitutes an exceptional circumstance for the purpose of paragraph 6.5.5 of PPW, particularly as the identified harm is reversible and the setting of the scheduled monuments will revert back to their present state once the scheme is decommissioned.
>
> 67. Therefore, I disagree with the Inspector's recommendation …

11. The statement of facts and grounds which supports this proposed statutory review identifies two grounds upon which it is said that the Defendant's decision was arguably unlawful, although conceptually, at least, the first ground has two distinct strands. Ground 1 asserts that the Defendant misconstrued or misinterpreted the phrase 'exceptional circumstances' in paragraph 6.5.5 of PPW. Additionally or alternatively, it is suggested that the Defendant's decision to the effect that exceptional circumstances existed within that paragraph is irrational. Ground 2 asserts that the Defendant failed to provide adequate reasons for her decision.

12. I remind myself that at this stage of the proceedings my task is to determine whether the grounds of review identified by the Claimant are arguable in the sense that they give rise to a realistic prospect of a successful review. When, as in the instant case, three experienced lawyers deploy their advocacy skills to good effect it becomes tempting to conclude that the threshold for permission is bound to be reached. However, in cases of this sort, in particular, it is necessary to scrutinise the grounds with a degree of rigour; the judge at the permission stage should avoid falling into the trap of concluding that a ground is arguable simply because it is presented attractively by an experienced advocate.

13. With that reminder to myself, I turn to consider the grounds in this case.

14. Underpinning Mrs Townsend's contention that the Defendant misconstrued or misinterpreted the phrase 'exceptional circumstances' in paragraph 6.5.5 of PPW is the contention that she did not distinguish between the need to identify exceptional circumstances on the one hand and what might be described as the balance of benefits and harm which, necessarily, must be assessed when a decision-maker is determining whether or not planning permission for a particular project

should be granted. She submits, correctly, in my judgment, that the requirement that exceptional circumstances should be found to exist as a pre-requisite for the grant of planning permission demands that the decision maker do more than simply assess the balance of benefit and harm. According to Mrs Townsend, the Defendant, at least arguably, failed to appreciate this was the correct approach.

15. Mrs Townsend submits that this alleged error upon the part of the Defendant has its genesis in the way that Hendy presented its case at the inquiry before the Inspector and, as a consequence, neither the Inspector nor the Defendant examined whether the prevailing circumstances were exceptional as opposed to determining whether the balance of benefits and harm associated with the proposal pointed to the conclusion that permission should be granted.

16. As I have said, there are passages in the Inspector's report which apparently demonstrate that Hendy did invite the Inspector to the view that exceptional circumstances could be demonstrated provided the balance of the benefits of the proposal outweighed its detrimental impacts – see, in particular, paragraphs 135 and 136 of the Report. That said, I am not convinced that there is any real indication in the Inspector's report which suggests that he concurred with that view. My judgment upon the approach taken by the Inspector is set out at paragraph 7 above.

17. What is clear is that the Inspector did accept that in a particular case the benefits of a proposal might be sufficiently significant so as to constitute exceptional circumstances within paragraph 6.5.5. Correctly, in my judgment, Mrs Townsend does not seek to suggest that such an approach, in a particular case, could not be open to a decision maker.

18. In any event, whatever may have been the approach of the Inspector, the crucial issue is whether the Defendant, arguably, fell into error when interpreting or construing paragraph 6.5.5.

19. When analysing this issue it is crucial to read individual sentences or paragraphs within her decision letter in the context of the letter as a whole. In my judgment, paragraph 66 of her decision, read in the context of the decision letter as a whole (including, in particular, paragraph 62), demonstrates that the Defendant did not misinterpret or misconstrue paragraph 6.5.5 of PPW. She understood, fully, that there was a need to identify exceptional circumstances to justify the grant of permission if, as she was prepared to find, the proposal had a significant impact on the setting of the SAMs. She found that such circumstances existed and, in so doing, she was not simply weighing the benefits of the proposal against the harm which, she acknowledged, would be caused by the development. As Mr Lewis said more than once in oral argument, the Defendant chose her language very carefully in paragraph 66 of the decision letter and, it seems clear to me that she was saying no more and no less than that the benefits associated with the proposal before her constituted exceptional circumstances for the purposes of the Policy.

20. Was that decision irrational? I do not think it can be so categorised, even arguably. There was no dispute about the benefits of the proposal. They were set out in the Inspector's report and they are repeated at paragraphs 41 and 62 of the Defendant's decision letter. Whether those benefits properly constituted exceptional circumstances was, quintessentially, a matter of judgment for the decision-maker. It would not have surprised me if the Defendant had concluded that the benefits did not amount to exceptional circumstances. After all, that is what the Inspector found. However, I do not consider that there is any basis for categorising the Defendant's decision as irrational.

21. Mrs Townsend seeks to persuade me otherwise by suggesting that the Defendant has categorised as exceptional that which, in reality, was no more than the inevitable consequence of a development of the type in question. I do not consider that is correct. The Defendant clearly focused upon the particular benefits in the particular case.

22. Mrs Townsend also submits that it was irrational for the Defendant, when assessing whether the circumstances prevailing were exceptional, to take account of the fact that the development had a finite lifespan. I do not see how that consideration can found an argument in favour of irrationality on the part of the Defendant. The duration of the development was, on any view, capable of being a material factor and, in those circumstances, it was capable of being a factor to be taken into account when assessing whether the prevailing circumstances were exceptional.

23. I can deal with Ground 2 much more succinctly. As I have indicated, the Defendant identified the exceptional circumstances, as she saw them, and concluded that they were sufficient to rebut the presumption against development contained within paragraph 6.5.5 of PPW. More generally, she concluded that the benefits associated with the development outweighed the harm which would be caused to visual amenity. Like the Inspector, the Defendant identified the main issues upon which her decision would be based and it is not suggested that she failed to address any of those issues in her decision letter. Applying the well-known principles upon which 'reasons challenges' are to be determined (see *South Bucks DC v Porter (No 2)* [2004] 1 WLR 1953), I have reached the clear conclusion that it is not arguable that the Defendant failed to provide appropriate reasons such that the informed reader of her decision letter could not understand the basis upon which she had reached her decision upon the principal issues. I accept that the summary grounds contained within the Defendant's acknowledgement of service and the points made in the skeleton argument presented on behalf of Hendy demonstrate, conclusively, that the reasoning of the Defendant was adequate and sufficient.

24. It follows that I have reached the conclusion that permission to bring this statutory review should be refused. I make it plain that I am in agreement, wholeheartedly, with the basis upon which Lewis J refused permission on the papers. Inevitably, this judgment is significantly longer than the reasons for refusal

provided by Lewis J at the paper application stage. Essentially, however, my reasons for refusing permission are no more than an elaboration of that which Lewis J provided at the paper application stage.

Costs

25. In the light of my decision on the permission issue, the Claimant accepts that the Defendant should be awarded the costs of and incidental to the preparation of her acknowledgement of service (AOS). The Claimant complains, however, that the amount of such costs claimed on behalf of the Defendant is excessive and that I should direct that a lesser amount should be paid.

26. My understanding is that the total amount claimed by the Defendant is £4,491. Having regard to the hourly rates charged by the Government Legal Department and Counsel (neither of which can be regarded as unreasonable) I would be entitled to reduce the sum claimed only if I regarded the work done in preparing the AOS to be unreasonable. The Defendant has provided an itemised breakdown. I do not consider it discloses any evidence that unnecessary work was undertaken in the preparation of the AOS. I reject the suggestion that the sum claimed is excessive, unreasonable or disproportionate.

27. However, I am also asked to determine an application by Hendy for its costs of preparing its AOS. The sum claimed is £10,164.

28. This application raises issues which are far from straightforward. At the permission hearing I invited submissions upon costs upon various hypotheses with the aim of reducing the possibility of there being additional costs incurred in arguments upon costs. However, with the benefit of hindsight, the issues arising were not dealt with as fully in oral argument as I would have liked. Since the oral hearing I have been sent a variety of documents and some authorities which bear upon whether I should make an order in favour of Hendy. It seems to me the following points arise. First, given that this is an Aarhus Convention case, does the costs cap set out in CPR 45.43 as amplified in Practice Direction 45, apply in this case? If yes, is the cap of £10,000 the limit of the costs which can be awarded regardless of whether costs are split between the Defendant and other parties? If not, what is the proper approach to an award of two sets of costs in Aarhus Convention cases?

29. In this unusual state of affairs I am not inclined to rule, definitively, upon the applications for costs. If the parties seek a definitive ruling I see no alternative but to convene a further oral hearing which, of course, may be wholly disproportionate in terms of the costs at stake. That being so, I am prepared to offer this provisional view, namely that in an Aarhus Convention case the limit under CPR 45.43 and Practice Direction 45 defines the total amount of costs for which a claimant may be liable. In this case the Claimant has been directed to pay £5,000 towards the costs of Hendy by the order made by Garnham J at a hearing relating to interim relief. Accordingly the balance of the cap available to be awarded against the Claimant either in favour of the Defendant or split between the Defendant and

Hendy is £5,000. Again on a provisional basis, my instinct is that the Defendant should have first bite at that particular cherry in which case virtually nothing remains for Hendy.

30. Ultimately the parties may reach the conclusion that this may not be the type of case in which it is appropriate to sort out some difficult problems given that, in order to do so, Hendy and the Defendant may have to engage in the payment of significant legal costs which will not be recovered.

31. In the result, the order which I make has two stages. First, I direct that the parties have liberty to apply as to further directions as to costs. Any such application must be made within 14 days of the date of the order giving effect to this judgment. If no party has made such an application within the specified time limit I direct that the Claimant shall pay to the Defendant the costs of and incidental to the preparation of the Defendant's AOS which are assessed in the sum of £4,491. If the liberty to apply provision is invoked there will have to be a further hearing at which all the issues arising can be addressed.

32. I would be grateful if the parties could agree a form of order to give effect to this judgment.

Comment

2. The case is interesting as it goes to show that the benefits of the proposal in terms of delivering renewable electricity were found to outweigh the impacts on the landscape, visual amenity and the setting of scheduled monuments. The view was also taken that the proposal's contribution to renewable energy targets constituted an exceptional circumstance for the purpose of paragraph 6.5.5 of Planning Policy Wales, particularly as the identified harm was reversible and the setting of the scheduled monuments will revert back to their present state once the scheme had been decommissioned. It seems plain that the threshold for permission was not reached. Indeed, the claimant got nowhere near showing that the decision-maker had misdirected herself or that her decision was irrational. As the judge put it at [20], whether the benefits of the proposal constituted exceptional circumstances was, quintessentially, a matter of judgment for the decision-maker and he did not consider that there was any basis for categorising the defendant's decision as irrational. This was, I think, a case that could so easily have gone a different way before another inspector.

CASE STUDY VI

Varying Conditions whose Effect was to Change the Description of the Development (Concerning Two Wind Turbines)

Finney v Welsh Ministers [2019] EWCA Civ 1868 (5 November 2019)

1. Appeal against a decision concerning the scope of LPAs' powers under section 73 of the TCPA 1990 to grant permission for a development when the applicant had not complied with the conditions subject to which a previous permission had been granted.

2. Permission was granted to the developer for a development described as two wind turbines 'with a tip height of up to 100m'. The permission contained a condition that the development was to be carried out in accordance with a plan which showed a wind turbine with a height of 100m. The developer applied under section 73 to amend the condition to permit a tip height of up to 125m. The LPA refused the application and the developer appealed to the Welsh Ministers. The inspector appointed by the Welsh Ministers allowed the appeal and granted planning permission with the amended condition. The words 'with a tip height of 100m' were excised from the original grant. The appellant sought to quash that decision, but the High Court upheld it, following the approach taken in *R (Wet Finishing Works Ltd) v Taunton Deane BC* [2017] EWHC 1837 (Admin), [2018] PTSR 26, [2017] 7 WLUK 443. It found that on an application to vary a condition to a previous planning permission under section 73, a different condition could be imposed if it did not amount to a fundamental alteration of the original proposal.

3. The issue therefore was whether, on an application under section 73, it was open to an LPA, or the Welsh Ministers on appeal, to alter the description of the development contained in the operative part of the planning permission.

4. Appeal allowed.

5. The Court of Appeal found that section 73(1) was limited to permission for the development of land 'without complying with conditions' subject to which a previous planning permission had been granted. In other words, the purpose of an application under section 73 was to avoid committing a breach of planning control of the second type referred to in section 171A.

6. On receipt of a section 73 application, section 73(2) indicated that a planning authority had to 'consider only the question of conditions'. It could not, therefore, consider the description of the development to which the conditions were attached. The natural inference was that the planning authority could not use section 73 to change the description of the development.

7. It was notable that if the planning authority considered that the conditions should not be altered, it could not grant permission with an altered description but subject to the same conditions. On the contrary, it was required by section 73(2)(b) to refuse the application.

8. That requirement emphasised the underlying philosophy of section 73(2) that it was only the conditions that mattered. If the inspector had left the description of the permitted development intact, there would have been a conflict between what was permitted (a 100m turbine) and what the new condition required (a 125m turbine). A condition altering the nature of what was permitted would have been unlawful. That was undoubtedly why the inspector changed the description of the permitted development, but that change was outside the power conferred by section 73. The inspector's decision was accordingly quashed because it was beyond her powers (see [42]–[43], [46]–[47] of the judgment).

9. The Supreme Court refused Welsh Ministers permission to appeal.

Comment

10. It now seems plain that if an operator wishes to amend the scope of its permission it will have to do so either: (a) by resorting to the power of a planning authority under section 96A to amend an existing permission by making non-material changes (which includes power to impose new conditions or to remove existing conditions); or (b) by bringing a fresh planning application for a different scheme. In other words, the section 73 power cannot be used in a wind farm case as a means of granting permission for a different development as, for example, by increasing the height of the consented turbines in what could well be an area of landscape importance.

11. The section 73 power is quite different in that it gives an express power to apply for planning permission without complying with conditions attached to the earlier permission. It confers power to amend or remove conditions only, but not to amend the description of the development, and results in the grant of a new planning permission. In this case the alteration of the condition changed the nature of the development, whereas section 73 is limited to permission for the development of land 'without complying with conditions' and so avoid a breach of planning control. Section 73 is not a mechanism for interfering with conditions which impact on the description of the authorised development.

CASE STUDY VII

Community Benefits as Material Considerations – Appeal Against a Decision to Uphold the Quashing of a Grant of Planning Permission for a Wind Turbine

R (Wright) v Resilient Energy Severndale Ltd [2019] UKSC 53 (20 November 2019)

1. The LPA had granted the developer permission for the change of use of agricultural land to allow the erection of a wind turbine. The turbine was to be run by a community benefit society. The application included a promise that an annual donation of 4% of the turbine's turnover would be made to a local community fund. The LPA took the promised donation into account as a material planning consideration and imposed a condition that the development should be subject to the scheme. The respondent, a local resident, succeeded in having the permission quashed on the basis that the LPA had acted unlawfully in taking the donation into account because it was not a 'material consideration' for the purposes of section 70(2) of the TCPA 1990 and section 38(6) of the Planning and Compulsory Purchase Act 2004. The Court of Appeal upheld that decision. The appeal to the Supreme Court was dismissed.

Approach to identifying 'material considerations'

2. The scope of the concept of 'material considerations' was considered in *Newbury DC v Secretary of State for the Environment* [1981] AC 578 and is to be equated with the scope of a power to impose planning conditions where there exists a three-fold test, namely: (a) does the consideration fairly and reasonably relate to the provisions of the development plan and to planning considerations affecting the land; (b) can it be said to fairly and reasonably relate to the development; and (c) is it such that a reasonable planning authority could have properly imposed? The equation of the ambit of 'material considerations' with the ambit of the power to impose planning conditions was logical because if an LPA had power to impose a particular planning condition as the basis for its grant of permission, it would follow that it could treat the imposition of that condition as a material factor in favour of granting permission. It had long been recognised that a consequence of the approach of relying on the *Newbury* criteria to identify 'material considerations' was that planning permission could not be bought or sold.

3. A principled approach to identifying material considerations in line with the *Newbury* criteria was important as a protection both for landowners and for the

public interest. It prevented a public authority from extracting money or other benefits from a landowner as a condition for granting permission to develop its land in cases where such payment or the provision of such benefits had insufficient connection with the proposed use of the land. It also prevented a developer from similarly offering to make payments or provide benefits as a way of buying a planning permission which it would be contrary to the public interest to grant according to the merits of the development itself. The protection for landowners on the one hand and for the public interest on the other hand had been established by Parliament through statute. It was a question of law on which the courts had already provided authoritative rulings. Statute could not be overridden or diluted by general policies laid down by central government. The meaning of the concept of 'material considerations' did not change according to what was said by ministers in policy statements. The interpretation given to the statutory term by the courts provided a clear meaning which was principled and stable over time: *Bradford City Council v Secretary of State for the Environment* (1987) 53 P&CR 55, *R v Plymouth City Council ex parte Plymouth and South Devon Cooperative Society* (1994) 67 P&CR 78 and *Tesco Stores Ltd v Secretary of State for the Environment* [1995] 1 WLR 759 applied; *Newbury* and *Aberdeen City and Shire Strategic Development Planning Authority v Elsick Development Co Ltd* [2017] UKSC 66, followed (see [16]–[17], [32]–[34], [37]–[42], [45] of the judgment).

Were the community benefits material considerations?

4. The community benefits promised by the developer did not satisfy the *Newbury* criteria and therefore did not qualify as a material consideration within section 70(2) of the TCPA 1990 and section 38(6) of the Planning and Compulsory Purchase Act 2004. The benefits were not proposed as a means of pursuing any proper planning purpose but for the ulterior purpose of providing general benefits to the community. Moreover, they did not fairly and reasonably relate to the development for which permission was sought and did not affect the use of the land. Instead, they were proffered as a general inducement to the LPA to grant planning permission and constituted a method of seeking to buy the permission sought, in breach of the principle that planning permission could not be bought or sold. That was so whether the development scheme was regarded as commercial and profit-making in nature, or as a purely community-run scheme to create community benefits. The planning permission had rightly been quashed ([44], [58]).

Comment

5. It is now plain, following *Good Energy Generation Ltd* and *Resilient Energy Severndale Ltd*, that community benefits, if proffered as an inducement to the LPA to grant planning permission, are not material considerations, nor can they

be relied on to justify the imposition of conditions. Such benefits are wholly separate from the planning process and breach the principle that planning permission cannot be bought or sold. Planning conditions and matters falling within the statutory concept of 'material considerations' must have a sufficient connection with the proposed development as arose, for instance, in *R (Working Title Films Ltd) v Westminster City Council* [2016] EWHC 1855 (Admin). This case concerned a challenge to the grant of planning permission for the erection of a building for mixed uses, including the provision within it of a community hall in accordance with a planning obligation undertaken by the developer. A ground of challenge relied on was that the LPA was wrong to have had regard to the community benefit from the provision of the community hall as something which compensated for under-provision of affordable housing in the residential part of the development. The challenge was rejected as it was held that this was a planning judgment which the LPA was entitled to make. The planning obligation had been one which clearly related to the use of the land and justified the acceptance of such a planning obligation.

6. It is certainly possible that Parliament might one day decide that the offer of community benefits by a promoter of a renewable energy development would count as a 'material consideration'. In view of the present urgency arising from climate change it hardly seems objectionable in principle that community benefits should not be taken into account in the grant of planning permission for onshore wind development and that communities should be rewarded for hosting wind projects, especially where this might help to overcome objections. There is surely little doubt that the urgent demand for low carbon electricity generation will mean that the government will have to take a fresh look at the planning restrictions that have held back the onshore wind sector. The government clearly needs more new onshore wind development, yet planning is still greatly restricted by the WMS of 18 June 2015 which dictates that LPAs should only grant planning permission if the development site is in an area identified as suitable for wind energy development in a local or neighbourhood plan.

7. Reference should perhaps be made to the general guidance published by the DECC in October 2014, *Community Benefits from Onshore Wind Developments: Best Practice Guidance for England.* The object of the DECC guidance was to set out principles of good practice applicable through the preparation and planning phases and on to the operational phase for onshore wind energy developments, with the aim of securing local community acceptance and support for such developments. The DECC guidance was considered by Lord Sales in *Resilient Energy Severndale Ltd* at [12]–[16]:

> 12. The Ministerial foreword to the DECC Guidance included the following: 'Communities hosting renewable energy play a vital role in meeting our national

need for secure, clean energy and it is absolutely right that they should be recognised and rewarded for their contribution'.

13. The Introduction stated: 'Communities have a unique and exciting opportunity to share in the benefits that their local wind energy resources can bring through effective partnerships with those developing wind energy projects'.

14. Under the heading 'What are community benefits?', the Introduction continued:

> Community benefits can bring tangible rewards to communities which host wind projects, over and above the wider economic, energy security and environmental benefits that arise from those developments. They are an important way of sharing the value that wind energy can bring with the local community. Community benefits include:
>
> 1. **Community benefit funds** – voluntary monetary payments from an onshore wind developer to the community, usually provided via an annual cash sum, and
> 2. **Benefits in-kind** – other voluntary benefits which the developer provides to the community, such as in-kind works, direct funding of projects, one-off funding, local energy discount scheme or any other non-necessary site-specific benefits.
>
> In addition to the above, there can also be:
>
> 3. **Community investment (Shared ownership)** – this is where a community has a financial stake, or investment in a scheme. This can include co-operative schemes and online investment platforms.
> 4. **Socio-economic community benefits** – job creation, skills training, apprenticeships, opportunities for educational visits and raising awareness of climate change.
> 5. **Material benefits** – derived from actions taken directly related to the development such as improved infrastructure.
>
> This document contains guidance on community benefit funds and benefits in-kind (points 1 and 2). The provision of these community benefits is an entirely voluntary undertaking by wind farm developers. They are not compensation payments.
> Material and socio-economic benefits will be considered as part of any planning application for the development and will be determined by local planning authorities. They are not covered by this guidance …

15. Prior to October 2014, many onshore wind developers already provided voluntary contributions in various forms over the lifetime of their projects. The DECC Guidance stated:

> The wind industry through RenewableUK has consolidated this voluntary approach by coming together to produce a protocol which commits developers of onshore wind projects above 5mW (megawatts) in England to provide a community benefit package to the value of at least £5,000 per mW of installed capacity per year, index-linked for the operational lifetime of the project.
>
> Community benefits offer a rare opportunity for the local community to access resources, including long-term, reliable and flexible funding to directly enhance their local economy, society and environment.
>
> The best outcomes tend to be achieved when benefits are tailored to the needs of the local community …

It referred to a number of case studies where community benefit funds have been set up by wind farm developers, e.g. by RWE Innogy UK in respect of the Farr Wind Farm in Scotland (£3.5m over the lifetime of the wind farm).

16. However, the DECC Guidance makes clear the relationship between the guidance it gives in the context of renewable energy policy, and the planning regime. Under the heading 'Preparation phase guidance: Background to community benefits', it states:

> This document contains guidance on community benefit funds and benefits-in kind. The provision of these community benefits are entirely voluntary undertakings by wind farm developers and should be related to the needs of the local community.
>
> These community benefits are separate from the planning process and are not relevant to the decision as to whether the planning application for a wind farm should be approved or not – i.e. they are not 'material' to the planning process. This means they should generally not be taken into account by local planning authorities when deciding the outcome of a planning application for a wind [farm] development.
>
> Currently the only situation in which financial arrangements are considered material to planning is under the Localism Act as amended (2011), which allows a local planning authority to take into account financial benefits where there is a direct connection between the intended use of the funds and the development.
>
> And Planning Practice Guidance states that, 'Local planning authorities may wish to establish policies which give positive weight to renewable and low carbon energy initiatives which have clear evidence of local community involvement and leadership'.

> Socio-economic and material benefits from onshore wind developments are types of benefit that can be taken into consideration when a planning application is determined by the local planning authority and are not covered by this Guidance.

This explanation is in accordance with the general object of the DECC Guidance, which is to set out ways in which the support of local communities for wind energy development in their area might be promoted, rather than to provide policy guidance regarding the operation of the planning system. The distinction was emphasised again later in the document, under the heading 'Planning phase guidance: Planning and the role of local authorities':

> Local authorities can play an important role in supporting community benefit negotiations by supporting the development of neighbourhood, community or parish plans and having positive local plan policies.
>
> Community benefits should be considered separately from any actions or contributions required to make a development acceptable in planning terms.
>
> The primary role of the local planning authority in relation to community benefits is to support the sustainable development of communities within their jurisdiction and to ensure that community benefits negotiations do not unduly influence the determination of the planning application.
>
> There is a strict principle in the English planning system that a planning proposal should be determined based on planning issues, as defined in law. Planning legislation prevents local planning authorities from specifically seeking developer contributions where they are not considered necessary to make the development acceptable in planning terms. Within this context, community benefits are not seen as relevant to deciding whether a development is granted planning permission.

8. In short, the DECC's guidance makes it clear that community benefits are separate from the planning process and are not relevant to a decision about whether a planning application should be approved. Lord Sales JSC said that the foregoing represented 'an accurate statement of the conventional and well-established rule of planning law ...' (at [17]).

CASE STUDY VIII

Permission for Onshore Substation to Support Major Offshore Wind Farm

Planning appeal reference CIN-ELN-001 (22 February 2019)

1. On 22 February 2019 Scottish Ministers approved an application made to East Lothian Council which had been called in by Ministers for determination. The application involved efforts to introduce a major offshore wind farm in the North Sea some 15km off the Angus coast. The decision concerned a planning application in principle for an onshore substation and infrastructure on a 98-hectare coastal site at the former Cockenzie Power Station site, East Lothian, which had been acquired by East Lothian Council in 2018 to promote economic growth in the area. Allison Coard, a reporter appointed by the Scottish Ministers, stated in her report that the benefits of the proposal were:

> significant in terms of overall investment, support for climate change and the government's renewable energy targets as well as for employment opportunities in the construction phase. In particular … the significant investment and employment opportunities associated with the Inch Cape Offshore Wind Farm are dependent on onshore transmission works. Clearly sustainable economic development is an objective of the strategic and local development plan as well as national planning policy.

CASE STUDY IX

Approval of Wind Farm Despite the Turbines Exceeding Local Policy Height Restrictions

Planning appeal reference PPA-300-2052 (25 February 2019)

1. In a decision dated 25 February 2019 under planning appeal reference PPA-300-2052 by Richard Hickman, a reporter appointed by the Scottish Ministers dealing with an appeal against a decision of Moray Council, planning permission was granted for five wind turbines (maximum height 130m to blade tip) along with associated works and infrastructure. The proposed development would contribute up to 15MW of energy. Permission had been refused primarily because of adverse landscape character, cumulative effect arising from further wind energy close and visual impacts owing to the size of the turbines on a site considered inappropriate for large turbines (80–130m) in line with local policy guidance on wind energy. It was the view of the council that the 130m turbines would dominate the scale of buildings, woodlands and farmland. It was council guidance that turbines of less than 100m in height would minimise effects on adjacent settled landscapes and formed the starting point for the consideration of wind energy proposals.

2. It was the overall conclusion of the reporter that the proposed turbines would form a well-sited and arranged cluster that would sit comfortably in their landscape setting, without appearing intrusive in most of the existing views. He also considered that their relationship with existing and approved turbines would be acceptable, both in terms of visual separation and apparent height. There were 30 properties within 2km of the proposed development (some of which were uninhabitable) and it was the reporter's overall view that the turbines would not have a significant adverse visual impact on the residential enjoyment of these properties, nor would the turbines appear overbearing and certainly not to the extent that any of them would become unattractive places to live. The reporter also noted (and attached weight) to local policy PP1, which stated that proposals 'which will contribute towards the transition of Moray towards a low carbon economy will be supported where the quality of the natural and built environment is safeguarded and the relevant policies and site requirements are met'. This support for renewable energy sources was, as he also noted, in line with national policy, which was a material consideration.

Comment

3. The proposal site accommodated large turbines and local policy supported renewable energy.

CASE STUDY X

Proposal for Eight Wind Turbines Fails on Adverse Landscape and Visual Impacts

Planning appeal reference PPA-370-2066 (1 March 2019)

1. In a decision dated 1 March 2019 under planning appeal reference PPA-370-2066 by Amanda Chisholm, a reporter appointed by the Scottish Ministers dealing with an appeal against the decision of South Ayrshire Council, a proposal for planning permission was rejected for eight wind turbines (131m to blade tip) including access tracks and associated infrastructure. The total installed generating capacity would be 27.2MW and the operational life of the wind farm would be 25 years. The site was 1km from an existing settlement and close to three other operational wind farms.

2. Although the appeal site was identified as the preferred area of search for turbines of this height given its large scale and low levels of settlement, the ES identified significant adverse effects on the South Ayrshire Scenic Area which the reporter accepted would be the case. It was her view that the proposal would introduce a new and large-scale intrusive element into the landscape which would break the skyline and be out of scale and character with what was, as she found, a small-to-medium-scale landscape. She also found that adverse visual impacts extended to residential properties within the nearby settlement and further afield resulting in new and large-scale intrusive elements into views. It meant that, despite the contribution which the proposal would make to climate change, renewable energy and greenhouse gas emissions targets, the proposal did not conform with development plan policies relating to wind energy, landscape quality and protecting the landscape which were, as she found, too significant to be outweighed by other environmental and economic benefits (the appellant was, for instance, proposing to invest £3.4 million in a Community Benefit Fund over the lifetime of the wind farm).

Comment

3. The proposal for eight large turbines and associated development close to three other operational wind farms was found to be too large and intrusive in a sensitive landscape despite the contribution to climate change, renewable energy and greenhouse gas emissions' targets.

CASE STUDY XI

Proposal for Five 125m High Wind Turbines Allowed on Orkney

Planning appeal reference PPA-330-2023 (18 April 2019)

1. In a decision dated 18 April 2019 under planning appeal reference PPA-330-2023 by Malcolm Mahoney, a reporter appointed by the Scottish Ministers dealing with an appeal against the decision of Orkney Islands Council, planning permission was allowed for five wind turbines (125m to blade tip with a maximum capacity of 20.4MW), substation and associated infrastructure typical of a wind farm. The operational life of the wind farm is to be 25 years. The reporter considered that the negative seascape, landscape and visual impacts of the development, although significant, were nonetheless acceptable. The wind farm also lay within a favourable area for development within the Spatial Strategy Framework for wind farm development. The reporter also accepted the advice of Scottish Natural Heritage that the impact of the turbines, either on their own or in combination with other wind farms, on breeding peregrine falcons was unlikely to be of national significance or constitute grounds for refusal of the application.

2. The reporter also attached weight to the potential economic and employment benefits of the proposal. The proposal would also add to the case for a new sub-sea cable transmission link to the Scottish mainland on which further commercial renewable energy generation in Orkney would be dependent and had been a stated strategic priority for the Orkney Islands Council for many years. The appellant also offered benefits to the local community in the form of a shared ownership scheme with a low minimum buy-in to maximise local participation. The reporter also considered that the project's displacement of more than 449,500 tonnes of CO_2 over the 25-year lifetime of the project would be a useful contribution to the Scottish government's renewable and carbon targets.

Comment

3. The proposal site was found to be suitable for wind farm development. Approval also gave an impetus to the case for a new sub-sea cable link to the Scottish mainland, which had been a strategic priority for many years.

CASE STUDY XII

Lifetime of Wind Farm Extended on Basis that the Proposal Involved Repowering and was not a Fresh Application

Planning appeal reference APP/M0933/W/18/3204360 (29 July 2019)

1. In a decision dated 29 July 2019 (under planning appeal reference APP/M0933/W/18/3204360), Philip Ware, an inspector appointed by the SoS, gave planning permission for 12 wind turbines and dispensed with an earlier condition which required the existing wind farm (Kirkby Moor Wind Farm) to be removed within 25 years of being brought into use. The site, which is in the Lake District, had been established under a permission granted in 1992. The application under appeal from a refusal by South Lakeland District Council (under application reference SL/2017/0687) sought to remove and vary the original 25-year limited period condition to extend power generation until March 2027 followed by period of decommissioning to March 2028.

2. The NPPF does not define the meaning of 'repowering', and the issue was whether the proposal involved an application for repowering existing turbines such that in policy terms the appellant would not need to demonstrate that the appeal site was in an area identified for wind energy development, nor that the planning impacts identified by the affected local community had been fully addressed and that the proposal had their backing. The LPA (with the support of a rule 6 party, Kirby Moor Protectors) argued that this was not a repowering scheme but a proposal for a new wind farm on the site.

3. The inspector considered that the proposal involved repowering and attached weight to the appellant's submission that within the wind industry 'repowering' is an umbrella term covering replacement, replanting and extension of life and that there was nothing in the scheme which suggested that repowering necessarily meant the physical replacement or enlargement of the turbines. The inspector was also concerned that the LPA did not intend to identify any suitable areas for renewable or low carbon energy for at least five years. The implication of this is that no wind farm developer wishing to extend the life of an existing scheme would be able to comply with footnote 49 in the NPPF (where there is a saving in the case of repowering when it comes to the acceptability of impacts), which he considered to be incompatible with the intention underlying the footnote, although he said that footnote 49 did not mean that it would reduce the weight to be given to development plan policies or that the varied views of local people should be ignored.

4. The site is not in a nationally designated area and although the turbines are visible from many places in and around Kirby Moor, the inspector considered that the landscape was more than capable of continuing to assimilate the wind farm without significant harm to its essential character. Local policy also places the site as being within an area categorised as having a medium/high capacity for wind energy development with, it is assumed, additional capacity for further turbines of significantly greater height. There was no objection to the proposal from the Lake District National Park or Natural England. Although the proposal was also one that would lead to less than substantial harm to the significance of three designated heritage assets, the view taken by the inspector was that this would be outweighed by the very substantial public benefit arising from the continuation of sustainable energy generation from a site which provides enough energy to power 2,700 homes along with a much-enhanced decommissioning proposal and a new restoration scheme.

Comment

5. This is a repowering case and was not treated as a proposal for a new wind farm on the same site where turbines had been in situ since 1992. The inspector had little difficulty varying the original 25-year limited period condition to allow power generation to continue until 2027.

CASE STUDY XIII

Approval Given to 14-Turbine Wind Farm Despite Concerns about 19km Access Track

Planning appeal reference PPA-270-2183 (22 August 2019)

1. In a decision dated 22 August 2019 under planning appeal reference PPA-270-2183 by Claire Milne, a reporter appointed by the Scottish Ministers, permission was granted for the erection of 14 wind turbines and associated infrastructure (having a likely overall capacity of around 42MW with tip heights of 115.5m in the case of four turbines with the remaining turbines proposed at 130.5m) (Dell Wind Farm) overcoming a refusal of permission for such development by The Highland Council. The critical issue on the appeal was with regard to the landscape and visual impacts of a proposed 19km access track on a site extending some 577 hectares to the east of Loch Ness on the western edge of the Monadhliath Mountains with the turbines being arranged across a flat, gently rolling upland plateau. The site is regarded as being generally remote from existing settlements and properties.

2. The LPA doubted whether the design mitigation would overcome the expected visual impact of the track. The appellant submitted that the question of harm needed to be considered in the context of the improvements to the existing track and the proposed mitigation which included inverting the track away from external views and grading so as to leave a rounded and vegetated berm and adopting a technique which rolls back the turf and topsoil which is then regraded and replaced to assist with a more rapid re-vegetation. The appellant also suggested that the LPA's engineer could be more directly involved or that more scope could be given to agree the duties of the Ecological Clerk of Works to oversee such works.

3. The inspector took the view that the character of the area was already affected to some degree by existing tracks. Although new sections of tracks would need to be formed and areas of moorland and heath displaced, the proposal sought to lessen the impact and included various measures which, over time, were likely to reduce its visual effect. Although the light colour of the proposed crushed stone surface might initially contrast with the surrounding vegetation, particularly during and immediately post-construction, it should become darker and partially covered in grass and moss. Further, the reporter found that 1km of existing hill access track was going to be removed and the landscape restored, providing some visual improvement to the scheme overall. Best practice techniques were to be deployed in the construction of the track and, based on her own observations, the

reporter expressed herself satisfied that the visual impact of the proposed track would be acceptable and that any harm would be at the lower end of the scale, albeit subject to the proposed mitigation measures, and would not give rise to any conflict with the development plan, which meant that she did not have to consider an alternative route. Indeed, even the EIA regulations did not require all alternatives, or even all reasonable alternatives, to be studied and it was sufficient for the appellant to deal with the practical and commercial reasons as to why the suggested alternative had been ruled out.

4. The reporter considered that paragraph 33 of Scottish Planning Policy was engaged and was a significant material consideration, given that the local development plan was more than five years old. The reporter considered that the planning balance was tilted in favour of the proposed development and that the presumption in favour of granting permission to sustainable development should prevail. In balancing the benefits and dis-benefits she cited, on the one hand, the contribution to the Scottish government's renewable energy targets (the wind farm had the capacity to generate 2,500GW hours of electricity over a period of 25 years), employment during the construction phase and indirect employment through local spend and as part of the supply chain, along with supporting wider economic benefits, road improvements, contributions to the local eagle population, positive habitat management through improvement of some 10.5 hectares of degraded blanket bog to be set against, on the other hand, the loss of trees, habitats and areas of peatland and some visual effects at higher elevations and temporary road impacts. Drawing all the relevant considerations together, the reporter expressed herself to be satisfied that any adverse impacts of the proposal would not significantly and demonstrably outweigh its benefits.

Comment

5. The mitigation was sufficient to overcome the adverse impacts of a 19km access track. The planning balance also favoured allowing the proposal as paragraph 33 of the Scottish Planning Policy was engaged and was regarded as a significant material consideration as the local development plan was more than five years old.

CASE STUDY XIV

Ten-Turbine Wind Farm Approved despite Landscape Objections

Planning appeal reference PPA-170-2138 (4 September 2019)

1. In a decision dated 4 September 2019 under planning appeal reference PPA-170-2138 by Allison Coard, a reporter appointed by the Scottish Ministers, permission was granted for the erection of up to ten wind turbines (each with an overall height from base to tip of up to 149.9m) along with associated works and infrastructure. The issue on what was a non-determination appeal was whether the landscape, visual and other impacts were acceptable.

2. It was the overall view of the reporter that the landscape effects would not be significant (although it was accepted that there would be some limited localised effects, including cumulative effects arising within the same landscape from other operational turbines which the reporter deemed acceptable) in the case of a site characterised by gently rolling upland moorland with commercial forestry and would also be compatible with local policies (albeit subject to appropriate mitigation through conditions in the case of identified landscape and other impacts). She also noted that the surrounding hills provided some containment and that the nature of the landscape appeared not untypical of that often associated with wind farm development which was consistent with the description of the area in the council's capacity study which referred to the medium to large scale of the landscape, its generally simple land cover of forestry and moorland and sparse population.

3. The reporter also attached weight in the planning balance to the Scottish government's Scottish Energy Strategy and the Onshore Wind Policy 2017, which provided support in principle for the scheme arising on this application which gives rise to renewable energy provision and carbon reduction. The reporter considered that the scheme not only conformed overall to the local and national planning policies, but was also appropriately sited, could help to deliver national energy objectives and could reasonably be considered to contribute to sustainable development.

Comment

4. The proposal site for ten 150m high turbines was in a suitable location and weight was attached to the Scottish government's energy strategy and onshore wind policy.

CASE STUDY XV

Single Wind Turbine on Green Belt close to Heathrow Rejected

Planning appeal reference APP/K3605/W/19/3228083 (12 September 2019)

1. In a decision dated 12 September 2019 (under planning appeal reference APP/K3605/W/19/3228083) Tim Crouch, an inspector appointed by the SoS, dismissed an appeal against a decision by Elmbridge Borough Council to refuse consent for the erection of a single small Britwind wind turbine (25m to tip) on a farm estate.

2. The site was in the Green Belt and it was agreed that none of the exceptions applied which meant that the appellant was forced to rely on the test of 'very special circumstances' in NPPF, paragraph 143. It was the appellant's case that the proposal would not be unduly prominent or obtrusive in the local landscape and would give rise to only limited harmful impact on the visual amenity of the area. However, it was the view of the inspector that the turbine would have an adverse impact on openness in the Green Belt as it would introduce new development into the area. The appeal also failed as it would be detected by air traffic control radar where the turbine, being within a controlled airspace, would appear as 'clutter' and had the potential to risk the safety of air traffic. Although it might be possible to introduce mitigation measures to overcome the issue of 'clutter' on the radar, this would involve 'a modification to the radar configuration' for which NATS required funding and a commercial agreement to be entered into with the appellant. No such agreement was advanced on the appeal, or details of the precise mitigation, or its likely costs, timings or other influencing factors to implementation. A *Grampian* condition (i.e. a condition which prevents the start of development until off-site works have been completed on land not controlled by the applicant) was also rejected as there was no prospect at all of it being fulfilled within the time limit imposed by the permission.

3. The inspector recognised that NPPF, paragraph 147, acknowledges that renewable energy projects in the Green Belt have to demonstrate very special circumstances to proceed. He also gave significant weight to paragraph 148, which identifies that the planning system should support renewable and low carbon energy. However, he found that these considerations did not outweigh the substantial weight to the harm to the Green Belt and to other harm arising from the proposed development. It followed that the very special circumstances

necessary to justify the development did not exist and was thus contrary to local and national policies and the appeal was dismissed.

Comment

4. This was always going to be a difficult application in a Green Belt location, which failed on openness and air safety issues. The 'very special circumstances' threshold is a good deal higher than this.

CASE STUDY XVI

Five Wind Turbines Refused on Significant Environmental Grounds

Planning appeal reference PPA-270-2212 (23 October 2019)

1. In a decision dated 23 October 2019, under planning appeal reference PPA-270-2212, Keith Bray, a reporter appointed by the Scottish Ministers, dismissed an appeal against the decision of The Highland Council and refused planning permission for the erection of five wind turbines with a tip height of up to 125m and associated infrastructure.

2. The reporter considered that the presence of such high turbines on coastal hills (in contrast to other wind farms in the area which are set back from the coast) would become prominent features and would detract from the distinctiveness of the localised landscape character at the Ord of Caithness (considered a gateway location) which is recognised as the boundary between Sutherland and Caithness. Criterion 2 of the Onshore Wind Energy Supplementary Guidance aims to ensure that at gateway locations wind turbines do not overwhelm or detract from the landscape characteristics which contribute to distinctive transitional experiences at gateway locations. It was therefore the view of the reporter that the siting of the turbines on the coast increased the local prominence of the turbines and were out of character with other nearby wind farms. Further, because the turbines also appear to be dominant over the hills that are visible from the A9 (a transport corridor identified and promoted for tourism development in the local plan) the inspector also concluded that the distinctiveness of the localised landscape character was affected by the siting of the turbines so close to the coast which gave rise to a tension with criterion 10 of the Onshore Wind Energy Supplementary Guidance which aims to ensure that the distinctiveness of landscape character is respected. The reporter also determined that the proposed wind farm would also diminish key attributes of the nationally important Causeymire to Knockfin Flows Wild Land Area which covers a large area of the landscape from the proposed site in the south to Ben Alisky in the north. It was also a material consideration that Scottish Planning Policy stated that Wild Land Areas have little or no capacity to accept new development and development plans were expected to safeguard the character areas of wild land which, as the inspector found, had not been overcome by the siting, design, scale or any other mitigation offered by the development. The inspector also found that there would be significant effects on an area of Class 1 peatland habitat (which would be lost), which could not be mitigated within the site by siting and design (there was a lack of clarity over the potential net impact arising from off-site peatland restoration).

Overall the inspector did not consider that the benefits arising from the proposal, including a positive carbon balance, would be of greater importance than the negative environmental effects and consequential non-compliance with a number of development plan policies.

Comment

3. This was another difficult application involving five turbines (125m high) on an unsuitable site close to the coast where the turbines would give rise to serious impacts in an extremely sensitive landscape and was also non-compliant with a number of local and national policies.

CASE STUDY XVII

Single Turbine Allowed where Area of Outstanding Natural Beauty Landscape and Visual Impacts Found to be Minor (Involving Heritage Issues and Local Planning Authority's Declaration of Climate Emergency)

Planning appeal reference APP/Y2620/W/15/3134132 (3 February 2020)

1. In a decision dated 3 February 2020, under planning appeal reference APP/Y2620/W/15/3134132, Paul Griffiths, an inspector appointed by the SoS, allowed an appeal against the decision of North Norfolk District Council to refuse planning permission for the erection of a single wind turbine with a maximum hub height of 40m and a minimum tip height of 66m along with associated infrastructure, a single-storey substation building, access tracks and crane hardstanding in accordance with the terms of the application under reference number PF/14/0925.

2. The main issues involved harmful landscape and visual impacts (the proposal site was located in an AONB), including the impact on the setting of designated heritage assets. There was a specific development plan policy which stated that proposals which were significantly detrimental to the special qualities of the AONB would not be permitted. There was also a policy which encouraged proposals for renewable energy where there were no significant adverse effects on landscape, townscape and historical features/areas, residential amenity (noise, fumes, odour, shadow flicker, traffic, broadcast interference), highway safety and designated nature conservation or biodiversity considerations.

3. The inspector found that although the AONB was clearly a valued landscape, the area of the appeal site was not and he saw no justification for conferring protection on it that went beyond the development plan. Consistently with NPPF, paragraph 193, the inspector also determined that when considering the impact of a proposed development on the significance of a designated heritage asset great weight should be given to the asset's conservation. He also referred to NPPF, paragraph 148, and the need for the planning system to lend its support to renewable and low carbon energy proposals except that, in the case of a proposed wind energy development involving one or more turbines, a proposal would not be considered acceptable unless it was in an area identified as suitable for wind energy development in the development plan and, following consultation, that it could be demonstrated that the planning impacts identified by the affected local

community had been fully addressed and the proposal had their backing (see footnote 49 in the NPPF).

4. The appeal site was located in a landscape which was said to be characterised by generally open and rolling/undulating rural farmland with some elevated plateau and a rich diversity of minor settlements, woodland and historic estates. The presence of some of the highest land in the district gave rise to what the inspector described as long range, uninterrupted, panoramic views and a prominent skyline. The area classified as Wooded Glacial Ridge, to the north, much of which lies within the AONB, is frequently visible on the horizon and was said by the inspector to exert a strong influence on the landscape. This classification related to a terminal glacial moraine, the Cromer Ridge, which is said to form a dramatic, distinctive and influential landscape feature, characterised by a steep, north-facing wooded scarp slope and a more gently sloping, largely arable southern side. The Wooded Glacial Ridge also has a significant influence on the visual character of adjacent landscapes to the north, and south. The valued features and qualities of the area of Tributary Farmland (and the proposal site lay within an area classified in the 2018 update of the North Norfolk Landscape Character Assessment as Tributary Farmland) were described as having a strong rural character with a sense of remoteness and tranquillity, and comprised historic parklands, historic field patterns, woodland cover, hedgerows and hedgerow trees, remnant semi-natural habitats, rural historic villages and vernacular buildings, rural lanes, and long range views with prominent landscape features. It was said that many of these valued features contributed positively to key qualities of natural beauty of the Norfolk Coast AONB. These included strong and distinctive links between land and sea, diversity and integrity of landscape, seascape, settlement character, sense of remoteness, tranquillity and wildness and richness of archaeological heritage and historic environment, particularly that relating to the coast and its character. It was contended that such a tranquil, rural landscape would be particularly sensitive to increases in built development such as wind turbines. Indeed, the LPA had also published, in draft, the North Norfolk Landscape Sensitivity Assessment with particular reference to renewable energy and low carbon development in which the Tributary Landscape classification outside the AONB was said to have moderate to high sensitivity to medium-scale wind turbines (i.e. those with a hub height of up to 60m – the proposal would have a hub height of 40m).

5. It was the view of the inspector that, whilst recognising the intrinsic character and beauty of the countryside, the starting point was that a wind turbine with a 40m hub height and blades spinning to a maximum height of 66m was bound to have somcthing of a harmful impact on the landscape. He said that the true question was not whether harm to landscape character and visual amenity would be caused, but the extent of that harm. He noted that the appeal site would

be on land in agricultural use that rises up to a summit where the Cock Point communications mast, a man-made structure of around 65m, was already located, whereas the proposed wind turbine would be about 8m below the summit but would still be on a site that was elevated above most of the surroundings. There was also an existing solar array to the north-west of the appeal site. The wind turbine would be situated within a large field designed to accommodate modern, mechanised farming practices. Nevertheless, from the footpath that passed north–south to the east of the appeal site, and that to the west which ran in a similar direction, the wind turbine would appear as a prominent feature. It would be similarly noticeable from a local National Cycle Route to the north of the appeal site. The inspector also noted that an undertaking made provision for some screen and other forms of planting which would assist but would take some time to become established. However, because of the nature and scale of the appeal site and the presence of the Cock Point communications mast and the solar array, the proposed wind turbine would not appear as an isolated piece of infrastructure or would be particularly incongruous.

6. The inspector opined that while the proposal would cause some harm in terms of landscape character and visual amenity, the overall impact of the wind turbine would be limited and would also be temporary and reversible and would have no detrimental impact on the landscape character or visual amenity of the area classified as Wooded Glacial Ridge or the special qualities of the AONB or its setting.

7. The inspector accepted that the proposed wind turbine would bring about change to the setting of a number of designated heritage assets but he said that the change would not necessarily lead to harm to significance of these assets. He said that in dealing with the impact on the setting, and thereby the significance of designated heritage assets, visibility from, or in juxtaposition with, an asset, did not necessarily equate to harm to significance.

8. He said that the heritage assets all derive a part of their significance from their position in or close to the rural settlements they serve. At the distances involved, the ability to see the proposed wind turbine from the environs of the churches would not affect that relationship or an understanding of it. He considered that the wind turbine would be an isolated feature and would not mark the position of a settlement. In that way, while it would still be a prominent feature in the landscape, it would very clearly have a different function to a church. As such, it would not diminish the status of the church towers as landmarks and would have no harmful impact on their significance as a result, nor was it his view either that the proposal would harm the respective settings, and thereby the significance, of two conservation areas. He said that as parts of rural settlements, these conservation areas derived some significance from their settings in the

countryside. However, the presence, in some views, of a wind turbine, some distance away, would not, in his view, affect relationships with the surrounding countryside in any detrimental way.

9. However, the inspector did accept that, in the case of two groups of heritage assets, there would be an impact of setting that would lead to a diminution of significance. The first was in the case of Baconsthorpe Castle which is located in a low-lying position, about 1km to the north of the village of Baconsthorpe. It comprised the remains of a late-medieval fortified manor house. The entire complex, which covers a rectangular area of around 250m x 200m, is a Scheduled Ancient Monument (SAM) and the remains of the three surviving structures within the area of the SAM are listed buildings: the remains of Baconsthorpe Castle (the original fortified manor house) are Grade I; the remains of Baconsthorpe Hall (the outer gatehouse) are Grade II; and the tithe barn at Hall Farm is also Grade II.

10. The late medieval fortified manor house sits in the north-west quadrant of the SAM and is surrounded by a moat. The moat had been expanded on the east side of the manor house to form a mere in the north-east quadrant. To the south of the moat, in the south-west quadrant, are the remains of the outer courtyards of the fortified house that evolved into Baconsthorpe Hall and Hall Farm. In the south-east quadrant, there are earthworks forming the remains of a formal garden associated with Baconsthorpe Hall. As the inspector put it, all this added up to a designated heritage asset of the highest order of significance. That significance lay predominantly in the architectural interest of the remaining fabric and in the below-ground archaeology. Notwithstanding that, he found that the complex derived significance from its setting in three main ways. First, the castle in its earliest form was a moated enclosure that depended upon ready access to water and the ability to impound the water around the castle for defensive purposes. This has dictated the position of the castle on the southern edge of a shallow valley floor close to a stream. This position made it possible to more easily create a water-filled moat and secure dry access to the site from the higher ground to the south. The locational logic remained readily discernible and contributed to an understanding of the asset. Second, throughout its history, Baconsthorpe Castle was at the centre of an agricultural estate. The landscape around the asset is much changed from the medieval period and there are many modern features in it, but the agricultural surroundings allow an appreciation of the functional relationship between the complex and its surroundings, and how the wealth that underpinned its development was generated. Third, the complex is experienced in a series of views within the complex itself and from rights of way around it. The shorter-range views facilitate an appreciation of the architectural sophistication of the remains and allow the observer to visualise what the complex must once have been like and to take in planned outward views, in particular across the mere. The

longer-range views allow the place of the asset in the wider landscape, and its isolation from Baconsthorpe, to be discerned.

11. The inspector accepted that the proposed wind turbine could be seen from various places on the approach to the complex and would also be visible from points within the complex itself. However, he said that while it was important that the proposed wind turbine would lead to a change in the setting of the complex, that change need not have a harmful effect on its significance. For instance, the presence of the wind turbine at the separation distances involved would not undermine the ability to appreciate the locational logic of the castle complex. He opined that the nature of the surrounding agricultural landscape had much changed from medieval times which had significant man-made interventions already, such as the present-day field pattern, hedged field boundaries, blocks of woodland, relatively large agricultural sheds, silos, the communications mast near the Pond Farm site, the water tower at Baconsthorpe and the car park adjacent to the complex. The inspector questioned whether the presence of the wind turbine, some distance away, would really mask an understanding of the way the complex functioned in an agricultural hinterland and how the wealth that underpinned its development was generated. The inspector did not consider that, in terms of longer-range views along the approaches, or from elsewhere, the wind turbine would harm the setting or the significance of the designated heritage assets affected. However, he did accept that in terms of views from within the complex itself, and close to it, the wind turbine, while not dominant, and screened by trees to a degree, would still be visible alongside the Cock Point communications mast. It would, in his view, still intrude into the views across the mere and the formal gardens and its presence would undermine the appreciation of the architectural sophistication of the remains in relation to their immediate surroundings and make it a little more difficult for the observer to visualise what the complex must once have been like. In that way, the wind turbine would still have a negative impact on the setting of the complex, and thereby harm the significance of the individual designated heritage assets involved (the three listed buildings and the SAM), as well as the complex as a whole. However, the wind turbine would be far less of a distraction to one's appreciation of the architectural sophistication of the remains, and their arrangement in relation to their immediate surroundings, or one's ability to visualise what the complex must once have been like, than the distractions presented by visitors and their activities, especially when numbers are high or in the case of cars moving in and out of the car park. Put this way, the degree of harm that would be caused by the wind turbine to the setting and thereby the significance of Baconsthorpe Castle, and the designated heritage assets that constitute the whole, would be very slight and at the lower end of the scale of less than substantial harm which again would only be temporary and reversible.

12. The second group of assets which the inspector considered that there would be an impact of setting that would lead to a diminution of significance was at Barningham Hall which is a Grade I listed building. The grounds of Barningham Hall are also included on Historic England's Register of Parks and Gardens of Special Historic Interest in England at Grade II. Barningham Hall dates from 1612, but the current layout of the grounds and the buildings dates back to 1805 when the main house was also extended. The creation of the park also incorporated the medieval Church of St Mary, Barningham Winter, a Grade II listed building, and just beyond, Dairy Farmhouse, which dates from the 17th century and is a Grade II listed building. There are also other listed buildings within the overall complex too, namely the Coach House and Stables to Barningham Hall. The inspector considered the listed complex to be of the highest order of significance. Despite this, the inspector considered that there were only three views of the wind turbine which were likely to affect setting and thereby impact on the significance of the listed assets. The inspector considered, however, that the degree of harm that would be caused by the wind turbine to the setting and thereby the significance of complex of designated assets at Barningham Hall would only be very minor and at the lower end of the scale of less than substantial harm, and while not matters that attracted significant weight in the planning balance he reiterated that the harmful impact would only be temporary and reversible. He concluded the proposal was acceptable in heritage terms. The inspector also considered that there would be no significant impact either on the living conditions of local people and any matters of concern in this regard could be addressed through conditions.

13. The inspector did, however, attach very great weight to the public benefit arising from the fact that the proposed wind turbine would generate around 2,400MWh of electricity annually (net) from a renewable source sufficient to power 600 average sized homes, or 550 in the East of England, and saving over 9,000 tonnes of CO_2 emissions over the lifetime of the scheme. He considered these to be very weighty public benefits which easily outweighed the limited and less than substantial harm that the proposal would cause to the designated heritage assets affected. He found that the proposal complied with Core Strategy Policy EN7, which he said was specifically directed towards renewable energy projects and he regarded it as the lead development plan policy for the purposes of determining the appeal.

14. As a material consideration the inspector noted that on 24 April 2019 the North Norfolk District Council agreed a motion declaring a climate emergency. With the motion, the council acknowledged: the devastating impacts that climate change and global temperature increases will have on the lives and livelihoods of people around the world, including on the health, safety and well-being of North Norfolk residents; the urgent need for action to be taken fast enough for there to

be a chance of further climate change being limited to avoid the worst impacts of drought, floods and extreme heat; the opportunity for individuals and organisations at all levels to take action on reducing carbon emissions, from both production and consumption; the need to enable low carbon living across society through changes to laws, taxation, infrastructure, policies and plans; and the council's responsibility to help secure an environmentally sustainable future for residents and in relation to the global effects of climate change. The inspector further noted that the council had already supported many policy-compliant renewable energy schemes onshore and was playing an active part in NSIPs. He considered that that was, as he put it, laudable, but in light of the matters the council acknowledged in declaring a climate emergency, he said it would be something of a contradiction to resist further policy-compliant schemes in the district. He also said that the proposal readily complied with the council's development plan policy on renewable energy – a policy that was adopted after an open process in which residents of the district had the opportunity to participate in. The appeal was accordingly allowed. Reference should be made to the appeal decision for the conditions imposed on the appellant.

Comment

15. This is a very detailed decision and the inspector's careful analysis of a number of issues typical to wind farm applications is extremely useful. This was a proposal involving one turbine in an AONB. The planning balance was in the appellant's favour when it came to landscape and heritage issues. The inspector also attached weight to the general benefits accruing from a renewable energy project. He also considered it a material consideration that the council had recently passed a motion declaring a climate emergency in which, among other things, it acknowledged the impacts of climate change and the need for action to reduce carbon emissions and for the council to help secure an environmentally sustainable future for residents within its area. The council was noted to have already supported many policy-compliant renewable energy schemes onshore and the inspector considered that that it would be something of a contradiction for it to resist further policy-compliant schemes in the district. The appeal was allowed and the decision is useful as it incorporates the conditions which were imposed on the appellant. It is probable that a number of councils will have passed motions declaring a climate emergency and those acting on behalf of applicants seeking renewable energy consents should investigate this.

CASE STUDY XVIII

Benefits Associated with the Generation of Renewable Energy and Climate Change Considerations still Insufficient to Outweigh Adverse Impacts on Landscape and Visual Effects Could Not Satisfactorily be Mitigated

Planning appeal reference PPA-140-2068-1 (6 February 2020)

1. In a decision dated 6 February 2020, under planning appeal reference PPA-140-2068-1, Mike Shiel, a reporter appointed by the Scottish Ministers, dismissed an appeal against the decision of Scottish Borders Council to refuse planning permission for the erection of a 25-year lifespan wind farm comprising seven turbines 126.5m high to tip, associated infrastructure, ancillary buildings and temporary borrow pits.

2. This was the re-determination of an appeal decided on 7 February 2019 when a previous reporter allowed the developer's appeal and granted planning permission for the development, a decision that was later quashed by the Court of Session on the appeal of Heriot Community Council.

3. As well as the turbines themselves and associated foundations, hard standings and laydown areas, there would be approximately 3.9km of new access tracks connecting to the main highway along with underground cabling underneath the access tracks linking the turbines to a proposed substation. Two borrow pits (i.e. pits resulting from the excavation of materials for use in embankments) were also proposed.

4. The development plan provided broad support for renewable energy proposals provided there were no relevant unacceptable significant adverse impacts or effects which could not be satisfactorily mitigated. If there were then the relevant policy stated that the development would only be approved if the LPA was satisfied that the wider economic, environmental and other benefits of the proposal outweighed the damage arising from it which would require consideration of current national planning and energy policies.

5. In terms of landscape impact, strategic guidance suggested that the landscape character was such that because of existing wind farm developments the area had a low capacity for further wind turbines of all sizes, especially of the large size proposed. The ES also concluded that the effect of the development on landscape character would be adverse. Although local landscape designations did not preclude wind farm developments, they did indicate a degree of landscape

sensitivity which meant that they should be protected where appropriate. The reporter also found that the scheme would be likely to have significant adverse cumulative landscape and visual impacts in combination with nearby wind farm developments comprising a total of 78 turbines with a maximum height of 76m giving rise to potential visual ambiguity created by the differences in size between the proposed and existing turbines (rather than being a coherent enlargement of an existing cluster). The reporter also found that such large turbines would have a significant visual impact on the local landscape and the proposal was addressed from a number of different viewpoints. In terms of its unacceptable adverse landscape and visual impacts (including cumulatively when added to other wind farms in the area), the reporter considered that the proposal could not be satisfactorily mitigated and was contrary to local wind energy policy.

6. In terms of impacts on residential amenity (visual, noise and shadow flicker), the view taken by the reporter was that the effect on visual amenity and the level of predicted noise from the wind farm was not such as to warrant a refusal of permission, nor were any properties located within the area of potential shadow flicker incidence. In terms of ecological impacts, the area was undoubtedly a very sensitive site, but the reporter was satisfied that subject to the good practice and mitigation measures included within a Construction Management Plan, the proposed wind farm would have no significant adverse non-avarian ecological impacts, nor would it have a significant adverse ornithological impact and as such would not be in conflict with local policies. The same applied in the case of impacts on the cultural heritage of the area within which there were a number of archaeological features where it was possible for mitigation measures to be secured through appropriate conditions such that any direct impacts would be of only minor significance. The same also applied to the risks of pollution to watercourses and groundwater during the construction stage and in relation to traffic impacts which would only be short-lived. The position was the same in relation to aviation safety impacts which would be conditioned. The reporter also found that there would be no significant impacts on tourism or local recreation and that the local economy would benefit from the contribution of £5,000 per megawatt of electricity generated to a community fund and from the landowner's rental receipts from the turbines' operator which he appears to have accepted would be of benefit in diversifying and sustaining the rural economy in the area. He did not, however, consider that the short-term economic benefits generated by the construction projects (including contributions towards a community fund – now a common practice for wind farm proposals, although not a material consideration in its own right) carried significant weight.

7. Ultimately, the reporter found that, contrary to relevant provisions within the development plan, none of the economic benefits or general environmental benefits associated with the generation of renewable energy and climate change

considerations (the wind farm was, in this instance, predicted to displace 2,333.5 tonnes of CO_2 per annum – in line with the targets for renewable energy generation of the Scottish and UK governments) outweighed the significant adverse impacts in terms of its landscape and visual effects, including cumulatively when its effects were added to the present baseline of wind farms in the area, impacts which, as the reporter found, could not be satisfactorily mitigated. The reporter was at pains to point out that when it came to energy needs and the need to decarbonise electricity generation, a balance still had to be struck with environmental impacts. He stressed that the current approach still reflected the need to undertake an assessment of the balance between environmental benefits and dis-benefits on a case-by-case basis which, for the time being, until the government altered the planning balance to place greater weight on the environmental benefits as against any adverse impacts, was still based on the pre-eminence of the development plan in arriving at planning decisions (i.e. should still reflect local policies). On this application the appeal was dismissed and planning permission was refused as the reporter found that although the proposal would be of benefit in contributing towards government targets for the generation of electricity from renewable sources, in the circumstances these benefits would not outweigh the unacceptable environmental impacts. The reporter also cited from a Landscape Capacity Study mentioned in the development plan, which contained specific advice that larger scale wind farm development should be located away from sensitive locations, including visually prominent outer slopes, as he found would be the case on this proposal.

Comment

8. This decision is covered in some detail as the reporter analyses the benefits and dis-benefits of the scheme with some care, which are again typical of this sector. The application failed on landscape grounds on what was always going to be a difficult application despite the renewable energy and climate change considerations. One notes that it was also a case involving cumulative impacts in view of nearby wind farm developments comprising a total of 78 turbines with a maximum height of 76m giving rise to potential visual ambiguity created by the differences in size between the proposed and existing turbines rather than, as the reporter put it, being a coherent enlargement of an existing cluster. The seven turbines in this instance were 126.5m high to tip.

CASE STUDY XIX

Renewable Energy Benefits still Insufficient to Outweigh Adverse Landscape Impacts

Planning appeal reference PPA-370-2077 (16 April 2020)

1. In a decision dated 16 April 2020, under planning appeal reference PPA-370-2077, Amanda Chisholm, a reporter appointed by the Scottish Ministers, dismissed an appeal against the decision of South Ayrshire Council (application reference 14/00764/APPM) refusing planning permission for the erection of five wind turbines (up to 110m high to blade tip and having a capacity to generate up to 15MW of electricity annually), meteorological mast, ancillary infrastructure and the formation of associated access tracks. The reporter determined that the five wind turbines would be too prominent in a coastal landscape. There were also going to be unacceptable impacts on the amenity of 14 residential properties located within 2km of the appeal site.

CASE STUDY XX

Permission Refused for a Development Consent Order Extending the Thanet Offshore Wind Farm on the Ground of Navigational Risks

DCO reference EN10084 (1 June 2020)

1. On 1 June 2020 the SoS for the DBEIS disallowed an application by an operator for a DCO to extend the Thanet Offshore Wind Farm.[1] The operator sought consent under the PA 2008 for an offshore wind station generating up to 340MW comprising an extension to the existing offshore wind farm in waters adjacent to the entrance to the Thames estuary in Kent. The SoS accepted the conclusions of the ExA that consent should be withheld for the proposed development.

2. The operator wanted to add another 34 wind turbines to its existing development of 100 turbines, which was completed in September 2010. The 250m high turbines would have added up to 340MW of renewable energy to the grid. The proposal included up to one meteorological mast and up to one offshore substation. The onshore works consisted of cables running from Pegwell Bay to a new onshore substation at Richborough Port then onward through an underground connection to the grid substation at Richborough Energy Park in Kent.

3. The SoS was required to have regard to the relevant NPS (namely NPS for Renewable Energy Infrastructure (NPS EN-3)) which applied to offshore wind energy generating station development. The SoS also had regard to NPS Ports (NPSP), which applies to the development of major ports infrastructure. Although it was not an application under NPSP, the application was treated as though it was as it affected major ports and the prospective development of ports within the Thames estuary.

4. The SoS also had regard also to the Infrastructure Planning (Decisions) Regulations 2010 (SI 2010/305) as the draft DCO included a deemed marine

---

[1] A DCO is the means of obtaining planning permission for developments categorised as NSIPs. This includes energy, transport, water and waste projects. Introduced by the PA 2008, DCOs are intended to simplify and speed up the process of obtaining planning permission for the larger NSIPs. Such applications were originally decided by the Infrastructure Planning Commission but by the Localism Act 2011 this role passed to PINS, as the ExA (the appointment of examiners to conduct Examinations into applications for development consent under the PA 2008 is a matter for PINS), and for decision by the SoS.

licence. Under these Regulations, if a DCO (and thus the deemed marine licence) was granted, regulation 3A would require the SoS to have regard to the need to prevent interference with legitimate uses of the sea which gave rise to a need to address the reduction of navigation risks to the As Low As Reasonably Practicable (ALARP) range.

5. The SoS considered that the claimed DCO would not be in accordance with his obligations under the PA 2008 in relation to the policies within NPS EN-3 relevant to shipping, maritime navigation risk and ports, nor under NPSP in the case of policies relevant to port development. The SoS also agreed with the ExA that the planning balance under section 104(7) of the PA 2008 (as to whether the strategic benefits of the proposed development would outweigh the negative effects) was unfavourable to the application.

6. NPS EN-3 policy precludes the SoS from giving his consent to applications which posed unacceptable risks to the safety of navigation after all possible mitigation measures had been considered. It was the conclusion of the ExA that the applicant had failed to demonstrate sufficient mitigation of the risks to safety of navigation so as to make them ALARP. The impact of the proposed development on navigational safety of shipping traffic in immediately adjacent waters and the resilience of facilities and services (including ports and pilotage) accessed by that shipping traffic were the main issues on the application. The ExA considered that the applicant had also failed to comply with policy which required early stakeholder engagement to ensure that solutions were sought which allowed offshore wind farms and navigation uses of the sea to successfully co-exist.

7. The SoS noted that the applicant had failed to address to the ExA's satisfaction questions as to how much additional spatial allowance should be made for vessels turning around the NE Spit Racon buoy as well as other vessels crossing in the sea area, being a fishing ground and a location passed by a high density of service craft. The ExA concluded that the expert evidence submitted by the applicant revealed a lack of effective understanding with that of the regulators and other stakeholders (which included locally experienced mariners) which, as it was found, presented a practical level of expertise and specific local knowledge and local operational experience that was not matched by the applicant's experts. The ExA had regard to likely effects of the proposal on pilot transfer operations (which constituted an important part of the navigation activities in the sea area under consideration) and found that the proposal would be likely to produce an obstruction to navigation in the space between the existing Thanet Offshore Wind Farm and the NE Spit Racon buoy and the east–west shipping route to and from the Princes Channel resulting in an increased risk of danger to navigation or effects to the shipping industry. The ExA found that such obstruction would increase the likelihood of collision by reducing the time

available for encounter resolution because of traffic compression in a reduced sea area would accordingly increase the risk attending navigation and pilot transfer operations with a consequential adverse impact to shipping in what was a confined sea space with complex patterns of use.

8. In deciding the application in accordance with section 104(3) of the PA 2008, the SoS agreed with the recommendation of the ExA that approving the application would not be in accordance with NPS EN-3 policies relevant to shipping, navigation and ports because the proposed development did not reduce the increased navigational risk to ALARP.

Comment

9. This may not be the last we hear of an extension to the Thanet Offshore Wind Farm. Clearly, new generating capacity is required if the government's target of quadrupling offshore wind capacity to 40GW by 2030 is to be achieved, bearing in mind the time it takes to obtain approval for NSIPs.

CASE STUDY XXI

Development Consent Granted for 158 Wind Turbines off the Norfolk Coast (Decision recently quashed and subject to re-determination)[1]

DCO reference EN010079 (1 July 2020)

1. On 1 July 2020 the SoS for the DBEIS allowed an application by the Swedish energy group Vattenfall for a DCO for the Norfolk Vanguard Offshore Wind Farm some 40 miles off the Norfolk coast, comprising up to 158 wind turbines and other associated infrastructure (involving onshore and offshore areas covering the wind farm including the export cable route, onshore cable route and substation locations) with a claimed generating capacity of up to 1.8GW. Powers of compulsory acquisition for both land and new and existing rights over land were also sought by the applicant to support the delivery of the project. This project included infrastructure works and impacts arising from the proposed Hornsea Project Three Offshore Wind Farm (Hornsea Project Three) comprising 231 turbines with a capacity of up to 2.4GW which will extend the Hornsea Project One and Project Two Offshore Wind Farms farther into the North Sea) which the SoS has said he is 'minded to approve' in 2020 (despite the ExA recommending that consent be refused), and Vattenfall's 1.8GW Norfolk Boreas Offshore Wind Farm which is also scheduled for decision by the SoS in 2020. It has been predicted that the Norfolk Vanguard and Hornsea Project Three Offshore Wind Farms will generate enough electricity to power almost 4 million homes.

2. It had been the conclusion of the ExA that a DCO should not be granted because of potential impacts on habitats and species afforded protection under the Habitats Directive. However, it had been the ExA's view that none of the other matters raised during the Examination process were of such a magnitude, either alone or in combination with other factors, to justify withholding consent. In other words, setting aside all seabird-related matters, the ExA's overall conclusion, with which the SoS agreed, was that the impacts of the proposal were not so great as to offset its significant benefits, particularly in respect of its contribution to the decarbonisation of the electricity generation sector.

1 See page 197.

Matters considered by the ExA during the Examination process

Need for the development

3. The PA 2008 sets out a process for decision-makers to follow in considering applications for NSIPs. In the first instance, the decision-maker needs to consider whether the proposed NSIP is in accordance with the relevant NPSs. The project is an NSIP as defined in sections 14 and 15 of the PA 2008 by virtue of being an offshore generating station with a generating capacity of greater than 100MW. Section 104 of the Act sets out that decisions on NSIPs where an NPS has effect must have regard to the relevant NPS and any other matters that are both important and relevant to the decision. Any decision must be taken in accordance with the relevant NPS except where doing so would lead to a breach of the UK's international obligations, lead to the SoS being in breach of any duty imposed on him/her by or under any enactment, be unlawful by virtue of any enactment, or where the adverse effects of a development outweighs its benefits (the last at section 104(7) of the Act). NPS EN-1 (Overarching NPS for Energy (NPS EN-1)) and NPS EN-3 set out a national need for development of new nationally significant electricity generating infrastructure of the type proposed by the application. NPS EN-1, in particular, sets out that the assessment of development consent applications should start with a presumption in favour of granting consent.

4. The ExA noted the strong need case for renewable energy projects that is set out in NPS EN-1 and NPS EN-3. The ExA also considered the onshore and offshore cables and substations against the tests set out in the NPS for Electricity Networks Infrastructure (NPS EN-5). The SoS considered that the development was in accordance with NPS EN-1 and NPS EN-3 (and NPS EN-5) and benefitted from the presumption in favour of electricity generating stations in general and in favour of offshore wind farm generating stations in particular. In addition, granting development consent for the development would be consistent with government policy and would contribute to the delivery of low carbon and renewable energy, ensuring a secure, diverse and affordable energy supply in line with legal commitments to 'net zero' and the need to address climate change.

Consideration of alternatives

5. The applicant's consultation efforts and its consideration of alternatives (particularly in respect cable landfall, the onshore cable route and the location of the grid connection for the development) were raised by many interested parties as sources of concern. The main focus, when it came to alternative routes, was the cable route from Happisburgh to Necton and the siting of the project substation and an extension to the existing National Grid substation in the same general location (close to Necton). The ExA found that concerns had been raised

by many local people about the consultation process followed by the applicant, along with the applicant's failure to respond to ideas and worries that had been submitted to it as a result of the consultation. However, it was the view of ExA that the consultation undertaken by the applicant was sufficient to comply with the requirements of the PA 2008 and the SoS agreed with this conclusion.

6. As far as the consideration of alternative site locations was concerned, the ExA noted that the applicant had set out its rationale for the choices it made about offshore and onshore locations for the proposed development in its 'Strategic Approach to Selecting a Grid Connection Point' document. The applicant's decision-making on site locations came under scrutiny during the Examination with views being expressed that an offshore ring main, which would consolidate a number of grid connections for wind farms proposed off the Norfolk and Suffolk coasts into a single connection point, should be adopted for the Norfolk Vanguard, Norfolk Boreas and Hornsea Project Three projects. The SoS received representations on this from three Norfolk MPs. There were also suggestions from interested parties that it would be beneficial if the grid connection points for the proposed development (at Necton) and for the proposed Hornsea Project Three (at the Norwich Main substation) could be swapped between the projects. The ExA noted the applicant's approach to site selection for the onshore and offshore elements of the projects and the part that was played by the National Grid in narrowing down the range of options, particularly in respect of the onshore substation at Necton. The ExA noted that the consideration of an offshore ring main was a strategic matter involving many interested organisations and was not suitable for consideration by the ExA in a forum which was considering a DCO for a single site. The ExA also concluded that suggestions about a grid connection swap between the proposed development and Hornsea Project Three were not matters to be considered during the Examination. In the circumstances, the ExA concluded that the applicant undertook a reasonable alternatives process in finalising its site options. The ExA considered that the SoS should be aware of the strongly held views that, in view of the number of offshore wind farm projects coming forward in this region, there should be a strategic approach in terms of contributions towards the development of an offshore ring main. The SoS's view about this was that while acknowledging the views expressed both during and after the Examination, NPS EN-3 states that 'When considering grid connection issues, the IPC should be mindful of the constraints of the regulatory regime for offshore transmission networks'. The SoS considered that the offshore transmission proposal for the development had been brought forward in line with the existing regulatory regime. However, whilst discussions were taking place in respect of the future shape of the offshore transmission network, such discussions were only at the preliminary stage. The SoS therefore considered that he had to assess the development in accordance with current policy as set out in the NPSs. He did not consider that his decision should be delayed to await the outcome of

the discussions on the offshore transmission network given the urgent need for offshore wind development.

Landscape and visual assessment

7. The applicant assessed the potential visual impacts of the proposed development in relation to the offshore wind farm itself, the onshore cable corridor and the substation and extension to an existing substation at Necton. Given their distance from the shore, the offshore wind farm areas were scoped out of the environmental assessment process under this heading.

8. Paragraph 5.9.18 of NPS EN-1 sets out the following guidance for decision-makers: 'All proposed energy infrastructure is likely to have visual effects for many receptors around proposed sites. The SoS will have to judge whether the visual effects on sensitive receptors, such as local residents, and other receptors, such as visitors to the local area, outweigh the benefits of the project.'

9. NPS EN-1 and NPS EN-3 also set out that developers of NSIPs should use good design wherever possible to mitigate any impacts on landscape and visual impacts. The NPPF sets out that policies and consent decisions should contribute and enhance the natural environment by recognising the 'intrinsic character and beauty of the countryside'.

10. The ExA noted that the relevant Development Plan policies for each of the local authorities which had an element of the development within its jurisdiction generally required that infrastructure should enhance, or at least should not diminish, landscape features.

11. The applicant carried out various studies of the potential landscape and visual impacts of the onshore works. In relation to the impacts of the proposed substation works at Necton, there were concerns from local councils, individuals and an MP about the scale of what was being proposed across the two sites and that it would be completely disproportionate to the size of the village (Necton) near to where they would be located and would be a major visual blight. Other concerns were expressed about the removal of hedgerows and trees along the onshore cable route, although agreement was subsequently reached about the inclusion of a suitable condition for replacement planting in any DCO that might be issued. There were also concerns from residents of Happisburgh about the potential impact of the works at the landfall site of the offshore export cable. The ExA noted the continued opposition to the proposed onshore works throughout the Examination process because of visual impact concerns and concerns about related matters such as the time period that should be allowed for replacement planting to take effect.

12. The SoS sought views on this matter. North Norfolk District Council re-stated the need for a ten-year period of remedial work to ensure that proposed vegetation had the chance to establish itself. The applicant's response to this was that it would not be able to undertake remedial work over a ten-year period because it did not, by and large, have land access rights for plots of land for more than a five-year period and it would not, therefore, be possible to work to a ten-year period unless it could secure voluntary agreements with relevant landowners. Where that was the case, the applicant would work to a ten-year window as secured in the Outline Landscape and Ecological Management Strategy and therefore secured through Requirement 18 of the DCO.

13. North Norfolk District Council made the point that this proposal was not secured in the DCO and suggested additional wording for the order to ensure suitable coverage. In response, the SoS accepted the arguments put forward by the applicant and decided to maintain the planting period of five years on the face of the DCO while noting that the period of ten years is maintained in the Outline Landscape and Ecological Management Strategy.

14. The ExA noted that the substation buildings would have a height of 19m with lightning protection masts being 25m tall. The applicant had prepared visualisations of the built structures on the basis of 25m-high buildings to represent the worst case 'Rochdale Envelope' of the substations. However, during the Examination, the ExA asked the applicant to produce revised visualisations to show more accurate representations of the building heights.

15. The ExA carefully considered the position at Necton which would accommodate an extension to the existing National Grid substation as well as a new project substation. The ExA noted that the proposed infrastructure would introduce significant additions to the built environment and that there was no guarantee that it would be possible to screen it to avoid it being seen. It further noted that the development in Necton would represent a material change to the landscape character and visual characteristics of this locality. The ExA considered the extension of the National Grid substation and the removal of one overhead line pylon tower and its replacement with two towers each with a maximum height of 50m. It noted that the maximum height of the extension would be 15m and that it would more than double the floor area of the nine existing substations to cover in excess of 50,000m^2. The ExA also considered the effect of highways access points at the substation extension and noted that the need to clear vegetation from these areas would increase the visibility of the infrastructure for road users along the A47 trunk road which passed within reasonable proximity of the extension to the National Grid substation.

16. As far as the project substation was concerned, the ExA noted that the permanent footprint of the development would have dimension of around 300m x 250m. The applicant had proposed that planting of trees and shrubs around some of the substation (including on top of a 2m high bund along its western edge) would mitigate the impacts to some extent although the degree of mitigation was not guaranteed. Assessments had therefore been based on precautionary growth rates.

17. In considering the effects on landscape of the two developments at Necton, the ExA noted that the substation location was not within any designated landscape areas. The ExA set out that the landscape was typically rural with hedgerow framed roads and that much of the area was productive farmland. The ExA also noted that the location or the proposed new project substation would benefit from existing hedgerow and plantations of trees which would help to reduce potential visual and landscape impacts, although some of the hedgerows would be removed during construction and would be replaced once construction had finished.

18. In respect of the extension to the existing substation at Necton, the ExA noted that the existing National Grid substation was a noticeable feature in the local landscape with the development being slightly incongruous within it. The ExA went on to say that the extension to the substation would add to the impression of a large-scale energy development. This would be exacerbated for some vantage points by the removal of hedgerows during construction. However, the ExA considered that, over time, the initial significant effects would reduce.

19. The ExA noted that for many viewpoints in the village of Necton the views of the substations would be screened by vegetation and the undulating topography. Similarly, in the small hamlet of Ivy Todd, there would be views of the upper parts of the new substation from certain properties on the north edge of the hamlet. The ExA concluded that the most significant impacts would be for walkers and drivers on certain local routes. The ExA's overall conclusion for Necton and Ivy Todd was that there would be no significant impacts on the views of residents within those villages. In regard to the cumulative impacts of the two proposed substation developments, the ExA's view was that someone walking around the Necton area would be conscious of two large-scale energy plants. It concluded that these views would be localised, that there would be no open views of the whole of the project infrastructure and mitigation planting would reduce the impacts over time.

20. The onshore cable route would run 60km from Happisburgh on the Norfolk coast to Necton. As indicated, the cables would be underground for their entire length. The proposed works would also include the ducting within which any

cables from the proposed Norfolk Boreas Offshore Wind Farm would be laid for use in the event that it was consented and taken forward to development. The cable corridor would be 45m wide along its length and would include room for the cable trenches, a 'running track' (which allows construction equipment to move along the cable route) and spoil heaps of the excavated earth. There would also be along the length of the cable route various compounds (including 'mobilisation areas' with an area of around 10,000km^2) that would be used to provide storage and working space for the activities that would be needed to dig the cable route and install the cables within it. At the end of the construction period, the land over the cable route would be re-instated. In addition, for the duration of the operation of the onshore cables, there would be link boxes (of 1.5m x 1.5m dimensions) set into the ground every 1.5km along the cable route. These would generally not be visible. In terms of the onshore cable route's impact on landscape character is concerned, the ExA's view was that the flat landscape and the enclosed nature of the cable route meant that there would be only limited visibility of the cable works. The ExA also noted that the short-term duration of the works and the fact that they would be reversible would limit the significance of the impacts.

21. The ExA drew attention to concerns from Broadland District Council in its Local Impact Report about the loss of hedgerows and trees in hedgerows along the cable route – particularly at road crossing points – and the effect this would have on landscape character. The council highlighted one particular crossing point where the loss of the trees would result in a significant detrimental impact on the landscape character and visual amenity. The council suggested that a trenchless crossing technique (where the cable route would be tunnelled underneath the road in question – a technique which is used at a number of points along the cable route) should be utilised to minimise disturbance. The ExA agreed with the council and the location in question has been added to the list of trenchless crossing points in the DCO.

22. The SoS noted that there were competing arguments about whether trenched or trenchless crossing techniques should be used at Colby Road. He decided that, on balance and with the exception of one road crossing, a trenched crossing would be the most appropriate for this location. The ExA also considered the potential impacts of the onshore cable route on two designated landscapes – Salle Park and Blickling Hall – which would lie quite close to the cable route. Both landscapes feature in Historic England's Register of Parks and Gardens of Special Historic Interest in England. The ExA concluded that the impacts on both landscape areas would be short term and reversible.

23. In concluding its assessment of the onshore cable route's effect on landscape character areas (LCAs), the ExA considered that, while there would be harmful

impacts, these would be limited and temporary. The impacts on the designated landscapes mentioned above would not be significant.

24. The ExA next considered the impacts of the onshore cable route on visual amenity. The loss of hedgerows and trees along the cable route would have some impacts for local residents and travellers using routes along the cable route until the replanting had taken effect. The ExA's conclusion on hedgerow removal was that there would be some localised harm to visual amenity. The ExA also looked at the potential visual impacts of the users of a number of designated footpaths along the onshore cable route – particularly the Wensum Way, the Marriott's Way and the Paston Way. In respect of the Wensum Way, the ExA noted the potential for significant detrimental visual effects along a 550m section of the path following removal of hedgerow and trees. Replacement planting would fill the gaps, but only over a long period of time. The ExA concluded that impacts would be moderate, localised and of medium-term duration. There would be impacts on the Marriott's Way, but these would be limited, short term and reversible. Lastly, the ExA considered that the onshore cable route would have limited impacts on the Paston Way. Overall, the ExA concluded that the Wensum Way would be significantly affected over localised sections, but the other routes would not be affected to the same extent.

25. There are a number of major and minor roads that run either alongside or across the onshore cable route. There would be a range of impacts arising from the onshore cable route with some roads having extended lengths of exposure to the construction works. However, in general terms, the ExA considered that the impacts would be time-limited and reversible.

26. The ExA also considered the potential impacts of the offshore cable landfall to the south of Happisburgh on the Norfolk coast. There would need to be construction works at the Happisburgh site (inland rather than on the beach) to ensure the onshore and offshore cables were joined together. The works would necessitate two 60m x 50m compounds within which two transition pits would be constructed. There would be no workings on the beach as the export cables would be drilled under the coastal strip from an offshore location to a point inland.

27. The ExA considered the impact of the landfall works on landscape character. While noting that the works would be visible within what is a largely agricultural landscape, the ExA concluded that any impact would be modest and reversible once the construction works had been removed.

28. The ExA also considered the impacts of the landfall works on visual amenity and noted that they would be visible for some residents of Happisburgh and nearby Eccles-on-Sea, with the former being significantly affected. The ExA

noted that walkers along a section of the Norfolk Coast Path would clearly notice the works, which would be an unexpected intrusion in landward-facing views. The ExA noted again that this was limited to a short stretch of the Coast Path and would be reversible, although some residual impacts would remain until replacement planting took hold.

29. The ExA noted the proximity of the onshore cable route to the Norfolk Coast AONB (1.7km away at its closest point) and the Broads National Park (less than 1.2km away at its closest point). The ExA considered that given topography and vegetation cover between the onshore cable route and those designated areas, there would be only limited visibility of the works from those areas. Natural England also agreed that there would be no adverse effects on the designated areas.

30. The applicant identified the potential for cumulative visual and landscape effects to arise in relation to the onshore cable route for the development and the onshore cabling works for the proposed Hornsea Project Three. In particular, the crossing point for the two cable routes just outside the small town of Reepham in Norfolk. For a short stretch of the path, walkers along the Marriott's Way would be able to see both sets of construction works. However, the ExA noted that, while there would be some significant effects, they would be localised, short term and reversible.

31. The applicant also noted cumulative effects from the construction compounds for the proposed development and the proposed Hornsea Project Three, which would be located close to the village of Oulton. The ExA considered that while the compounds were reasonably close together, there would be no materially harmful cumulative effects on landscape character or visual amenity arising from them. The ExA also considered whether there would be any cumulative impacts arising from the construction compounds in respect of Salle Park and concluded that there would be no significant adverse effects because of the dense woodland enclosing the Park.

32. The ExA noted that, while the applicant's Landscape and Visual Impact Assessment included the proposed 1.8GW Norfolk Boreas Offshore Wind Farm project (where the Examination closed on 12 October 2020), it was not considered by the ExA because of the limited information available on that project. The ExA concluded that this was a matter which should be considered in the future as part of the Examination of the development consent application for the Norfolk Boreas Offshore Wind Farm.

33. The ExA also considered changes to the DCO to include new or modify old mitigation conditions in respect of landscape character and visual impact. In

concluding its assessment of the impacts of the development on landscape character, the ExA considered that with mitigation measures enacted, there would be significant local effects in the vicinity of the onshore substations which would lessen over time and affect only a small part of the overall LCA. In respect of visual amenity, the ExA concluded there would be localised but significant effects during construction along parts of the A47 trunk road and some minor roads. In terms of the onshore cable route and landfall location, there would be local but short-term harm to landscape character which would not be significant. There would be significant but short term and reversible effects along some roads and footpaths. Considering all these matters in the whole, the ExA's overall conclusion was that the proposed development would accord with the policy requirements of NPS EN-1 and NPS EN2 and would not cause material harm to key characteristics of Norfolk County Council's relevant development plans and policy strategies covering the onshore cable route and the cable landfall. The ExA noted that the impacts of the proposal would be generally acceptable except in respect of the harm to visual amenity in relation to the substation works. The proposal would not, therefore, fully conform to relevant policies in Breckland Council's Core Strategy documents. However, given the localised nature of the harm that would arise, the ExA gave this matter limited weight in the overall planning balance.

34. The SoS noted the opposition to the development's onshore substations at Necton which has driven calls for an offshore ring main to provide a single infrastructure connection point. The substations are very large and local people in Necton (and their local MP) consider that the scale of development would be completely out of keeping with the local setting. However, it was the view of the SoS that the ExA's analysis of the landscape character and visual amenity impacts was sound and he saw no reason to disagree with its conclusions.

The historic environment

35. The ExA noted that NPS EN-1 sets out the cultural heritage/historic environment issues that should be addressed by an applicant for a DCO in submitting its application for development consent and considered by the SoS in determining any application. The ExA noted the presumption in favour of the conservation of designated heritage assets and that any significant impact on those assets should be weighed against the public benefit of the development in question.

36. The applicant assessed both the onshore and offshore areas covering the wind farm, export cable route, onshore cable route and substation locations. The applicant's assessment for onshore areas showed that with one exception – the Blickling Conservation Area – the area of the proposed development and the

proposed works would avoid direct physical impacts on designated heritage assets. However, there could be indirect impacts on designated assets though mitigation measures would avoid significant adverse impacts. Similarly, indirect impacts would be avoided.

37. During the Examination, the applicant produced further information on possible impacts on heritage assets – the Grade I listed St Andrew's Church at Bradenham and the Cawston Conservation Area in the town of Cawston. The assessment of St Andrew's Church indicated that, while the onshore project substation and the extension to the National Grid substation would be visible from a part of the churchyard, there would be a less than significant impact. As far as the Cawston Conservation Area is concerned, the assessment concluded that changes to the town through highway mitigation measures would affect the character and appearance of the Cawston Conservation Area. In addition, there would be harm – identified as short term and reversible, once construction traffic had finished passing through Cawston.

38. As far as offshore areas were concerned, the applicant's study showed potential archaeological resources within the boundary of the proposed development, but noted that these could be avoided with mitigation, including micrositing of assets. The applicant's conclusion was that there would be no significant adverse impacts.

39. Broadland District Council raised concerns about the impact that heavy goods vehicles (HGVs) travelling along Cawston High Street might have on listed buildings in the Cawston Conservation Area. Cawston Parish Council and local people raised similar concerns. Broadland District Council welcomed some of the traffic control measures that would be put in place, but had a concern about whether the widening of a footpath in the High Street would increase the risk of a listed building – Whitehouse Farm – being struck by passing vehicles. North Norfolk District Council indicated the impacts from the development on heritage assets would be less than significant and the benefits of the development would outweigh any harm to those assets. Historic England was generally content that any harm to designated historic assets – St Andrew's Church, Salle Park, Blickling Hall and the Blickling Conservation Area – would be limited in duration and be less than substantial. Residents of Happisburgh raised concerns about potential impacts on the Grade II listed Happisburgh Lighthouse and Cottages and on the Grade II listed Bradenham Hall. There were no real concerns about the impacts of the proposed development on offshore heritage assets.

40. In its analysis of the above issues, the ExA noted the need for a Written Scheme of Investigation to be put in place to inform mitigation strategies. There would also be engagement with the National Trust about its Blickling Estate and

mitigations and archaeological activities that might be put in place. Overall, the ExA considered that matters relating to onshore and offshore archaeology have been satisfactorily addressed. The ExA did, however, note the potential harm to the properties and Conservation Areas outlined above, particularly on the Cawston Conservation Area (through an increase in HGV traffic through the village) and on St Andrew's Church at Bradenham (from the proximity of the substation).

41. In reaching its conclusions, the ExA considered NPS EN-1's presumption in favour of the conservation of heritage assets and noted the legal requirements which needed to be considered on applications for development consent where the setting of heritage assets might be affected. However, the ExA concluded that any impacts on onshore and offshore archaeology would be mitigated by measures in the Written Scheme of Identification which would need to be provided by the applicant. There would, however, be no impacts on the setting and heritage significance on the majority of onshore and offshore heritage assets. The ExA did not, however, consider that the setting of St Andrew's Church at Bradenham would be preserved and that this harm had to be considered against the public benefit of the proposed development which the ExA concluded (in light of the policy support in the NPS for renewable energy electricity generation) would outweigh the less than significant harm that is identified. In the result, the ExA concluded that the effect on the historic environment carried limited weight in the planning balance.

42. The SoS noted that on 8 November 2019, Historic England had notified the Planning Inspectorate of the Designation Decisions under the Ancient Monuments and Archaeological Areas Act 1979 (as amended) for two vessels – The Seagull and Xanthe – lying off the Norfolk coast. These vessels were added to the Schedule of Monuments after the close of the Examination. The SoS was aware that these vessels are located close to the offshore cable route for the development. The SoS also noted that the applicant was proposing to avoid heritage features by way of Archaeological Exclusion Zones and micrositing during detailed design of the development and that embedded mitigation had been incorporated into the detailed project design and that this would be set out in an Outline Written Scheme of Investigation for consideration by Historic England and other relevant authorities.

43. The SoS noted the potential impacts on the historic environment and that weight had to be given to those impacts in relation to St Andrew's Church at Bradenham. However, he also had regard to the ExA's overall conclusion in respect of the historic environment – 'In terms of onshore and offshore heritage assets any impact on onshore and offshore archaeology would be adequately

addressed and mitigated through the measures secured in the DCO' – and agreed that the matters set out above carried limited weight in the planning balance.

Traffic and transport

44. The consideration of traffic and transport impacts arising from the proposed development was a major issue throughout the Examination. The ExA noted that consideration of the impacts was made more difficult by the need to factor in the impacts arising from the proposed Hornsea Project Three where development consent has not yet been determined by the SoS. It also appeared, as the ExA noted, that discussions between the applicant and relevant councils about traffic and transport impacts and mitigations were taking place throughout the Examination process. The ExA noted the position set out in NPS EN-1 in relation to the information to be provided by the applicant about traffic and transport assessments and mitigation measures to support an application and the way that information should be considered by the decision-maker.

45. The applicant's methodology for traffic assessment and cumulative impacts was agreed with Highways England and Norfolk County Council. The main areas for consideration of traffic and transport impacts were the cable landfall at Happisburgh, the onshore cable route and the traffic access to the onshore substation construction sites at Necton (from the A47 trunk road). There was considerable discussion about the substation access points off the A47, with particular emphasis on the safety of vehicle movements both accessing the sites and using the road for other, non-construction, purposes. The applicant worked closely with Highways England and Norfolk County Council during the Examination to address issues about access to the substation sites. The ExA concluded that, with mitigation being set out in an Access Management Plan which would need to be agreed with the LPA in consultation with the relevant highways authority, the access arrangements were satisfactory.

46. The B1145 road runs across Norfolk to link King's Lynn to Mundesley on the north-east coast of the county. Part of the road runs through the village of Cawston. Concerns were expressed by the local parish council, local residents and Broadland District Council about the potential impacts of construction traffic related to the onshore cable route for the development – particularly in relation to the number of HGVs that would need to drive through the village along the B1145. The concerns were compounded because of the cumulative impact of vehicles associated with the construction of the onshore cable route for the proposed Hornsea Project Three using the same road through the village. The concerns revolved around whether the narrow main road through Cawston (effectively the High Street) would be able to cope with the extra traffic, with implications for local amenity and the safety of pedestrians and other road users.

As indicated above, there were also concerns about the impact of HGV movements through Cawston on the village's Conservation Area. During the Examination, there were extensive discussions between various parties to try to address the issues, including the possibility of using a route that would avoid using the road through the village.

47. The ExA noted the mitigation proposals which the Hornsea Project Three operators had put forward for their works. The ExA also noted that the applicant had committed itself to reducing the number of the proposed development's daily HGV movements through Cawston from a peak of 144 to 112. The ExA sets this in the context of 127 daily HGV movements for the proposed Hornsea Project Three works. Norfolk County Council was of the view that it would be possible to produce a mitigation scheme for Cawston, but that it needed more information to do so. However, there would be caps on the numbers of HGV movements using the Cawston route, which would mean the peak flow would happen only over a limited period rather than throughout the construction phase.

48. In considering the issues related to traffic impacts in Cawston, the ExA assessed two scenarios: one with the traffic related to the Hornsea Project Three included and one without. In the event that Hornsea Project Three did not proceed, then the ExA considered that the traffic impacts at Cawston would be acceptable subject to suitable mitigations being put in place. The ExA acknowledged the complications that arise in the event that a development consent for Hornsea Project Three is granted by the time the SoS determines that Application. The ExA assessed the combined HGV traffic that would use the road through Cawston and noted that on a worst-case scenario there could be a maximum of 222 HGV movements associated with the two projects using the village daily. (The existing baseline HGV flow through the village would add another 100 plus vehicles to the traffic flow.) The ExA noted that there would be 34 HGV movements an hour through the village over the 12-hour construction working day – one every two minutes (or more frequently).

49. The ExA was sceptical that the mitigation measures proposed by the applicant in the scenario where the onshore cable route required by both the proposed development and Hornsea Project Three was constructed at the same time would avoid a material harm to highway safety.

50. The ExA's rationale for this is that the narrowness of the roadway, the narrow footways, parked vehicles along the route and the volume of 17 HGV traffic would impact on pedestrian and walker safety and increase the prospects of delays and blockages of the carriageway. The ExA also noted that Norfolk County Council was of the view that an acceptable mitigation scheme could come forward from the applicant. However, the ExA concluded that it disagreed with

both the applicant and Norfolk County Council and considered that material revisions would be needed to the proposed mitigation measures to make the scheme acceptable. In the circumstances, the ExA recommended to the SoS that the applicant should be made to secure a revised mitigation scheme 'which considers each project in combination and the overall scheme context'.

51. The SoS consulted on this matter on 6 December 2019, seeking views on the inclusion of a provision in the DCO that would provide additional mitigation for traffic impacts that might arise at Cawston in the event that both the development and the proposed Hornsea Project Three were granted development consent. In light of the responses received, the SoS considered that amendments should be made to the DCO which required further mitigation measures to be agreed between the applicant and relevant local authorities should Hornsea Project Three and the Norfolk Boreas Offshore Wind Farm be granted development consent.

52. The ExA also considered potential impacts on other sections of road that might be affected by traffic associated with the onshore works – The Street at Oulton (where there would be potential cumulative impacts from works that would be undertaken for Hornsea Project Three), the B1149 at Edgefield, the B1149 at Horsford, the B1436 at Felbrigg, a local road at Happisburgh, and Blickling Road close to the Blickling Estate. In these cases, the ExA considered that mitigation measures would satisfactorily remediate any significant harm. The ExA also considered the use by construction traffic for the proposed development of a number 'sensitive junctions' along the A47 road and the cable crossing of the A47 at Scarning. In each case the ExA noted agreement with the mitigation measures that would be put in place. Although there was disagreement between the applicant and Norfolk County Council over the need for trenchless crossings for the onshore cable route in respect of the A1067 and B1149 roads, agreement was reached that trenchless crossing would be utilised in respect of the A1067.

53. There was, however, considerable debate about the best way for the onshore cable route to cross the B1149 north of Cawston, which would be used by construction traffic for the onshore cable route for the proposed development and the proposed Hornsea Project Three. Norfolk County Council was adamant that trenchless crossing techniques should be used while the applicant sought to utilise its trenching option supported by changes to traffic management measures. The ExA concluded that the B1149 should be subject to trenchless crossing for the onshore cable route. However, the ExA did note that the need for trenchless crossing of the B1149 would be avoided if consent for Hornsea Project Three was not granted as it would be easier to manage the traffic from a single development.

54. The ExA made a number of suggestions to modify the DCO that might be granted by the SoS. In its conclusion, the ExA pointed out that the construction

of such projects will always generate an increase in traffic movements – often HGVs. However, the ExA considered that these impacts would be acceptable subject to the adoption of suitable mitigation measures to be set out in the proposed DCO to be submitted to the SoS by the ExA.

55. The SoS acknowledged that the traffic impacts from the development on local people and their villages and the ability to move around the local area were of concern to many parties potentially affected by them and that such impacts would be spread over many months. However, in light of the ExA's conclusions, the responses to the SoS's consultation and the inclusion of suitable wording in the DCO, the SoS considered that there was no reason why traffic impacts should prevent the grant of consent.

Socio-economic impacts

56. Discussions about socio-economic impacts concerned the potential for community benefits, job creation and the potential (adverse) impacts the project would have on tourism. The ExA noted that NPS EN-1 requires that applicants for development consent should make an assessment of socio-economic impacts and of the existing socio-economic setting. The ExA also noted that there were a number of local policies on socio-economics which also needed to be considered.

57. The applicant provided a socio-economic analysis of the impacts of the proposed development. On employment opportunities, the applicant estimated the proposed development might create more than 1,000 full-time equivalent jobs during its construction and around 290 full-time equivalent jobs during its operation: the jobs would generally be filled by workers from the East Anglian jobs market. The onshore cable route would employ between 250 and 420 people in the summers of 2022 and 2023. More generally, the applicant was working with local businesses and representative bodies to look at local economic benefits arising from the development.

58. On community benefits, the ExA noted that there were strong local calls for a community fund to be set up but that the applicant had argued these were not directly related to planning issues and so should not be dealt with as part of the Examination process. On tourism, the applicant recorded moderate adverse short-term impacts in the vicinity of the landfall works (at Happisburgh) although there were claims that there would also be an impact on some holiday lets in the vicinity of the substations.

59. North Norfolk District Council made strong representations during the Examination about the potential harm that the proposed development would have on the local tourist sector. The council sought the inclusion of a Requirement in

any DCO that might be made to require the applicant to contribute to organisations that aimed to boost local tourism to increase tourist footfall across the area. The applicant disputed the rationale for such a requirement, arguing that it was unnecessary and unlawful.

60. In considering the various issues raised under the socio-economic heading, the ExA noted that the wording of the council's proposed Requirement was not justified in light of the absence of any authoritative information that there would be an actual or perceived impact on tourism and the case has not been made for its inclusion in a DCO. In respect of the other socio-economic matters mentioned above, the ExA concluded that the jobs and skills package proposed by the applicant would be capable of supporting the region's aspirations and achieving sustainable economic growth. The SoS saw no reason to disagree with the ExA's conclusions under this head.

Contamination and ground conditions

61. This issue was a major concern for local people, with particular focus on the possibility of residual impacts from the crash of a Royal Danish Air Force F-16 fighter plane in 1996 which came down in the vicinity of Necton, close to the proposed site of the substation and over part of the cable corridor. In line with the requirements of NPS EN-1, the applicant produced an assessment of potential risks from contaminated land. The applicant's overall conclusion was that, provided embedded and proposed mitigation measures were put in place, there would be only minor adverse effects arising from the development.

62. However, the crash site was not included in the applicant's risk assessment. The particular concern for local people was the possibility that some of the remains of the plane and its various contaminants might remain below ground and could be disturbed by the construction work on the substation and onshore cable route. The concern covered the possibility that the crash site had not been cleared properly leaving radioactive contaminants, hydrazine (which is highly toxic and unstable), oil and shards of carbon fibre in situ. One member of the public raised the possibility of a cancer cluster in the vicinity of the crash (although the cluster had not been investigated by Public Health England).

63. The Environment Agency stated during the Examination that it had not been established whether the land around the crash site was contaminated by radioactivity. The Environment Agency also said that based on the records kept by the RAF, there was little risk of contamination of water courses or aquifers and any impacts were likely to be localised and risks appeared to have been addressed and mitigated. The Environment Agency did not, therefore, see the need for a site investigation prior to the commencement of the development, but stated that a

discovery strategy should be in place during the works in case contamination was discovered. Necton Parish Council was also content that the applicant's commitment to produce a Contaminated Land and Groundwater Plan as part of its Code of Construction Practice was adequate to deal with potential contamination at the site. The ExA acknowledged the concerns of local people about the potential for contamination of the land at the site of the plane crash. However, it was satisfied that appropriate mechanisms for the discovery and remediation of any discoveries would be secured in a DCO that might be granted by the SoS. Overall, the ExA concluded that any adverse impacts would be mitigated by conditions in the DCO and that there would be no significant adverse impacts. The ExA considered, therefore, that the development would accord with NPS EN-1 and with the NPPF. The SoS acknowledged that the question of possible contamination at the crash site had generated strong feelings among people living in proximity to the site. However, the ExA's analysis of the issue was considered robust and mitigation would be put in place in the event any contamination was discovered, and the SoS saw no reason to disagree with the ExA's conclusions.

Coastal change

64. This was an important matter for residents of Happisburgh where cable landfall would be made in a context of an increasing rate of coastal erosion along that section of coastline. The matter was also of concern to North Norfolk District Council, Natural England and Happisburgh Parish Council and there were discussions throughout the Examination about it. The applicant's case was that its approach to horizontal drilling of the cable under the beach and cliffs adopted a conservative approach which took account of the retreat of the coast and cliff lines over time. The applicant also argued that the development would not have any impact on the coastal erosion processes. There was, however, agreement that the applicant's design of the cable landfall at Happisburgh appropriately factored in coastal retreat and that mitigation measures secured in the DCO would provide further comfort. The ExA concluded that the cable landfall as proposed would neither exacerbate coastal erosion nor be affected by it and that the development would be in accord with the relevant provisions of NPS EN-1. The SoS saw no reason to disagree with the ExA's conclusion under this head.

Flood risk and water resources

65. The ExA noted a policy requirement in NPS EN-1 in relation to the potential impacts of national significant energy infrastructure projects on the water environment and the need for applicants to assess these impacts and for the decision-maker to consider them against a range of relevant issues (e.g. flood risk, requirements of the Water Framework Directive, etc).

66. The applicant's assessment recorded that most of the development (including the onshore project substation and the extension to the National Grid substation) would lie within the low-risk Flood Zone 1 designation, although some parts of the onshore cable route would be in areas with Flood Zone 2 and Flood Zone 3 designations. Various mitigations were proposed which would be secured by requirements in the DCO. Norfolk County Council, as Lead Local Flood Authority initially had concerns about the design of the onshore substation and the wording of some of the proposed Requirements in the DCO, but was in agreement with the applicant on these issues by the end of the Examination. The Environment Agency also had concerns about certain aspects of the development. More specifically, there were concerns from members of the public and landowners about the possibility that all the onshore components of the proposed development would increase the risk of flooding – with an existing flooding issue near Necton (in the vicinity of the onshore substations) being mentioned as a particular issue.

67. In considering the issue, the ExA noted that the applicant's assessment methodology for flood risk and water resources was agreed with Norfolk County Council and the Environment Agency. The ExA also noted that various mitigation measures would be included in any DCO that might be made. As far as the flooding near Necton was concerned, the ExA concluded that the drainage systems that would be put in place at the onshore substations would mean the presence of those structures would not exacerbate the existing risk of flooding. The ExA concluded that it was unlikely the development would cause any significant impacts on flood risk or water resources. It meant that the development would accord with the requirements of NPS EN-1 and that this matter should not weigh against a DCO being made. The SoS saw no reason to disagree with the ExA's position.

Noise and vibration

68. This topic covered the noise and vibration arising from the construction and operation of the onshore elements of the development. Airborne noise from the construction operation and decommissioning of the offshore wind farm element of the development were scoped out of the noise and vibration assessment. The ExA noted that NPS EN-1 highlights the adverse effect that excessive noise and vibration can have on human health and that development consent should not be granted unless significant impacts on health and quality of life can be avoided. NPS EN-5 refers to noise from substations and sets out that where an applicant has demonstrated that appropriate mitigation measures can be put in place then it should be possible for the decision-taker to give limited weight to residual noise impacts.

69. The applicant identified some areas where there would be significant noise impacts in a worst-case situation. However, it would be possible to mitigate those impacts to reduce them to negligible. It was noted that there were proposals for 24-hour working at some locations along the onshore cable route. There were many concerns about the potential impact of the development's onshore elements, particularly in respect of construction noise, noise and vibration from HGV movements (especially at Cawston and Oulton, where there would be considerable numbers of such movements because of the cumulative impacts of the development and the proposed Hornsea Project Three) and noise from the operational substations. Residents of Necton had concerns about the potential impact of the construction of the substations near their village, having experienced the impact of the construction of the substation that services the Dudgeon offshore wind farm.

70. The ExA noted the range of concerns that had been expressed about the noise and vibration impacts of the development and acknowledged the adverse impacts that excessive noise and vibration could have on human health. However, the ExA also noted the extensive mitigation measures that would be put in place by the applicant requiring approval from the relevant planning authorities to limit those impacts and considered that these measures would provide adequate safeguards for residents and others potentially affected by the construction and operation of the development. While there would be some minor adverse effects, the ExA concluded that impacts would be minimised and mitigated in accordance with the provisions of NPS EN-1 and attracted only limited weight in the planning balance.

71. Notwithstanding the ExA's general position, the SoS did consult about how mitigation measures in this matter might be given effect and suggested amended wording for the DCO to do this. In light of responses received, the SoS incorporated his suggested wording into the DCO and agreed with the ExA's overall conclusion in this matter.

Air quality

72. This topic covered air quality impacts from the construction and decommissioning of the onshore elements (the offshore elements and the onshore operational impacts were scoped out of the applicant's assessment as they were negligible).

73. NPS EN-1 sets out that large infrastructure projects can have adverse effects on air quality which may lead to impacts on health. Significant weight is to be given to air quality issues in situations where a deterioration in air quality was likely to result or where national air quality limits would be breached. The

applicant considered that air quality impacts could arise from the construction and decommissioning of the onshore works, with the primary sources being dust and vehicle emissions. The applicant had identified a suite of mitigation measures which would form part of an Air Quality Management Plan that would sit within a Construction Code of Practice, which would be secured by a condition in the DCO. The applicant noted that the Swaffham Air Quality Management Area would be 1km south of the A47 road, but anticipated that as no construction traffic would be going through Swaffham there would be no increase in pollution concentrations in the Air Quality Management Area. The applicant's overall conclusion at the time of application was that mitigation measures would mean any air quality impacts (for the project alone and in combination with other plans or projects) would not be significant.

74. Emissions of dust from construction activities and emissions from vehicles engaged in those activities were raised as concerns by a number of interested parties to the Examination, including Cawston Parish Council (with concerns about pollution from vehicle movements) and Oulton Parish Council. While noting concerns about adverse air quality impacts arising from the development, the ExA was satisfied that the applicant had appropriately addressed air quality matters and that suitable mitigation would be put in place to limit any air quality impacts arising from the development. The ExA concluded that local air quality objectives would not be breached and predicted pollution levels would be below air quality objectives for all receptors. There would also be adequate mitigation for dust emissions. Accordingly, the ExA concluded that the development would be in accordance with NPS EN-1 and that air quality matters should not weigh against the DCO being made. The SoS saw no reason to disagree with the ExA's conclusions under this head.

Human health

75. The Examination considered impacts on human health in respect of the onshore works only as it was not considered there were any sensitive receptors in close enough proximity to the offshore works to trigger any human health impacts.

76. Large energy infrastructure projects have the potential to affect the health of people in their vicinity. The ExA noted that NPS EN-1 sets out that significant health impacts arising from those projects are likely to be subject to separate legislation which would constitute effective mitigation. It was unlikely, therefore, that health impacts would constitute a reason to refuse consent or require mitigation. However, the decision-taker would need to consider health impacts when looking to set conditions relating to potential impacts.

77. The ExA further noted that NPS EN-5 refers to electromagnetic fields generated by electric cables and their potential impacts on human health. While primarily an issue for overhead lines (the potential for electromagnetic fields is diminished by the undergrounding of electric cables), NPS EN-5 requires the decision-taker to be satisfied that any infrastructure proposal was in accordance with the International Commission on Non-Ionizing Radiation Protection (ICNIRP) Guidelines. NPS EN-5 concludes that where exposure to electromagnetic fields was within ICNIRP reference levels, then mitigation is unlikely to be required.

78. The applicant produced an assessment of potential health effects arising from the onshore elements of the development. With the implementation of mitigations, the assessment concluded that the health impacts on the general population would be negligible though with an increased potential for minor adverse effects on older people and those with existing health conditions. The assessment also looked at impacts from electromagnetic fields in light of guidelines from Public Health England, which identified a threshold above which there could be potential health effects. The applicant concluded that the level of electromagnetic fields produced by the development, even taking account of the potential impact of the cables for the Hornsea Project Six Offshore Wind Farm, would still be well below the level set in the Public Health England Guidelines. Many interested parties, including Cawston Parish Council and Oulton Parish Council, raised concerns about the health impacts of the electromagnetic fields associated with the cabling. Several interested parties also raised concerns about the levels of stress that had been generated by the proposals for the proposed development's onshore works. The ExA concluded that the electromagnetic fields produced by the cabling for the proposed development would be within the ICNIRP Guidelines and the in combination effects at the crossing point for Hornsea Project Three would also meet those tests. It accordingly concluded that the development would, therefore, meet the requirement of NPS EN-5. Overall, the ExA also concluded that the development would not give rise to any significant mental or physical health impacts and would, therefore, comply with NPS EN-1. Health impacts should not, therefore, weigh against a DCO being granted. The SoS saw no reason to disagree with the ExA's conclusions about these matters.

Onshore ecology and ornithology

79. The NSPs provide extensive references to the considerations that the applicant must address in framing applications for development consent for energy NSIPs and that the decision-taker must weigh in the balance in considering whether to grant development consent. The NPPF takes a similar line. Relevant

UK and European legislation and local development plans must also be considered.

80. The applicant submitted a wide range of documents as part of its ES which formed part of its application. Potential impacts on a broad range of potentially affected flora and fauna were considered and mitigation measures were proposed. All statutory and non-statutory sites within the Order land had been avoided except for the River Wensum Special Area of Conservation and Site of Special Scientific Interest (SSSI) which would be avoided by the use of the trenchless crossing technique. There would be impacts on hedgerows with consequential impacts on bats. However, these were expected to be of temporary duration until the hedgerows were reinstated.

81. The key matters considered during the Examination were: impacts on groundwater; bird features of SSSIs; the sand martin colony at Happisburgh Cliffs; nesting birds; monitoring; and air quality and Felbrigg Great Wood SSSI. There were some concerns about whether enough ecological surveying had been carried out over some parts of the onshore cable route, but the ExA considered that sufficient baseline information had been provided to allow an assessment of impacts to be undertaken.

82. In considering the potential impacts on onshore ecology and ornithology, the ExA noted that there was agreement with relevant parties about mitigation proposals. The ExA further noted that all ecological management proposals put forward by the applicant were set out in the Outline Landscape and Management Environmental Strategy and these would be further secured by inclusion in an Environmental Management Plan, which would need to be approved by the relevant LPA in consultation with Natural England. The Environment Management Plan would be conditioned in the DCO. In the event consent was granted, there would also be surveying of those areas which had not been covered in the application process.

83. The ExA concluded that the mitigations proposed by the applicant in its pre-application consideration of alternative routes/locations for the development's onshore works and in any post-consent DCO would avoid significant harm to onshore ecological interests. There would be some adverse impacts on bats through hedgerow loss, but these would be short term in nature. In general, relevant policy considerations had been met and the Assessment Principles set out in NPS EN-1 had been followed. The SoS noted that a representation from the Necton Substation Action Group had been submitted to him on 26 June 2020 drawing attention to the sighting of a red kite close to the location of the electricity substation at Necton. The representation was accompanied by an email from the British Trust for Ornithology stating that red kites were 'increasing in Norfolk

and breeding is more widespread than just a few years ago … and it is likely that a pair are now breeding in your area'. The SoS noted that the submission from the Necton Substation Action Group did not provide evidence that the development would have an impact on red kites and that the ExA did not make any reference to impacts on red kites having been raised by parties to the Examination (including by Natural England). The SoS therefore considered that this factor did not materially influence his consideration of the application. Overall, the SoS saw no reason to disagree with the ExA's conclusions on onshore ecology and ornithology.

Land use

84. The NSPs for Energy sets out that energy NSIPs should aim to minimise impacts on best quality agricultural land (classified as Grade 1, 2 and 3a under the Agricultural Land Classification (ALC)) and should instead use land of poorer quality (Grade 3b, 4 and 5 under the ALC). NPS EN-1 also requires developers to consider and minimise effects on uses of land including for recreational purposes.

85. The applicant claimed that the majority of the land that would be used by the onshore works was agricultural land with Grade 1–4 classification under the ALC though mainly between Grades 2 and 3. The onshore project substation would be located on ALC Grade 3 land. An assessment of impacts without mitigation measures in place ranged from 'no impact' to 'moderate adverse' (at the extension to the National Grid substation extension). There would also be impacts of moderate adverse significance on land drainage systems during construction of the development and the Hornsea Project Three proposal. As far as impacts on recreation were concerned, the applicant claimed that tourist sites had been avoided for onshore works. However, around 45 public rights of way would be intersected by the onshore works. There were also potential impacts in the coastal area where cable landfall would be made. The applicant had committed to working with Norfolk County Council to ensure any impacts were only temporary across the full range of the project. The updated Statement of Common Ground between the applicant and Norfolk County Council showed that all matters relating to recreation had been agreed. At the end of the Examination, the only outstanding matters related to concerns by the National Farmers' Union about certain compulsory acquisition matters (considered elsewhere) and potential impacts on farmland. In respect of the latter, the applicant amended its Outline Code of Construction Practice to address the issues.

86. In its consideration of these issucs thc ExA noted that, while there would be impacts on agricultural land – including the loss of some higher grade land – these would be set in the context of occurring over a very small proportion of

agricultural land of similar grade within Norfolk and generally being of temporary duration. The ExA noted that agreements would be in place with affected parties to minimise impacts, including with the developer of the proposed Hornsea Project Three. On recreational impacts, the ExA was satisfied that mitigation measures, including horizontal directional drilling where necessary to cross heavily used public rights of way, and the advertising of alternative routes while rights of way were closed by construction activity, would mitigate impacts. The ExA's overall conclusion was that land use impacts would be appropriately mitigated and any loss of good quality agricultural land would be justified by the benefits of the development. The SoS saw no reason to disagree with the ExA's conclusion under this head.

Commercial fisheries

87. The ExA noted that the applicant had identified some impacts on commercial fishing interests arising from the offshore cabling and wind farm elements of the development ranging from 'negligible' to 'minor adverse' for vessels from the UK and other countries. (There would be minor adverse impacts for UK beam trawlers and UK inshore fishing vessels.) A number of concerns about the development were raised by the UK (by the National Federation of Fishermen's Organisations (NFFO)) and foreign representatives of fishing interests. One of the NFFO's concerns was the possibility of floating wind turbines being used for the wind farm but the applicant discounted this option. The NFFO was also concerned about the likely spacing of wind turbines as this would affect the sort of fishing activity that might take place within the wind farm area. The applicant indicated it would be able to increase the spacing of turbines within the wind farm because of a reduction (to 180) in the number of turbines that would be deployed. The ExA noted that the applicant's proposed increase in spacing would still not meet the NFFO's desired spacings. (The applicant eventually revised down the number of turbines that would be deployed to a maximum of 158.)

88. Further concerns were expressed by fishing representative organisations about areas of the North Sea being closed to specific fishing activities and the cumulative impact the closures and the proposed development would have on the activities of fishermen. As a result, the applicant amended its assessment of potential impacts and concluded that for certain activities carried out by Dutch or Anglo-Dutch fishing vessels, the cumulative impact would be of 'moderate adverse' significance which was greater than first predicted. In considering commercial fisheries, the ExA noted that some commercial fishing activity would be possible within the wind farm array. The ExA also noted that the proposed closure of areas of the North Sea to fishing activity would have an impact, but that, given the relevant designations had not yet been made, only limited weight

could be given to the impact this might generate. At the close of the Examination, there was still disagreement between the NFFO and VisNed (the Dutch fishing representative organisation) about whether fishing would be possible within the wind farm array. The ExA concluded that while some commercial fishing would be possible, there would be an impact from the development combined with the closure of areas to fishing activity. The ExA concluded that the requirements of NPS EN-1 and NPS EN-3 had nonetheless been met and the SoS saw no reason to disagree with this.

Shipping and navigation

89. NPS EN-3 sets out very clearly that NSIPs should avoid or minimise disruption or impacts on commercial shipping interests. The NPS states that consent should not be granted for proposed developments if doing so would cause interference to the use of recognised sea lanes essential to international navigation.

90. The applicant undertook an assessment of the potential impacts of the development (offshore cabling and wind turbines) on navigation and shipping. The conclusion was that potential impacts would be tolerable with mitigation. Mitigation was offered as part of the design of the wind farm and cabling route. The ExA noted that most issues that formed the basis of disputes between the applicant and a small number of parties were agreed before the close of the Examination. The outstanding issues were the timing of notification by the applicant that a buried electric sub-sea cable had become exposed on the seabed (which had been raised as an issue by the Maritime and Coastguard Agency) and safety concerns raised by the NFFO and VisdNed. The ExA concluded that the timing of notification should be three business days rather than the five days proposed by the applicant and that mitigations in the proposed DCO would provide suitable mitigation for safety concerns. The ExA stated that the proposed development would not conflict with the relevant provisions of NPS EN-3.

91. The SoS consulted on the proposed amendment to the notification period for seabed cable exposure. In response, the applicant, the MMO and the Maritime and Coastguard Agency indicated they had reached agreement that three days was an acceptable period of time from the time when the exposure was discovered. Wording for a DCO was provided and this has been included in the DCO. Consultation discussions also covered further points in relation to the trigger for the notification to mariners and the timeframe for sending copies of notices to the MMO and the Maritime and Coastguard Agency. Agreement was reached on all these matters. The SoS agreed with the ExA's overall conclusion under this head.

Aviation

92. The ExA noted that NPS EN-1 and NPS EN-3 provide a robust framework for applicants and decision-takers to work within the terms of the potential impacts of NSIPs on aviation interests. In particular, the ExA noted that NPS EN-1 states that development consent should not be granted if the development in question would impede the safe and effective use of defence assets or have adverse impacts on civil aviation infrastructure.

93. The applicant assessed that apart from potential interference with defence and aviation radar systems, the worst-case scenarios assessed with appropriate mitigation would produce impacts that were not significant. The key issues for consideration during the Examination were the potential impacts on the Ministry of Defence's Air Defence Radar at Trimingham (a village on the Norfolk coast) and the NATS PSR at Cromer.

94. During the Examination, the Ministry of Defence agreed wording about suitable mitigation for inclusion in any DCO that might be made and withdrew its objection to the development provided that wording was used. As far as the potential impacts on the NATS PSR were concerned, NATS and the applicant discussed a contractual agreement to put in place mitigation measures for the PSR. By the close of the Examination, no agreement had been signed. However, NATS wrote to PINS on 6 November 2019 to indicate it would remove its objection to the development subject to the inclusion of specific wording in any DCO that might be made to mitigate impacts on the PSR.

95. The ExA was satisfied that subject to suitable wording being included in any DCO that might be granted by the SoS, aviation impacts would be satisfactorily addressed and thus meet the policy tests in NPS EN1. In light of the withdrawal of the objection from NATS, the SoS saw no reason to disagree with the ExA's conclusion in this matter.

Marine physical processes

96. The ExA noted that the applicant considered the potential impacts of the development to be negligible on its own and minor adverse in combination with other plans or projects. The applicant produced an updated Outline Scour Protection and Cable Protection Plan during the Examination which took account of changes to the development, including the reduction in turbine numbers from 200 to 180. The total amount of scour protection would be specified in any DCO that might be granted.

97. The MMO agreed with the methodology used by the applicant and to the conclusions it had reached in relation to project alone and in combination impacts.

However, Natural England disagreed with some of the conclusions on assessment of impact. Natural England was also concerned that material dredged from the seabed should be deposited with other seabed material of similar size. Natural England also had concerns about the fact that the area of scour protection had not been specified by the applicant and about the extent of cable protection within the Haisborough, Hammond and Winterton SAC.

98. In considering the issues raised during the Examination, the ExA noted concerns about the volume of inert material that would be disposed of and of how it would be monitored but was satisfied that conditions in the DCO would address these issues. One outstanding issue was the particle size of deposited material. Here the ExA followed the view of Natural England and considered that a suitable condition should be included in the DCO. The ExA proposed a form of words, but was not able to consider the formulation with the applicant and accordingly recommended that the SoS should do so. The SoS accordingly sought comments on the proposed wording in his letter of 6 December 2019.

99. The applicant considered that the practicality of sampling all dredged sediment and areas within the disposal site in order to determine 95% similarity was not feasible. There would be limitations in the extensive sampling of dredged sediment. The applicant understood that both Natural England and the MMO shared these concerns. The applicant further noted that the disposal principles in the Site Integrity Plan ensured appropriate sediment disposal which must be agreed with the MMO in consultation with Natural England which meant that a 95% condition was unnecessary or was even achievable.

100. While the ExA concluded that, subject to the inclusion of the 'particle condition' in any DCO that might be made, there would be no reason to withhold consent, the SoS considered that the applicant's position as set out above was acceptable.

Other considerations

101. The ExA noted that representations were received from interested parties who were concerned that the onshore substations might be the target of terrorism or be a fire risk. The ExA considered these matters and concluded that there was little evidence that a terrorist attack is foreseeable and that the design of the substations would meet health, safety and other regulatory matters. The ExA concluded that these were not matters that weigh against consent being granted. The SoS saw no reason to disagree with the ExA's conclusion on this.

102. The ExA also noted representations about the potential impacts of the onshore works on property values, but stated that this was not a planning matter and could not be taken into account in the planning process.

Offshore biodiversity, biological environment and ecology (see also Offshore ecology and requirements of the Marine and Coastal Access Act 2009 and the Habitats Regulations 2017 below)

103. There were a number of disagreements on ornithological methodologies for EIA between Natural England, the Royal Society for the Protection of Birds (RSPB) and the applicant at the end of the Examination. These issues centred on the level of precaution that should be applied to the EIA which led to interested parties arriving at different conclusions on the significance of impacts on seabird populations.

104. Natural England and the RSPB considered that the cumulative effect of the development and other projects would be moderate adverse for key populations of red-throated diver, guillemot, razorbill, kittiwake, gannet and great black-backed gull. In contrast, the applicant's calculations led to a conclusion of minor adverse effects for these populations. Natural England's and the RSPB's conclusions equate to significant impact in EIA terms and, noting the conservation status for some of these species, the ExA agreed with this conclusion.

105. A significant cumulative effect on these populations would weigh against the Order being made as it would not conform with NPS-1. However, in view of the development's small contribution to the cumulative numbers, the SoS considered that, on balance, this issue should not prevent the granting of a DCO in respect of the development. The SoS considered the precautionary nature of the positions of the RSPB and Natural England. He also considered the Habitats Regulations 2017 Assessment (HRA) specific mitigation which had been secured post-Examination, which will go further to reduce the cumulative effect for some species. The SoS was also aware of the potential for lower numbers of predicted seabird mortalities than previously calculated based on built scenarios as opposed to the assessed or consented scenarios ('headroom').

106. In addition to matters relating to seabirds, the ExA considered several other issues relating to marine ecology. The SoS agreed with the ExA's conclusions on these matters, notably that:

- whilst some affected marine habitats and communities of benthos, fish, shellfish, and marine mammals were not protected by Natura 2000 sites (because, for example, they are located beyond designation boundaries or they are not a named feature), HRA-specific mitigation would be used to manage impacts on these receptors to acceptable levels;

- in relation to at-sea piling, appropriate monitoring will be carried out to safeguard marine mammals through an Offshore In Principle Monitoring Plan. This document provides that if, in the opinion of the MMO (in consultation with Natural England), initial noise monitoring measurements show different impacts to those assessed in the applicant's ES or failures of mitigation, then piling activities must cease until an update to the Marine Mammal Mitigation Plan and further monitoring requirements have been agreed.

BIODIVERSITY AND HABITATS, HABITATS REGULATIONS 2017 AND THE PLANNING ACT 2008 PROCESS

107. The SoS noted that the ExA had asked the applicant to comment on compensatory measures for sites designated under the Habitats Regulations 2017. The applicant's position was that there would be no adverse effects on integrity (AEoI) on these sites and that, consequently, it did not identify compensatory measures.

108. The SoS asserted that the development consent process for NSIPs was not designed for consultation on complex issues, such as HRA, to take place after the conclusion of the Examination. On occasion, as a pragmatic response to particular circumstances, he may undertake such consultation, but no reliance should be placed on the fact that he will always do so. In this instance, he has exercised his discretion, and allowed the applicant to make further representations on the matter of possible compensatory measures for those sites. However, the SoS made it clear that, in order to maintain the efficient functioning of the development consenting system, he would not always request post-Examination representations on such matters. Indeed, it should be assumed that he will not do so, and he may, therefore, make decisions on the evidence in front of him following his receipt of the ExA's report.

109. It is, therefore, important that potential AEoI of designated sites are identified during the pre-application period and full consideration is given to the need for derogation of the Habitats Regulations 2017 during the Examination. He expected applicants and statutory nature conservation bodies (SNCBs) to engage constructively during the pre-application period and to provide all necessary evidence on these matters, including possible compensatory measures, for consideration during the Examination.

110. This did not mean that it was necessary for applicants to agree with SNCBs if SNCBs considered that there would be significant adverse impacts on designated sites. The final decision on such matters remains for the SoS (who reserves the right not to request further evidence from applicants following the Examination). Applicants should therefore be assured that where they disagree with SNCBs and maintain a position that there are no significant adverse impacts,

but provide evidence of possible compensatory measures for consideration at the Examination on a 'without prejudice' basis, both the ExA in the Examination and the SoS in the decision period will give full and proper consideration to the question of whether or not there are significant adverse impacts. It will not be assumed that the provision of information regarding possible compensatory measures signifies agreement as to the existence of significant adverse impacts. The ExA will be required to provide an opinion on the sufficiency of the proposed compensation even if it considers that compensation is not required (in case the SoS disagrees with that conclusion), but such measures would only be required if the SoS were to find that there would be significant adverse impacts (and that the proposed compensatory measures are appropriate).

OFFSHORE ECOLOGY AND REQUIREMENTS OF THE MARINE AND COASTAL ACCESS ACT 2009 AND THE HABITATS REGULATIONS 2017

111. The Habitats Regulations 2017 and the Conservation of Offshore Marine Habitats and Species Regulations 2017 (SI 2017/1013) ('the Offshore Regulations') require the SoS to consider whether the development would be likely, either alone or in combination with other plans and projects, to have a significant effect on a Natura 2000 site, as defined in the Habitats Regulations 2017. If likely significant effects cannot be ruled out, then an appropriate assessment must be undertaken by the SoS pursuant to regulation 63(1) of the Habitats Regulations 2017 and regulation 28 of the Offshore Regulations to address potential AEoI on the site.

112. The SoS may only agree to the project if the SoS has ascertained that it will not adversely affect the integrity of a European site. This process is collectively known as an HRA.

113. The preparation of the HRA that accompanies this submission has been supervised by environmental specialists in the Energy Infrastructure Planning team in the DBEIS. The HRA concluded that a likely significant effect could not be ruled out in respect of 15 European sites when considered alone or with other plans and projects. It was, therefore, necessary to consider whether the development would have an adverse effect, either alone or in combination, on the integrity of those sites.

114. An appropriate assessment was, therefore, undertaken to determine whether an adverse effect on the sites could be ruled out in light of the sites' conservation objectives. The overall conclusion of the assessment was that the development would have no AEoI on any European sites. The SoS did not, therefore, consider that there was any breach of his duty under the Habitats Regulations 2017 and the Offshore Habitats Regulations in the event that consent was granted for the development.

115. The SoS's assessment differed from the ExA's conclusions on HRA in that, in agreement with the applicant, he considered that he had been presented with enough information to rule out an AEoI on two sites: the Alde-Ore Estuary SPA and the Flamborough and Filey Coast SPA. The key details of the SoS's assessment are provided below. Due to a large number of representations regarding the Haisborough, Hammond and Winterton SAC and the Southern North Sea SAC, key details of the assessment for these two sites are also provided below.

FLAMBOROUGH AND FILEY COAST SPA AND THE ALDE-ORE ESTUARY SPA

116. In relation to these SPAs, the ExA came to its conclusion in view of the potential for a range of seabird species, protected as features of these sites, to collide with the turbines or be disturbed and displaced from the array (depending on the species). On the advice of Natural England, the ExA's recommendation concluded that an AEoI could not be ruled out when the total number of birds impacted is added to the in combination total for other wind farms. The ExA's recommendation also warned that the applicant's in combination assessment was incomplete due to the use of incomplete seabird survey data from Hornsea Project Three. However, the SoS considered that a robust in combination assessment had been made in view of additional survey data provided by Hornsea Project Three. Furthermore, due to additional mitigation commitments made by the applicant during the post-Examination period, the SoS considered that the potential loss of a relatively very small number of birds through collision impacts did not contribute in a significant way to the total number of birds predicted to be impacted in combination (*de minimis*). On this basis the SoS concluded that the development would not have an adverse effect on the above SPA sites and, therefore, developmental consent should not be refused on Habitats Regulations 2017 grounds.

HAISBOROUGH, HAMMOND AND WINTERTON SAC

117. The SAC is designated for Annex I Sandbanks which are slightly covered by seawater all the time and Annex I Reefs (Sabellaria spinulosa). The ExA recommended that a conclusion of no AEoI could be reached on the basis of the information submitted during Examination. Having reviewed all representations received during and after Examination, the SoS agreed with a conclusion of no AEoI as the applicant had demonstrated that as the area of the site affected would be relatively small (in the case of reef, kept to a minimum through micrositing), any affected features are able to recover, and all cable protection will be removed at the time of decommissioning. On this last point, the SoS noted that the decommissioning of cable protection would be secured in the DCO to ensure that any effects are lasting (for the duration of the project) but temporary (repairable effect).

118. The SoS also noted in relation to this site the applicant's commitment to producing a Haisborough, Hammond and Winterton SAC Site Integrity Plan, which he considered to be an additional safeguarding mechanism, although it was not critical to the ExA's recommendation. The Site Integrity Plan committed the applicant to agree all works and potential mitigation measures associated with offshore cable installation (including seabed preparation works and cable protection) and maintenance within the Haisborough, Hammond and Winterton SAC, with the MMO in consultation with Natural England, in order to ensure there would be no AEoI. The SoS considered that it provided sufficient detail on potential mitigation measures at this stage, whilst granting the applicant a flexible approach until the extent and nature of mitigation became clear.

119. Lastly, the ExA's recommendation also included a change to the DCO that had not been agreed during Examination. This was made in order to meet Natural England's request that the applicant should commit to depositing any dredged material in location within the SAC that contain benthic material of similar particle size. The SoS consulted on this request post-Examination; however, the applicant has not been able to commit to ensuring that the particle size composition would be within 95% of the similarity to the particle size composition of the seabed at the disposal location. This is on the basis that it is not feasible to extensively sample all sediments to enable a realistic analysis of 95% similarity. However, the applicant committed to requiring the location and method for sediment disposal being agreed with the MMO in consultation with Natural England. This was to be secured in the Haisborough, Hammond and Winterton SAC Site Integrity Plan. The SoS was satisfied with this approach.

SOUTHERN NORTH SEA SAC

120. At the close of Examination a number of matters remained unresolved in relation to in combination disturbance to the harbour porpoise feature of this site. Of particular note were the residual concerns from Natural England, Whale and Dolphin Conservation and The Wildlife Trusts over the effectiveness of the applicant's Southern North Sea Site Integrity Plan. Nevertheless, the ExA was satisfied that with this plan secured, the applicant would use the most appropriate mitigation measures based on best knowledge, evidence, and proven available technology at the time of construction in order to avoid adversely affecting this SAC. Having reviewed this plan, the SoS considered that it provided sufficient detail on potential mitigation measures at this stage, whilst granting the applicant a flexible approach until the extent and nature of mitigation becomes clear. On this basis, the SoS considered that in combination disturbance would not have an AEoI of the Southern North Sea SAC.

121. In relation to this site, the ExA's recommendation included a change to the DCO that had not been discussed during Examination with regard to the use of

vibropiling or 'blue-hammer' technology. In response to the SoS's post-Examination consultation, the applicant highlighted that during the Examination, alternative text had been proposed that referred to all piled foundations irrespective of the technology used to install them. The SoS was content that the text proposed by the applicant included all possible installation scenarios involving piling and so specific mention of those techniques in the condition was not required. The applicant informed the SoS that the MMO and Natural England were in agreement with the applicant's position.

122. For the protection of marine mammals, the ExA also recommended that a maximum hammer energy should be secured in the deemed marine licences and the DCO. Following the ExA's recommendation, the SoS included a provision in the deemed marine licences that limits the maximum hammer energy to 5,000KJ. Lastly, the SoS noted that the French Biodiversity Agency participated in the Examination because of the potential impacts of the development on birds from two sites in French waters designated under the Habitats Directive. The ExA did not consider that the development, either alone or in combination with any other projects, would give rise to any significant effects on the French sites (or any other trans-boundary sites) but suggested that the SoS might want to consider whether any further information was needed from the Agency.

123. The SoS considered that no further information was needed in relation to this matter. Further details could be found in the SoS's HRA.

MARINE AND COASTAL ACCESS ACT 2009

124. The SoS noted that the ExA considered the potential impact of the development on the Cromer Shoal Chalk Beds Marine Conservation Zone. The ExA noted that the embedded mitigation measures in the application meant that the offshore cable route avoided the Cromer Shoal Chalk Beds. The SoS did not consider that there was any evidence of adverse impacts arising from the development on the Cromer Shoal Chalk Beds Marine Conservation Zone.

Consideration of compulsory acquisition and related matters

125. The applicant was also seeking powers for the compulsory acquisition of land, rights over land and related matters including temporary possession. The applicant was seeking those powers, 'to acquire compulsorily land and interests and other related powers to support the delivery of the Project'.

126. The PA 2008, together with related case law and guidance, provides that compulsory acquisition can only be granted if certain conditions are met. By section 122, compulsory acquisition may only be authorised if:

- the land is required for the development to which the consent relates; or
- it is required to facilitate or is incidental to that development; or
- it is replacement land which is to be given in exchange for the Order land under section 131 or section 132 of the PA 2008; and
- there is a compelling case in the public interest for the land to be acquired compulsorily.

127. In connection with this:

- the land required to be taken must be no more than is reasonably required and be proportionate;
- there must be a need for the project to be carried out;
- all reasonable alternatives to compulsory acquisition have been explored;
- the applicant has a clear idea of how it intends to use the land and can demonstrate that funds are available to pay for the acquisition; and
- they are satisfied that the purposes stated for the acquisition are legitimate and sufficient to justify the interference with the human rights of those affected.

128. The ExA noted that the applicant had submitted documentation with the application to support the request for compulsory acquisition powers. The powers sought were set out in the DCO that the applicant had submitted with its application for development consent. The ExA considered a broad range of matters related to the request for compulsory acquisition powers and asked a considerable number of questions during the Examination.

129. One of the issues covered was whether the ducting related to the proposed Norfolk Boreas Offshore Wind Farm could be classed as associated development as defined in the PA 2008 and thus be subject to compulsory acquisition powers. The ExA considered relevant legislation (the PA 2008) and guidance (Department for Communities and Local Government, 'Guidance on associated development applications for major infrastructure projects', which was issued in 2013) before concluding that 'Boreas ducting' could be classified as associated development and would, therefore, benefit from the compulsory acquisition powers that the applicant sought. The SoS agreed with this conclusion.

130. Prior to and during the Examination, the applicant had sought to make some minor changes to the application and to the compulsory acquisition requirements which were accepted by the ExA as suitable for consideration during Examination. The applicant provided a Funding Statement to explain how the acquisition of land would be funded. The Statement confirmed that the applicant's parent company would provide sufficient funds to cover any requests for compensation arising from the acquisition of land and rights, from the creation of new rights and from statutory blight where compensation is claimed. The ExA

sought further information from the applicant about the overall cost of the development. In response, the applicant indicated that the owner of the parent company – Vattenfall AB – was 100% owned by the Swedish state and that necessary funding would be made available as required. However, specific costs of the project were not provided. The applicant further stated that it would not seek to implement the DCO or exercise any of the powers in it until a Final Investment Decision had been reached.

131. There were a considerable number of objections to the grant of compulsory acquisition powers over certain plots of land although many were withdrawn before the end of the Examination. Provisions in the PA 2008 permit developers of NSIPs to extinguish or relocate the rights of statutory undertakers where the SoS is satisfied that the use of those powers is necessary for the project in question. The ExA noted discussions between the applicant and a number of statutory undertakers with interests that were subject to the request for compulsory acquisition powers. In most cases, the parties reached agreement over the interests that were sought and/or any protective provisions that would be included in any DCO that might be granted. The exception was the discussion with Network Rail, which was not concluded at the close of the Examination, with Network Rail maintaining its objection. Notwithstanding this position, the ExA concluded that the powers sought by the applicant in relation to statutory undertakers were necessary to carry out the development and that the relevant PA 2008 provisions had been met. The SoS noted that Network Rail subsequently wrote to him to withdraw its objection. In light of this, the SoS agreed with the ExA's conclusions in this matter.

132. Crown Land is also subject to special provisions under the PA 2008 – the interests in Crown Land cannot be compulsorily acquired but third party interests can be. In the case of the development such land is held by The Crown Estate (TCE) only. Highways England owns land interests affected by the development, but these are not technically Crown Land although they are treated as though they are. Consent was granted by TCE under section 135(1) of the PA 2008 in respect of Crown Land on the foreshore. The consent was conditional on TCE being consulted if any variation to the Order was proposed which could affect other provisions of the Order subject to sections 135(1) and/or 135(2) of the PA 2008, and the inclusion of amendments to the DCO. These amendments were included in the DCO that was submitted to the SoS by the ExA and were incorporated into the DCO made by the SoS.

133. 'Open Space Land' was also considered by the ExA in relation to the applicant's compulsory acquisition requests with relevant land plots on the beach at Happisburgh and the Marriott's Way long distance path. The Open Space Land was owned by a number of interests including individuals but also Norfolk

County Council and North Norfolk District Council. The ExA noted that trenchless crossing techniques would be used to install cables and ducting under the Open Space Land so that it should not be affected by the development. The Open Space Land would, therefore, be no less advantageous than it was before for its owners, occupiers, tenants, members of the public, etc.

134. The development would use National Trust land which, in the absence of an agreement between the parties, would be permitted only under a special parliamentary procedure. The ExA noted that the National Trust and the applicant were discussing an agreement during the Examination but that these discussions had not concluded by the time the Examination closed. The Trust was still, therefore, formally objecting to the use of its land. However, the SoS noted that the National Trust wrote on 25 September 2019 withdrawing its objection. Although the ExA considered that there were still a number of issues outstanding at the close of the Examination, it was thought that these would be satisfactorily addressed.

HUMAN RIGHTS

135. As far as human rights in relation to the proposals for compulsory acquisition and temporary possession of land and rights over land were concerned, the ExA was satisfied that: (a) the Examination ensured a fair and public hearing; (b) any interference with human rights arising from implementation of the development was proportionate and struck a fair balance between the rights of the individual and the public interest; and (c) that compensation would be available in respect of any quantifiable loss. The SoS saw no reason to disagree with the ExA's conclusion that there was no disproportionate or unjustified interference with human rights so as to conflict with the provisions of the Human Rights Act 1998.

OVERALL CONCLUSION ON COMPULSORY ACQUISITION

136. Because the ExA concluded that development consent should not be granted, it consequently considered that the compelling case in the public interest for the land to be acquired compulsorily had not been made out. However, it was mindful that the SoS might conclude that development consent should be granted and so examined the case for compulsory acquisition and temporary possession on that basis.

137. The SoS considered that relevant legislation and guidance relating to compulsory acquisition and temporary possession had been followed by the applicant and that, given his overall consideration that development consent for the development should be granted, there was a compelling case in the public

interest to grant compulsory acquisition and temporary possession powers to facilitate the development.

SoS's consideration

138. The SoS noted that the ExA had determined that consent should not be granted for the development because of potential impacts on habitats and species afforded protection under the Habitats Directive. In determining that it was not possible on the basis of the information available to it to rule out an AEoI on two sites protected by the Directive, the ExA concluded that the development would not be in accordance with NPS EN-1 and could not therefore be granted consent. In other respects, however, the ExA concluded that, while there would be impacts arising from the development across a range of issues (including on local landscape and traffic and transport), those impacts were not of such significance or would be mitigated to such a degree as to be not significant as to outweigh the substantial benefits that would derive from the development of a very large, low carbon, infrastructure project. The ExA noted that, if one set aside the conclusion on habitats-related issues, then in all other matters, the development would be in accordance with the NPSs and national policy objectives. This conclusion was subject to some clarification on specific points, including mitigation proposals.

139. In view of the ExA's Report to the SoS, the SoS consulted a range of parties including the applicant about the habitats-related issues and other relevant matters that had been raised in the ExA's Report. On habitats, further information on potential bird impacts such that the SoS felt able to conclude that, on balance, there would be no AEoI for the Flamborough and Filey Coast SPA and the Alde-Ore Estuary SPA.

140. The SoS noted that there were a range of views about the potential impacts of the development with strong concerns expressed about the impacts on, among other things, the landscape around the substation, traffic and transport impacts and potential contamination effects at the site of the F-16 plane crash. However, he has had regard to the ExA's consideration of these matters and to the mitigation measures that would be put in place to minimise those impacts wherever possible. The SoS considered that findings in the ExA's Report and the conclusions of the HRA together with the strong endorsement of offshore wind electricity generation in NPS EN-1 and NPS EN-3 meant that, on balance, the benefits of the development outweigh its adverse impacts. He, therefore, concluded that development consent should be granted (the SoS made a number of modifications to the draft order which are unnecessary to repeat herein and which did not materially alter its effect).

Climate Change Act 2008 and the net-zero target

141. The SoS also mentioned that on 2 May 2019, the CCC recommended the UK reduce greenhouse gas emissions to net zero by 2050. This was proposed to deliver on the commitments the UK made by signing the Paris Agreement in 2016. On 26 June 2019, following advice from the CCC, the government announced a new carbon reduction 'net-zero' target for 2050, which resulted in an amendment to the Climate Change Act 2008 requiring the UK to reduce net carbon emissions by 2050 from 80% to 100% below the 1990 baseline. The SoS noted that the NPSs continue to form the basis for decision-making under the PA 2008. The ExA was unable to consider this matter as it occurred after the close the Examination. However, the ExA did conclude that:

> … the strong policy support for renewable energy generation and the benefits of the scheme in terms of the large-scale generation of renewable energy and its contribution to sustainable development objectives, substantially outweigh the limited harms which have been set out above. When considered as a whole the ExA concludes that the Proposed Development would be in accordance with all of the relevant NPSs.

142. The SoS did not consider that the amendment to the Climate Change Act 2008 had lessened the need for renewable energy generation and that the development was still in accordance with the NPSs in that respect.

Comment

143. The SoS's reasons are set out in detail as the application for a DCO involved a wide range of important matters which, in many cases, typically arise for consideration on decision-making under the TCPA 1990. This is a decision which should be read by anyone with an interest in large-scale offshore wind farms and is in line with the strong endorsement of offshore wind power in national energy policy.

144. It was noteworthy on this application that the SoS did not accept the recommendation of the ExA that a DCO should not be granted because of potential significant impacts on SPAs through seabird deaths from collisions with this and other wind farm projects. Apart from this, the ExA confirmed that the scheme's renewable energy benefits outweighed its visual, traffic and other impacts. However, after requesting further information and taking into account additional mitigation proposed by the applicants, the SoS found that collisions with the wind turbines would potentially result in the death of only a very small number of birds and would make only a *de minimis* contribution to the overall number of bird deaths cumulatively with other projects. He therefore took the view that a DCO should not be refused.

145. The decision followed hard on the heels of the decision of the SoS on 28 May 2020 when development consent was also given for the UK's largest solar farm at Cleve Hill Solar Park on the north Kent coast (see Chapter 10, Case Study X).

Decision recently quashed and subject to re-determination

On 18 February 2021, Holgate J quashed the decision of the SoS to grant development consent for this project on the ground that he failed to evaluate the combined landscape and visual impacts affecting the proposed onshore substations at Necton in Norfolk for both the Norfolk Vanguard (NV) application and the separate but closely related Norfolk Boreas (NB) application where a decision on development consent is expected in April 2021.[2] The SoS deferred consideration of the significant environmental impacts arising from the choice of the proposed substation site for both projects until consideration of the NB application. The court found that the SoS acted unlawfully in that where the cumulative effects were substantial he had no discretion to defer a decision on them until a later application. Under the applicable EIA regulations the SoS had to be satisfied (before granting development consent) that he had sufficient information to enable him to evaluate the likely significant environmental effects of the relevant proposal before him. To defer the assessment of the environmental impacts to the later application as the information he had in relation to NV's onshore grid connection was limited was irrational. The NV and NB applications were separate projects for the purposes of assessment under the EIA regulations and could not be treated as if they comprised a single project and assessed at the time of the NB application. The court also found that before any re-determination the SoS would have to allow a reasonable opportunity for interested parties to make representations on the environmental impacts affecting the proposed substations in Necton where there were objections to the selection of this location on both applications.

---

2 See *Pearce v Secretary of State for Business Energy and Industrial Strategy and Norfolk Vanguard Ltd* [2021] EWHC 326 (Admin).

CASE STUDY XXII

Development Consent Granted in Principle for 231-Turbine Hornsea Project Three Offshore Wind Farm in the North Sea, although a Final Decision was Delayed to Allow for Final Approval of Measures to Cover Adverse Impacts to the Kittiwake Population and Coastal Special Protection Area

DCO reference EN010080 (1 July 2020)

1. This application for development consent follows the decision on 1 July 2020 of the SoS for the DBEIS to grant development consent for the 158-turbine Norfolk Vanguard Offshore Wind Farm some 40 miles off the Norfolk coast. As indicated in Chapter 8, Case Study XXI, the latter project included infrastructure works and impacts arising from the proposed Hornsea Project Three which, with 231 turbines, had a capacity of up to 2.4GW.

2. The SoS indicated that he was minded to approve Hornsea Project Three (despite the ExA recommending that consent be refused owing to potentially significant adverse effects from the cumulative impacts of a number of offshore wind projects and cable route concerns) and the 1.8GW Norfolk Boreas Offshore Wind Farm project, where the Examination closed on 12 October 2020. The Norfolk Vanguard and Hornsea Project Three Offshore Wind Farms are predicted to generate enough electricity to power almost 4 million homes.

3. The final decision on the application was delayed where, exceptionally, the SoS allowed further time for the applicant to submit further information by 30 September 2020 and to allow for consultation with interested parties in relation to the cumulative impacts of a number of wind farms on SPAs. The SoS accordingly set a new deadline of 31 December 2020 for his final decision on the application.

4. The object of the consultation was to enable the applicant to formulate measures that would satisfy the Habitats Regulations 2017. SNCBs had previously advised that proposed compensatory measures to protect the kittiwake seabirds of Flamborough and the Filey Coast SPA would not satisfy the Habitats Regulations 2017. The SoS found that the concerns of the ExA were outweighed by the importance he attached to the substantial contribution which Hornsea Project Three would make towards the delivery of renewable energy. He also attached great weight to the socio-economic impacts arising from the creation of employment opportunities, both direct (400 jobs in Grimsby) and with hundreds

more in the supply chain and during construction. In the circumstances he determined that it would be appropriate to give the applicant an opportunity to submit suitable detailed measures to compensate for the harm to the kittiwake population and the coastal SPA.

CASE STUDY XXIII

Unacceptable Landscape and Visual Impacts Preclude 30-Turbine Wind Farm in an Area of Great Natural Beauty in Dumfries and Galloway

Case reference WIN-170-2004 (8 January 2021)

1. On 8 January 2021 the Scottish Ministers (under case reference WIN-170-2004) refused an application for consent under section 36 of the Electricity Act 1989 and for deemed planning permission under section 57(2) of the Town and Country Planning (Scotland) Act 1997 for the construction and operation of a wind farm development comprising 30 wind turbines (with a maximum blade to tip height of 149m) and ancillary development at a site in Dumfries and Galloway. The application site was not within any national designations but was partly located within a local landscape designation (the Thornhill Uplands Regional Scenic Area) and was adjacent to another (the Leadhills and Lower Hills Special Landscape Area). There were also some non-scheduled archaeological assets on the application site and the Wanlockhead Conservation Area lay some 2km to the south-east. The boundary of the Muirkirk and North Lowther Uplands Special Landscape Area (and underpinning sites of special scientific interest) was also located to the west of the site.

2. It was plain that there were significant environmental impacts, including landscape and visual impacts, including cumulative effects, arising from the proposed development. It was accepted that the proposal gave rise to benefits comprising renewable energy generation, greenhouse gas emissions savings and net economic impacts (arising from construction, operation and maintenance). In terms of the environmental impacts, the view taken was that they were unacceptable in view of the scale and distinctiveness of the landscape features and scenic quality of the area in which the turbines would be located.

3. In agreeing with the findings of the reporter, the Scottish Ministers concluded that the significant adverse effects on the natural beauty of the application site outweighed the energy and climate change benefits and the socio-economic impacts.

Comment

4. This was a highly sensitive landscape and although there were undoubted benefits arising from the onshore energy proposal (in terms of meeting emission reduction targets and reducing greenhouse gases), this was plainly a development

that was in the wrong place which could not be realised without detriment to an environment which was a distinctive Scottish landscape. The planning balance was very much against a consent in this case and it is not difficult to see why. (Readers should note that the report of J Alasdair Edwards, a reporter appointed by Scottish Ministers, and the decision letter of the Scottish Ministers runs to 223 pages.) Although it is accepted that UK and Scottish legislation and strategies bring more focus on renewable generation, none of this is going to be achieved without regard to the impacts on environmental quality where the bar is still set at a high level.

CASE STUDY XXIV

Single Wind Turbine Allowed in Close Proximity to Existing Wind Farm

Planning appeal reference PPA-110-2401 (14 January 2021)

1. On 14 January 2021, Nick Smith, a reporter appointed by the Scottish Ministers, allowed an appeal (under planning appeal reference PPA-110-2401) against a decision of Aberdeenshire Council (where the appeal proposal involved EIA development) and granted planning permission for a single wind turbine (hub height 77m, total height 135m), access track and associated infrastructure at a site in the countryside at Huntly.

2. The appeal raised a number of issues under local development plan policies.

3. In terms of visual impacts, the reporter concluded (based on his own views and on visualisations from six viewpoints) that the overall effect on visual amenity for most properties beyond 2km would not be significant. However, he did accept that it would be significant for three properties close to the site, although even then the visual effect of the development would be limited by window orientation and garden vegetation and the fact that the new turbine would be viewed as part of an existing wind farm.

4. Landscape impacts would be diminished by rolling hills, commercial forestry and the proximity to other wind turbines, which made it appear as though the additional wind turbine would be either part of or adjacent to existing turbines within the Cairnbarrow wind farm. The appeal site was not within an area designated for landscape reasons although it was close to an SLA and an area of great landscape value. However, a combination of the scale of the proposed development, along with its proximity to existing turbines and the screening effect of the landform, meant that it would not lead to unacceptable effects on the landscape or historic features.

5. The ecological impacts and detriment to protected species were subject to rigorous pre-commencement conditioning. It was also considered unlikely that the appeal proposal would have direct impacts on the setting of five historic buildings and cultural assets in the vicinity of the appeal site.

6. Noise impacts were mitigated by a condition which required the wind turbine to operate in a restricted mode at wind speeds which would result in noise

threshold breaches had they been unrestricted. Such a condition would enable the authority to take enforcement action in the event that during operations a threshold breach occurred. With such a condition noise impacts affecting nearby residents would be avoided. The operator's evidence was accepted that there would be a 5.2% reduction in output from implementing the noise restrictions.

7. The appeal proposal was also found to have only a negligible impact on local hydrology and would be mitigated by suitable conditioning. There were also no impacts on aviation safety or telecommunication links, although there would be mitigation through technical conditioning. There was some risk involving shadow flicker, and a pre-commencement condition was imposed which required an agreed protocol for the assessment and remediation of shadow flicker such that, in order to protect the amenities of three local properties, the turbine would be capable of being shut down during times and weather conditions when shadow flicker could occur. Highway impacts on the environment, mainly during the construction phase, along with the construction of an access track and road widening at various points along the public road network to accommodate the delivery of large turbine parts, were also found to be acceptable, albeit subject to pre-commencement conditioning.

8. The reporter's conclusion (in light of his consideration of the information contained in the EIA Report) was that none of the impacts mentioned above outweighed any of the social, economic or environmental arguments relating to mitigation of climate change arising from the proposed renewable energy development.

9. The reporter considered that although there were some significant impacts affecting primarily the three residential properties closest to the appeal site (such as visual impacts arising from the presence of a wind turbine, along with noise at higher wind speeds and shadow flicker in bright sunlight), these factors could be mitigated by means of conditions and would not give rise to unacceptable residual impacts. Accordingly, the reporter considered that the appeal proposed accorded with the relevant provisions of the local development plan and there were no material considerations which justified a refusal to grant planning permission.

Comment

10. The outcome on this appeal was a predictable one. It involved the erection of a single wind turbine close to an existing wind farm and the impacts on the amenity of just three dwellings close to the appeals site were accommodated by suitable conditions. What is particularly noteworthy on this appeal (which involved EIA development) is the volume of evidence with which the reporter was presented under a number of different heads. This goes to show the lengths (and cost) to which an operator has to go in order to justify a grant of planning

permission in an area which was not even designated for landscape reasons where there were already a number of existing wind turbines.

Chapter 9

Solar Energy

PHOTOVOLTAIC SYSTEM

9.1 Solar power is the conversion of energy from sunlight into electricity. The energy from sunlight is typically converted into electricity by means of photovoltaics (PV), which comprises an arrangement of several components including solar panels to absorb and convert the sunlight into electricity, a solar inverter to convert the output from direct to alternating current, as well as mounting, cabling and other electrical accessories to set up a working system. A solar array (a loosely defined term referring to a group of PV solar panels or cells arranged and linked in such a way as to operate as a single unit) encompasses only the solar panels (which is the visible part of the system) and does not include all the other components. PV systems should not be confused with other technologies such as concentrated solar power or solar thermal power which is used for heating and cooling.

SOLAR CELLS

9.2 The essence of a PV system is its solar cells. PV cells are packed together in a frame known as a solar panel. Solar cells are made of semi-conductors such as silicon, which absorb the sunlight and convert it into electricity. A solar array consists of one or many solar panels although the solar array does not encompass the entire system.

9.3 A typical 150 watt solar panel is about a square metre in size and has a power output of around 265 watts, although it can range anywhere from as little as 225 watts to more than 350 watts. The higher the wattage of a solar panel, the more electricity it can produce under the same conditions. The life of a solar panel is typically 25 years. The payback period for an investment in a PV solar installation varies, but is likely to be in the region of 10–20 years.

TYPES OF PHOTOVOLTAIC SYSTEMS

9.4 PV systems range from small, rooftop-mounted or building-integrated systems with capacities from a few to several tens of kilowatts, to large utility-scale power stations capable of generating hundreds of megawatts. Most PV systems are connected to the grid while those off the grid account for only a small portion of the market. PV systems rarely use battery storage although this will change as improvements in technology make it economically viable for smaller systems. Operating silently and without any moving parts or environmental emissions, PV systems have developed into a mature technology used for mainstream electricity generation. Solar energy is obviously important as the sun is a sustainable source of energy, whereas fossil fuels are finite and add to greenhouse gases.

9.5 As indicated above, PV systems are usually divided into three distinct categories:

(a) *Residential rooftop*: a solar array of a typical residential PV system is rack-mounted on the roof rather than integrated into the roof or facade of the building whose function is to supplement power within the dwelling. A typical small rooftop array mounted on a sloped roof may produce up to 10kW producing around 95% of clean net renewable energy over a 30-year service lifetime. Although rooftop-mounted systems are small and have a higher cost per watt than large commercial-scale installations, they account for the largest share of the market. There will usually be a connection to the grid so that any surplus energy produced by the PV system can be sold to the grid provider.

(b) *Rooftop, mobile and portable*: a small PV system is capable of providing enough electricity to power a single home or isolated devices such as street lights, construction and traffic signs, powering electric cars or solar-powered tents. Portable and mobile PV systems are also commonly used on recreational vehicles and boats.

(c) *Building integrated*: in urban areas, PV arrays are often used on rooftops to supplement power use and the building will usually have a connection to the grid, in which case the energy produced by the PV array can be sold back to the provider in some sort of net metering agreement. Some providers use the rooftops of commercial customers and telephone poles to support their use of PV panels.

PERFORMANCE

9.6 Key performance factors are set out in the following list:

(a) Weather fluctuations and changes in the Earth's position towards the sun throughout the year. If sunlight is not constant irradiance will vary throughout the day. The angle of the sun, passing clouds, hazy weather and air pollution can all affect irradiance levels. Temperature also affects the efficiency of solar cells and the warmer solar cells get, the less efficient they are. Snow also blocks production of solar energy. It is perhaps worthy of note that although one imagines that a sunny climate is essential, Germany leads the world in installed solar capacity.

(b) The efficiency of the solar panels. The more efficient the panel the more electricity it can create from sunlight. Solar panel efficiency is measured by how much sunlight a solar panel can convert into usable electricity. The majority of residential solar panels typically have an efficiency of 15–18% although premium models can reach over 21%. The most efficient solar panel on the market is currently rated at 23.8%.

(c) Losses due to shading and dirt, dust, grit and other debris settling on the surface of the solar panels will block sunlight from reaching the solar cells and will reduce performance. In areas with frequent rain soiling is not usually significant, whereas areas that experience long periods of dry weather will give rise to more soiling during the summer. The same applies in the case of systems located near to construction sites and other places that produce dust. Solar panels therefore need to be regularly maintained and cleaned.

(d) Defects in panels: the most common problems with solar panels are hot spots on the panels; micro-cracks; snail trail contamination; degradation in the crystalline PV modules; internal corrosion/delamination.

PHOTOVOLTAIC MOUNTING

9.7 PV modules (and a solar panel consists of a string of connected modules which are assemblies of packaged PV cells) are assembled into arrays on some kind of mounting system which may be classified as ground mount, roof mount or pole mount. For solar farms (also known as solar parks or solar fields) large racks are mounted on the ground and the modules are mounted on the racks. For buildings, many different racks have been devised for pitched roofs. For flat roofs, racks, bins and building integrated solutions are used. Solar panel racks mounted on top of poles can be stationary or moving. Side-of-pole mounts are suitable for situations where a pole has something else mounted at its top, such as a light fixture or an antenna. Pole mounting raises what would otherwise be a ground-mounted array above weed shadows and livestock and may satisfy regulatory requirements regarding inaccessibility of exposed wiring. Pole mounted panels are open to more cooling air on their underside which increases performance. A multiplicity of pole top racks can be formed into a parking carport or other shaded structure.

CABLING

9.8 Owing to outdoor usage, solar cables are designed to be resistant against ultra violet radiation and extremely high temperature fluctuations and are generally unaffected by the weather. Standards specifying the usage of electrical wiring in PV systems include the British Standard BS 7671, which incorporates regulations relating to microgeneration and PV systems.

SOLAR TRACKER

9.9 A solar tracking system tilts a solar panel throughout the day. Depending on the type of tracking system, the panel is either aimed directly at the sun or the brightest area of a partly clouded sky. Trackers greatly enhance early morning and late afternoon performance increasing the total amount of power produced by a system by about 20–25% for a single axis tracker and about 30% or more for a dual axis tracker, depending on latitude. Trackers are effective in regions that receive a large portion of sunlight directly. In diffuse light (under cloud or fog) tracking has little or no value. Because most concentrated PV systems are very sensitive to the sunlight's angle, tracking systems allow them to produce useful power for more than a brief period each day. Tracking systems improve performance for two main reasons. First, when a solar panel is perpendicular to the sunlight, it receives more light on its surface than if it were angled. Second, direct light is used more efficiently than angled light.

9.10 Trackers and sensors to optimise performance are often seen as optional, but they can increase output by up to 45%. Arrays that approach or exceed 1MW often use solar trackers. For large systems, the energy gained by using tracking systems can outweigh the added complexity. For very large systems, the added maintenance of tracking is a substantial detriment. Tracking is not required for flat panel and low-concentration PV systems, but for high-concentration PV systems, dual axis tracking is considered to be a necessity.

BATTERY

9.11 PV systems increasingly use rechargeable batteries to store a surplus to be later used at night. Batteries used for grid storage also stabilise the electrical grid by levelling out peak loads and play an important role in a smart grid as they can charge during periods of low demand and feed their stored energy into the grid when demand is high. PV systems with an integrated battery solution also need a charge controller as the varying voltage and current from the solar array requires constant adjustment to prevent damage from overcharging. Batteries for one's home or business are heavy and large.

SELLING SOLAR ELECTRICITY BACK TO THE GRID (DOMESTIC INSTALLATIONS)

9.12 In 2009, it was possible to install solar panels and start breaking into profit at some point in the system's lifetime. The first income stream involved the immediate savings on domestic energy bills. The second income stream came from selling energy back to the grid, typically through one's own supplier.

9.13 Selling energy to the grid was a somewhat bureaucratic exercise and involved the installation of an export meter and feeding power back to one's supplier. Customers were typically paid somewhere between 6 and 9 pence per kilowatt feed-back, which was a small fraction of the heavy cost of installing the system. Change came in 2010 with a scheme, underwritten by the government, known as the FiT, whose object was to stimulate renewable energy activity in the UK.

9.14 Under the FiT scheme customers could be paid for all the energy generated, whether or not they used it themselves, and they could also get money back when they generated a surplus, which they could export to their supplier. The scheme was guaranteed for 20 years and meant that domestic consumers could make money from their solar panels for at least that period.

9.15 One benefits from the FiT scheme in three ways. First, in terms of energy generation where customers receive payment for all the energy generated from their solar panels, even if they used it in their own home. Once their system was installed and registered under the scheme, payments could be received for 20 years. Second, surplus energy could be sold back to customers' supplier. Third, the savings made on customers' energy bills too, which depend on the size of their system, how much electricity they use and how effective the installation is.

9.16 The only drawbacks to the FiT scheme were: (a) that eligible installations had to be carried out by MCS accredited installers; (b) that the customer's home had to pass what was known as a Green Deal survey (which meant that the customer had to ensure that his home was optimised for energy efficiency, which could be costly); and (c) the progressively lower rates being paid by suppliers. By 2015, the FiT scheme was under extensive review by the government and payment rates began to drop for many technologies. For instance, the following table shows the FiT rates for PV solar on 31 December 2016, with the rates applicable as at 1 April 2020 in square brackets (FiT rates are adjusted annually in line with the Retail Price Index).

Description	*Installed capacity*	*Tariff (per kWh)*
Standard solar PV receiving the higher rate	0–10	4.58 [3.87]
	10–50	4.81 [4.11]
	50–250	2.22 [2.26]
Standard solar PV receiving the middle rate	0–10	4.12 [3.48]
	10–50	4.33 [3.70]
	50–250	2.01 [1.55]
Standard solar PV receiving the lower rate	0–10	0.62 [0.15]
	10–50	0.62 [0.15]
	50–250	0.62 [0.15]
Standard large solar PV	250–1,000	1.85 [1.35]
	1,000–5,000	0.62 [0.15]
Stand-alone solar PV	0–5,000	0.56 [0.05]

Note: These modest figures are to be compared with: (a) the average UK price per kilowatt hour in 2020 of 14.40p; (b) the average annual standing charge for electricity in the UK in 2020 of £75.11; and (c) the average annual domestic electricity bill in the UK in 2020 of £557.94.[1]

9.17 As indicated, the FiT scheme was under review after 2015 and by early 2016 the measures introduced meant that the scheme's costs were effectively controlled, providing value for money for the consumers who funded it through their electricity bills. The FiT scheme eventually closed to new applications on 31 March 2019 subject to a grace period and a number of time-limited extensions. Existing generating stations under the FiT scheme will continue to receive support for up to 25 years. The closure of the scheme was a big blow to small-scale solar generating capacity in the UK (i.e. up to 5MW capacity).

1 Figures provided by Power Compare on 15 June 2020.

HOW MUCH ELECTRICITY DO SOLAR PANELS PRODUCE AND HOW MANY PANELS MIGHT ONE NEED FOR A DWELLING?

9.18 The amount of electricity a solar panel produces depends on three important factors: (a) the size of the panel; (b) the efficiency of the solar cells inside; and (c) the amount of sunlight the panel gets. A typical silicon PV panel for residential use is around 1.5m tall and a little more than 1m wide. A panel comprises of individual solar cells which are linked together by wires. The cells are where electricity is made and the wires carry the electricity to a junction box where the panel is hooked into a larger array. The more solar cells working in tandem, the more power they will create.

9.19 Solar panels have been about this size for decades, but these days modern panels make more electricity because of improved cell efficiency. By 2019 the efficiency of the most advanced solar cells is closer to 23%, whereas average solar cells for residential use are around 18.7% efficient. Clearly solar efficiency relates to the amount of available energy from the sun which can be converted into electricity. If you combine the efficiency of the solar cells with the size of the panel, you arrive at a 'power rating' such that in the industry the panel would be rated to produce X watts.

9.20 Nowadays, a typical solar panel is capable of producing around 320 watts of power, but panels come in many different wattage ratings and finding one that produces exactly 320 watts is rare. Most residential panels are 250 watt rated. More efficient panels are more expensive and are usually only needed if there is limited space on the roof. The contractor installing the panels on the roof will normally ascertain how many panels are required to produce enough to cover the energy needs of the household as it normally will not matter how much each panel can produce provided the whole array satisfies demand. Solar panels will have a number listed on the back indicating how much power they will generate during ideal conditions. This is called the Standard Test Condition rating (or STC). The rating assumes the power which the panel is capable of generating in one hour under ideal conditions. It follows that with four panels, you would get a single kilowatt hour of electricity. Clearly, even if one lived at the equator one could not expect to replicate ideal conditions and the amount of electricity solar panels are able to generate depends on the average sunlight over the course of a year.

9.21 Using the example of a 250 watt STC rated panel, multiplying the 250 watts the panel produces by the number of hours of sun per day will give the amount of kilowatt hours which that panel produces per day, and multiplying by, say, 30 days will give the monthly kilowatt hours output for the panel. To illustrate the point, if a roof is getting 4 hours of usable sun per day, multiplying 250 watts by 4 hours gives 1kWh (or 1,000 watts) in a day per 250-watt panel. It follows that to ascertain how many solar panels are required to power an average house one would need to make a prediction of the household's energy requirements over, say, a period of one year. For example, if a household used on average 900kWh a month, one would need to divide 900kWh by the amount of kilowatt hours one solar panel produces over the course of a month (30kWh), in which case one might need at least 30 panels. In other words, 30 panels multiplied by 250 watts per panel equals a 7,500 watt system (7.5kW) having, as a rule of thumb, a probable effective lifespan of at least 25 years.

9.22 In summary, to determine the size of a PV system for one's home, four things need to be looked at: (a) the energy bill; (b) estimate how much electricity is used during daylight hours; (c) choose a PV system that will generate enough electricity to meet daytime demand; and (d) consider whether battery storage is required.

HOW MUCH DO RESIDENTIAL SOLAR PANELS COST?

9.23 Solar panels for the average household in the UK cost in the region of £4,000–£6,000. Obviously, the more efficient and powerful the panels, the more electricity will be generated. Solar panels are getting cheaper all the time. For example, in 2010, the average price of a 4kW solar PV system was around £20,000.

9.24 As most residential solar panels are around 250 watts, four panels would be required to create a 1kW peak (1kWp) system, eight panels to create a 2kWp system, 12 panels to create a 3kWp system, and so on. A single solar panel costs around £400–£500. The potential output will obviously vary depending on location. For instance, a 4kWp system in the south of England could generate about 4,200kWh of electricity each year, whereas in Scotland the figure is closer to 3,400kWh.

9.25 Cost is not the only criterion as more and more people are motivated to make their own personal contribution towards a low carbon future. Having said that, more than half of solar panel owners would not have bought their system without the FiT, according to a survey of *Which?* members in May 2019.

COMMERCIAL-SCALE GROUND-MOUNTED SOLAR PHOTOVOLTAIC – BULLET POINTS

Pre-application engagement

9.26 Consultation with the LPA and local community is encouraged at an early stage. Local people should be engaged by the developer at the pre-design, conceptual stage, ideally utilising a local exhibition/presentation where community views can be sought and recorded. Such development might not be EIA development as it may or may not have a significant effect on the environment. However, an ES is likely to be needed if the solar PV development is to be located in a particularly sensitive location and is likely to have significant landscape and visual impacts along with cumulative effects arising from other existing or approved developments. Advice should be sought from consultees (Historic England or Natural England) where there is any doubt about the significance of a development's likely effects on a sensitive area as defined in the EIA regulations.

Planning performance agreements

9.27 A planning performance agreement (PPA) is a project management tool which the LPA and applicants can use to agree timescales, actions and resources for handling particular applications. It should cover the pre-application and application stages, but may also extend through to the post-application stage. It is important for collaborative working. The idea is that it will minimise the risks and costs of an appeal and enable problems to be identified at an early stage.

Application requirements

9.28 The LPA will dictate the level of information necessary to support the application which should be sufficiently detailed to allow it to be determined. Should the proposal involve EIA development under the 2017 Regulations there may be further requirements that will be determined through a scoping assessment in consultation with the LPA.

9.29 Information and guidance likely to be required includes:

(a) A location plan (1:1250 metric scale).
(b) A site/block plan (1:500 metric scale).
(c) Plans and elevations.
(d) A planning statement. Planning statements are supposed to provide a balanced justification for the development. They should demonstrate local context, need for the proposed development, how the proposed

development accords with relevant national and local planning policies, whether emerging policies should be taken into consideration and should also set out other material considerations that should be taken into consideration. The statement should also give details of pre-application consultation with local community and relevant bodies. In the case of EIA development an ES will be required. This is a publicly available document setting out the developer's own assessment of the likely environmental effects of his proposed development. It is prepared by the developer and submitted with the planning application. While responsibility for preparing the ES lies with the developer, he is expected to consult with those public authorities with relevant information. Those bodies are required to make available to the developer such environmental information as may be relevant. All ESs must include a description of the project, the main effects it is likely to have on the environment, a description of the measures envisaged to avoid, reduce or remedy significant adverse environmental effects, an outline of the main alternatives studied by the developer and a summary, in non-technical language.

(e) Fencing specification and details.

(f) Details of connection to grid.

(g) Full details and plans of proposed ancillary works or necessary infrastructure (see scope of ancillary works in Chapter 10, Case Study IX).

(h) Impact and other assessments: landscape and visual impacts (with proposals for mitigation planting); ecological appraisals and habitat mitigation; effects on the water environment (for instance, whether the development is compliant with the Water Framework Directive[2]), flood risk assessment; agricultural assessment; heritage impacts and in the case of heritage assets with archaeological interest, to consider the need for archaeological investigation (namely by way of a desk-based assessment and, if necessary, a field evaluation); residential amenity; socio-economic effects (such as impacts on footpath and recreational use), environmental benefits, including climate change considerations; construction, operational and decommissioning impacts (including traffic impacts) and a completed 'Electricity Generating Capacity' form.

(i) Application fee where required (normally such applications fall within category 5 (erection, alteration or replacement of plant or machinery) of the Town and Country Planning (Fees for Applications, Deemed Applications, Requests and Site Visits) (England) Regulations 2012 (SI 2012/2920) (but this should be clarified with the LPA – outline permission cannot be granted for a planning application submitted in category 5 of the above fee regulations – only detailed applications will be validated)).

---

2 Directive 2000/60/EC (23 October 2000).

(j) Applicants should seek guidance on delineating site area on application plan. For instance, if the solar arrays are close to a field boundary and there is an existing or proposed fence, the application land should include field boundaries. If the solar panels are more than 50m away from field boundaries where separate fencing is proposed, the application boundary should extend around the proposed solar panels with a separate planning application area extending around the fenced area. Where no fencing is proposed and the solar panels are to be positioned in the middle of a field well away from field boundaries the planning application boundary should be drawn around the proposed arrays and any immediate ancillary works, for example, access tracks (it is for the applicant to ensure that all proposed development is included within the planning application boundary).

Further considerations on applications

Site levelling works

9.30 Consideration should be given to the existing site contours. These works should be discussed at the pre-application stage and detailed within the planning application.

Development in relation to current land use

9.31 Ground-mounted large-scale PV arrays should ideally utilise previously developed land/brownfield land or agricultural land falling within classifications 3b (moderate quality agricultural land), 4 (poor quality agricultural land) or 5 (very poor quality agricultural land).

9.32 It is unlikely that permission will be granted for ground-mounted large-scale PV arrays on: (a) agricultural land within classifications 1 (excellent quality agricultural land), 2 (very good quality agricultural land) or 3a (good quality agricultural land); or (b) on sites designated for their natural beauty or of archaeological or ecological interest. It follows that, in the case of proposals involving agricultural land, there should be an agricultural land classification. If the site is categorised as grade 3 then all the criteria for grade 3 land will need to be assessed to establish whether the land meets the criteria for grade 3a or 3b. It follows that permission will not normally be given for development on agricultural land of a higher quality and removing the application land from full agricultural use would need to be justified.

Agricultural assessment

9.33 An agricultural assessment is needed for the following reasons:

(a) to deal with agricultural land classification;
(b) to explain why the development needs to be located on the application site and not on land of a lesser agricultural classification within the area;
(c) to provide information on the impact of the proposed development on the local area's supply of farming land within the same classification;
(d) to provide information on the viability of the existing farm to continue trading with or without the development in place;
(e) to explain and analyse the cumulative impact of the proposed development and other permitted large-scale solar PV developments on the supply of agricultural land within the same classification across the local area;
(f) to propose a project end date to demonstrate the temporary nature of the solar farm.

9.34 No additional information is required unless the agricultural practice which the proposed development would replace makes a special contribution to the environment or local economy.

Ground maintenance

9.35 Consideration should be given to managing the land once solar arrays have been installed. This will facilitate the eventual restoration of the site to agriculture. Spraying should be avoided and mulching large areas may present technical challenges as well as give rise to adverse landscape or visual impacts. Unless mowing or strimming beneath the arrays is feasible, continuing agricultural use is encouraged in the form of grazing by sheep, in which event the solar panels should be positioned at least 700mm above ground level and all cabling suitably protected.

Storage compound during construction phase

9.36 A temporary compound will be needed to accommodate the delivery and storage of construction materials, plant, machinery and office/welfare accommodation. Compounds should be carefully sited to minimise environmental/amenity impacts and any planning application should contain details of their size and location. Topsoil and subsoil should be stripped from such areas and stored on site for replacement following the completion of construction works. Details of these matters should be contained within the planning application along with the duration of the construction compound.

Soil stripping, storage and replacement

9.37 Large-scale solar PV developments are likely to require the excavation of soils associated with construction compounds, access roads, cable trenching, etc.

Where soil stripping occurs topsoil and subsoil should be stripped, stored and replaced separately in order to minimise soil damage and to provide optimal conditions for site restoration. The application should contain a methodology for soil stripping, storage and replacement and this methodology should subsequently be adhered to during site development.

Permitted development in the case of solar panels[3]

9.38 The installation of solar panels and equipment on residential buildings and land may be PD. There are, however, important conditions and limits which must be met in order to benefit from PD rights.

9.39 The following conditions must be observed:

(a) the equipment on a building should be sited, so far as is practicable, to minimise the effect on the external appearance of the building and the amenity of the area; and

(b) when no longer needed equipment should be removed as soon as reasonably practicable.

9.40 The following limitations must also be met:

(c) panels should not be installed above the highest part of the roof (excluding the chimney) and should project no more than 200mm from the roof slope or wall surface;

(d) the panels must not be installed on a building that is within the grounds of a listed building or on a site designated as a scheduled monument;

(e) if the property is in a conservation area or in a World Heritage Site, panels must not be fitted to a wall which fronts a highway.

9.41 In the case of stand-alone solar equipment (i.e. panels not on a building but within the grounds of a house or a block of flats), the following conditions must be observed:

(f) the equipment should be sited, so far as is practicable, to minimise its effect on the amenity of the area; and

(g) when no longer needed the equipment should be removed as soon as reasonably practicable.

9.42 The following limitations must also be met in the case of stand-alone solar equipment:

---

3 GPDO, Pt.14, Class A.

(h) only the first stand-alone solar installation will be PD; further installations will require planning permission;
(i) no part of the installation should be higher than 4m;
(j) the installation should be at least 5m from the boundary of the property;
(k) the size of the array should be no more that $9m^2$ or 3m wide by 3m deep;
(l) panels should not be installed within the boundary of a listed building or a scheduled monument;
(m) if the property is in a conservation area, or in a World Heritage Site, no part of the solar installation should be nearer to any highway bounding the house than the part of the house that is nearest to that highway.

MINISTERIAL STATEMENTS AFFECTING SOLAR ENERGY (AS MATERIAL CONSIDERATIONS)

9.43 Speech of Gregory Barker, the Minister for Energy and Climate Change, to the Large Scale Solar Conference on 25 April 2013:

> It's a great pleasure to be here today to speak to you at the Large Scale Solar Conference. And how appropriate to be here in Cornwall. A county that has long been at the forefront of the UK's drive towards a greener economy.
>
> And with levels of solar PV deployment now at a terrific 2.5GW, it seems like the perfect occasion to reflect on the progress the sector has made in recent years, and to map out our hopes and ambitions for the future.
>
> There are three big points I want to get over today:
>
> 1. The Coalition Government is committed to placing solar PV at the heart of the UK's energy mix
> 2. We have an ambitious and hands-on strategy to drive it forward
> 3. Solar is rightly popular. But if we aren't careful, or if the sector expands inappropriately, that invaluable popular public support will slip through our fingers. We don't want solar to become a bone of public contention like onshore wind.
>
> And that is my key message today. Solar is a genuinely exciting energy of the future, it is coming of age and we want to see a lot, lot more.
>
> But not at any cost … not in any place … not if it rides roughshod over the views of local communities.
>
> As we take solar to the next level, we must be thoughtful, sensitive to public opinion, and mindful of the wider environmental and visual impacts.

But if we are smart, and there are plenty of smart people in this sector, there is no reason we can't do that successfully. Indeed, we have to.

Solar's progress so far

Now earlier this year, the Prime Minister re-iterated this government's commitment to green growth.

He said 'When I became Prime Minister I said I wanted Britain to have the greenest government ever and I am as committed to that today as I was then. But I want to go further.'

To me it is absolutely clear. If we want to go further, solar PV must be at the centre of that ambition.

This is why solar is now, for the first time, a priority industry in the government's renewables roadmap.

And solar, alongside other industries, will benefit from the coalition government's new Energy Bill.

The new energy framework will revolutionise our energy system through introducing measures to attract the £110 billion investment needed to replace current generating capacity and upgrade the transition and distribution grid by 2020.

But we should be very proud of the progress that's been made in the solar sector. Particularly over the last two years.

At times the journey has been difficult. Reforming the ill-thought through and clumsy FiTs scheme was tough for the market. But the UK is now firmly established as one of the top 10 markets for solar PV worldwide. Since January, almost 400MW of solar was deployed under the Renewables Obligation. Despite one of the worst winters on record!

We have now seen over 420,000 small-scale installations, totalling almost 1.5 GW under the Feed in Tariff alone. Up and down the country, solar is powering thousands of homes and businesses and supports some 15,000 jobs.

This progress includes fantastic new projects like the 5 MW array at the Bentley Motors Factory in Crewe, the UK's largest rooftop solar array …

… Over 1 MW in the country's largest 'solar bridge' at Blackfriars in London …

… and the 30 MW Wymeswold Solar Farm in Leicestershire, the UK's largest, built on a disused World War 2 airfield.

Making solar work for local communities
This is a technology that is clean, reliable, accessible and is becoming increasingly affordable …

… and solar power consistently rates as the renewable technology with the highest level of public support. DECC's own public opinion tracker gives it an 82% approval rating.

We want to keep it that way.

This means it must work for local communities, with sensible, sustainable design of new projects. And for larger deployments, brownfield land should always be preferred.

The solar farm at the former Wheal Jane tin mine, just down the road, is a good example of how this can be done.

In other parts of the country, solar has been installed on disused airfields, degraded soil and former industrial sites. This is the model for future solar projects.

But this is not a new position. I have been clear on this point from when I first entered government.

Back in 2010 I told the House of Commons that 'large field-based developments should not be allowed to distort the available funding for roof-based PV, other PV and other types of renewable.' I still stand by this.

Indeed, in January I reiterated this in the House of Commons. I said, and I quote:

> We need to be careful that we do not over-incentivise large-scale ground-mounted projects in inappropriate places – I am thinking of greenfield agricultural land – that could generate strong opposition to our community energy agenda … It needs careful design and thoughtful consideration. It certainly could not be a scheme about renewable energy at any cost. Impacts on the local community, on landscape and on consumer bills have to be a real consideration …

So our message is very clear. And it is consistent.

We have revised our subsidy structure, offering higher levels of support to building-mounted solar PV. And we will do our best to spread examples of best practice, focusing deployment on buildings and brown-field land – not green-field.

Where solar farms are not on brownfield land, you must be looking at low grade agricultural works with farmers to allow grazing in parallel with generation ...

… incorporating well thought out visual screening ...

… involving communities in developing projects and bringing them with you …

… all of these will be vital in creating a sustainable future for large-scale solar PV.

Taking solar further
But no one organisation can carry the solar PV revolution on which we are all embarking.

To do this the sector needs real champions …

… champions with the vision, the ambition and the resources to lead the charge on the next stage of solar PV's journey into the mainstream.

This is where the National Solar Centre comes in.

I was delighted to be asked to cut the ribbon at the NSC this afternoon. I believe it will be an essential component in underpinning the industry.

It will help establish an effective infrastructure for sustained growth through a wide range of activities:

… developing formal Technical Standards … due diligence … developing a range of best practise guidance and training … driving innovation through R&D.

It will also act as a nucleus to influence new markets, and to benefit from the global solar community.

The commitment the Building Research Establishment has shown in driving this forward will help lay the groundwork for more concrete links between the solar PV, building and construction sectors.

I also pay tribute to Ray Noble, who has worked unstintingly to promote and develop the solar sector in the UK. His vision and hard work has made the NSC possible.

So, what next?
In the early summer the coalition will be publishing the first-ever government Solar PV Strategy.

This will set out, in more detail, the work which needs to be done – both by government and the private sector – to capitalise on the sector's growth and take it to the next level.

An important part of this is the creation of a new Solar PV Strategy Group, jointly chaired by DECC and the National Solar Centre.

As the sector grows, we need to balance the huge opportunities with responsible growth. As a key part of our work on a solar strategy, we will work, in association with the sector, on how we can ensure that large-scale solar deployment is truly sustainable.

What criteria the sector should follow, how they can be most effectively implemented – and enforced. That way, we can achieve our twin aims of growth of solar PV and protection of our rural environment.

The Solar PV Strategy Group brings together industry and government to ensure that we work effectively to address the challenges facing the sector over the coming years.

We will be consulting this group as we finalise the Solar PV Strategy over the coming weeks.

And there are other DECC initiatives which will underpin that progress ...

... including our flagship Green Deal which policy is turning out to be a real motor for driving demand ...

... the new government and industry Solar PV Strategy Group ...

... reform of the electricity markets and the other measures set out in our Energy Bill ...

... and, of course, the recent changes to the FiTs scheme and the RO have put in place a stable foundation on which to build further deployment. And provide good projects with the type of return needed to secure investment.

Before I conclude I would like to mention something many of you will consider to be the 'elephant in the room'...

... the European Commission's anti-dumping investigation into PV imports from China.

I completely understand the difficulties and uncertainty this is already causing many of you.

I want to reassure you that the government is working hard to ensure the Commission's response and any measures imposed are proportionate and take account of wider effects on the industry.

We will have greater clarity on the Commission's intentions early in the summer and I would strongly urge you to continue to work through your trade associations. As I know you already do.

Conclusion
The UK already is one of the best places for green energy, for green investment and for green jobs across the world.

And it is right that we should be putting solar PV at the heart of our green energy policy.

And I want us to continue to work together – government and industry – because this is a shared endeavour.

You are the businesses who can continue to develop our expertise in solar technology. To use this technology to cut costs, compete internationally and boost jobs.

You are the experts who can help us build the future of this industry …

… through the new Solar PV Strategy Group which will help to inform our new Solar Strategy.

There is no doubt that there are challenges. But those challenges will be met by us all together and this is just the beginning of our journey.

I would like to end with another quote from the Prime Minister, this time from February this year. He said that green energy makes

> our energy sources more sustainable, our energy consumption more efficient and our economy more resilient to energy price shocks – those things are a vital part of the growth and wealth that we need.

Thank you.

9.44 WMS HWCS488, Solar energy: protecting the local and global environment, made by Lord Pickles on 25 March 2015 (extract from statement on solar energy):

I would like to update the House on further steps we are taking to streamline the planning system, protect the environment, support economic growth and assist locally-led decision-making.

Solar energy: protecting the local and global environment
Last year, the coalition government published a comprehensive solar photovoltaic strategy setting out our ambitions for the technology as an important part of the United Kingdom's energy mix. In doing so, the strategy underlines the importance of focusing growth on domestic and commercial roof space and previously developed land.

My department supported this by consulting on reforms to permitted development rights which will encourage the take up of much larger scale solar power generation (solar photovoltaic) on non-domestic buildings and complement the existing flexibilities for home owners. These reforms allow for a 20-fold increase in the amount of solar that can go onto the roofs of non-domestic buildings such as warehouses and offices without having to submit a full planning application, subject to strict safeguards to protect local amenity. The proposals have been widely welcomed by the solar industry, and the measure will come into force from 15 April 2015.

The National Planning Policy Framework includes strong protections for the natural and historic environment and is quite clear that local councils when considering development proposals should take into account the economic and other benefits of the best and most versatile agricultural land. Yet, some local communities have genuine concerns that when it comes to solar farms insufficient weight has been given to these protections and the benefits of high quality agricultural land. As the solar strategy noted, public acceptability for solar energy is being eroded by the public response to large-scale solar farms which have sometimes been sited insensitively.

Meeting our energy goals should not be used to justify the wrong development in the wrong location and this includes the unnecessary use of high quality agricultural land. Protecting the global environment is not an excuse to trash the local environment. When we published our new planning guidance in support of the framework, we set out the particular factors relating to large scale ground mounted solar photovoltaic farms that a local council will need to consider. These include making effective use of previously developed land and, where a proposal involves agricultural land, being quite clear this is necessary and that poorer quality land is to be used in preference to land of a higher quality.

We are encouraged by the impact the guidance is having but do appreciate the continuing concerns, not least those raised in this House, about the unjustified use of high quality agricultural land. In light of these concerns we want it to be clear that any proposal for a solar farm involving the best and most versatile agricultural land would need to be justified by the most compelling evidence. Of course, planning is a quasi-judicial process, and every application needs to be considered on its individual merits, with due process, in light of the relevant material considerations ...

9.45 Letter from Brandon Lewis MP, Minister of State for Housing and Planning to Simon Ridley, Chief Executive of the Planning Inspectorate, dated 27 March 2015:

Dear Simon

Landscape character and prematurity in planning decisions

I have become aware of several recent appeal cases in which harm to landscape character has been an important consideration in the appeal being dismissed.

These cases are a reminder of one of the twelve core principles at paragraph 17 of the National Planning Policy Framework – that plans and decisions should take into account the different roles and character of different areas, and recognise the intrinsic character of beauty of the countryside – to ensure that development is suitable for the local context.

While National Parks, the Broads, Areas of Outstanding Natural Beauty and Heritage Coasts quite rightly enjoy the highest degree of protection, outside of these designated areas the impact of development on the landscape can be an important material consideration. We are publicising some of these appeal cases more widely, with the help of the Planning Advisory Service, to promote greater understanding of how landscape character can be taken into account by local planning authorities in their decisions.

These cases also reflect the wider emphasis on delivering sustainable outcomes at the heart of the Framework, which means taking full account of the environmental as well as the economic and social dimensions of development proposals. And, of course, these roles should not be undertaken in isolation – the economic factors can secure higher social and environmental standards.

I would also like to take this opportunity to restate our position on prematurity, which I know is also an issue that causes debate in some cases. Paragraph 216 of the National Planning Policy Framework makes clear that weight can be given to relevant policies in emerging Local and neighbourhood plans, and the particular factors that need to be considered when doing so.

When arguments relating to prematurity of development are advanced, our planning guidance sets out the tests to be applied. The weight that can be attached to an emerging plan will need to be considered carefully when assessing whether a prematurity argument is justified. We will continue to consider whether this careful balance is best serving local communities.

Brandon Lewis MP

Comment on Ministerial Statements regarding solar energy

9.46 Despite the enthusiasm of successive governments towards renewable energy, the importance of landscape considerations is repeatedly emphasised in the planning balance, namely that the promotion of renewable energy should not invariably outweigh local environmental concerns. As Lord Pickles put it (see 9.44):

> Meeting our energy goals should not be used to justify the wrong development in the wrong location and this includes the unnecessary use of high quality agricultural land. Protecting the global environment is not an excuse to trash the local environment …

Chapter 10

Case Studies Involving Solar Power Development

CASE STUDY I

Whether the Effect that Development might have on Solar Panels on Neighbouring Residential Property was a Material Planning Consideration

R (McLennan) v Medway Council [2019] EWHC 1738 (Admin) (11 June 2019)

1. The claimant (C) was granted planning permission to install solar panels on the south-facing wall of his residential property in Rochester, Kent. In September 2018 his next-door neighbour (the second defendant (2D)) applied for planning permission to the first defendant (1D) to build a rear extension and dormer window to side. C objected to the proposal on the ground that it would adversely affect his ability to generate electricity from his solar panels. Despite C's objections, 1D granted 2D planning permission on 6 December 2018.

2. In an application for judicial review C sought to challenge 1D's grant of planning permission on the ground that (amongst other things), although the officer's report noted objections in respect of loss of sunlight, loss of privacy, deliberate impairment of solar panels, increase of carbon footprint and the fact that a number of properties in the road had been altered by adding dormers within the roof, it was not considered that the proposal would be unacceptable or introduce new features. The report indicated that no shadow would be cast into the rooms of C's property nor any shadow into its garden. The report also noted that the proposed extension would increase the height of the existing rear projections and, together with the side dormers, would result in an increased level of overshadowing. However, due to the orientation of C's property and rise and fall of the sun, the majority of this overshadowing would be over 1D's property

and was not considered to result in a detrimental impact on the neighbouring properties. Accordingly, whilst the proposal would alter the existing overshadowing, light and overlooking, it would not be significant or detrimental to warrant a refusal of permission and would be in accordance with Policy BNE2 of the Medway Local Plan 2003. For his part, C contended that the decision was in breach of this policy which stated that the design of development should have regard to privacy, daylight and sunlight. As against this, 1D claimed that the effect of daylight on C's solar panels was not a material planning consideration and that 1D was not required to consider the effect of the development on them.

3. In March 2019, after the grant of permission, 2D made a further application for planning permission. Although not identical to the first application, the outline and massing of the built form of the development proposed by the second application was identical to that of the development for which planning permission had already been granted by 1D. A different planning officer prepared a report for 1D's planning committee, which met in May 2019. The second officer recommended approval of the application which was allowed (the present proceedings were not a judicial review of the second grant of planning permission). She observed that although objections were received on the grounds of party wall matters and interference with solar panels, these were not considered to be material planning considerations. The second planning officer recorded that Policy BNE2 of the Medway Local Plan stated that:

> … all development should secure the amenities of its future occupants, and protect those enjoyed by nearby and adjacent properties. The design should have regard to daylight, sunlight and privacy, including noise and activity levels generated by traffic.

4. In terms of daylight and sunlight, the report accepted that whilst there would be some additional overshadowing to the north from the proposed extension, it would not be at unacceptable levels (whereas C considered that the overshadowing would be severe). In terms of overlooking and loss of privacy, the report concluded that the proposal would be acceptable. As far as the solar panels were concerned, the report said that officers did not consider that the potential interference with the solar panels on the neighbouring property was a material planning consideration as it involved a purely private interest which did not require protection in the public interest.

5. Lane J started by referring to section 38(6) of the Planning and Compulsory Purchase Act 2004 which requires that planning applications must be determined in accordance with the development plan unless material considerations indicate otherwise. With regard to the statutory scheme, he also referred to section 70 of the TCPA 1990 under which an LPA, in dealing with applications for planning permission, is required to have regard to the provisions of the development plan

(so far as material to the application) and to any other material considerations. Further, he also indicated that section 19(1A) of the Planning and Compulsory Purchase Act 2004 (as amended by the PA 2008) provided that development plan documents must (taken as a whole) include policies designed to secure that the development and use of land in an LPA's area contribute to the mitigation of, and adaptation to, climate change.

6. In dealing with the development plan, Lane J cited Policy BNE2 of the Medway Local Plan, adopted in May 2003, with which 1D contended the development would be compliant, in addition to Policy BNE1 which provided as follows:

> *BNE1: General Principles for Built Development*
> The design and development (including extensions, alterations and conversions) should be appropriate in relation to the character, appearance and functioning of the build and national environment by:
>
> (i) Being satisfactory in terms of use, scale, mass, proportion, details, materials, layout and siting; and
> (ii) respecting the scale, appearance and location of buildings, spaces and the visual amenity of the surrounding area; and
> (iii) where appropriate, providing well-structured, practical and attractive areas of open space.

7. Policy BNE2 (Amenity protection) also provided as follows:

> *BNE2: Amenity Protection*
> All development should secure the amenities of its future occupants, and protect those amenities enjoyed by nearby and adjacent properties. The design of development should have regard to:
>
> (i) Privacy, daylight and sunlight; and
> (ii) noise, vibration, light, heat, smell and airborne emissions consisting of fumes, smoke, soot, ash, dust and grit; and
> (iii) activity levels and traffic congestion.

8. Lane J also noted the following provisions of the Medway Local Plan:

> 3.4.20. Non-renewable fossil fuels such as gas, oil and coal are burnt to yield energy directly, or are used in power stations to produce electricity. A reduction in the demand for energy from these sources will help in reducing harmful atmospheric emissions. These emissions include greenhouse gases and gases which contribute to 'acid rain' and 'smog'.

> 3.4.23. The use of solar panels also provides a direct means of utilising the sun's energy. Whilst their wider use will generally be appropriate, particularly in new buildings, their visual impact will need to be taken into account …

9. C pointed to the following provisions of BNE4 (Energy Efficiency):

> Energy efficiency measures will be sought within development proposals, providing there is no detrimental impact on amenity. In particular, the proposals should have regard to
>
> …
>
> (iii) Energy efficient technology including solar panels, combined heat and power/district heating schemes and district wind power schemes …

10. C also pointed to various provisions of the NPPF 2018:

> 148. The planning system should support the transition to a low carbon future in a changing climate, taking full account of flood risk and coastal change. It should help to: shape places in ways that contribute to radical reductions in greenhouse gas emissions, minimise vulnerability and improve resilience; encourage the reuse of existing resources, including the conversion of existing buildings; and support renewable and low carbon energy and associated infrastructure.
>
> 153. In determining planning applications, local planning authorities should expect new development to:
>
> (a) comply with any development plan policies on local requirements for decentralised energy supply unless it can be demonstrated by the applicant, having regard to the type of development involved and its design, that this is not feasible or viable; and
> (b) take account of landform, layout, building orientation, massing and landscaping to minimise energy consumption.
>
> 154. When determining planning applications for renewable and low carbon development, local planning authorities should:
>
> (a) not require applicants to demonstrate the overall need for renewable or low carbon energy; and recognise that even small-scale projects provide a valuable contribution to cutting greenhouse gas emissions.

11. C also referred to the Glossary of the NPPF, which defines renewable and low carbon energy as including energy for heating and cooling as well as generating electricity. Renewable energy covers those energy flows that occur naturally and repeatedly in the environment – from the wind, the fall of water, the movements of the oceans, from the sun and also from biomass and deep geothermal heat.

12. 1D's counsel argued that they were correct not to treat the alleged interference with the claimant's solar panels as a material planning consideration in determining the application. He said that such interference was not prescribed, either expressly or impliedly, by the Planning Acts or any other relevant legislation, as a material planning consideration in the determination of applications. It followed that C could only succeed on this issue by demonstrating that the interference with the operation of his solar panels was a consideration which no reasonable decision-maker would have failed to take into account; in other words, C only had a rationality challenge where the bar is set high. 1D's counsel also argued that a planning policy cannot convert something which is immaterial into a material consideration for planning purposes. He also argued that any interference with C's solar panels constituted an interference with a private right and that only rarely would a private right be a material planning consideration, and the present case was not of this character. Lastly, 1D's counsel also relied on section 31(2A) of the Senior Courts Act 1981, suggesting that, even if the first planning officer had not made a mistake as to the alignment of the relevant properties, for the purposes of determining the sun's arc over them, the decision is highly likely to have been the same.

13. C's counsel asserted that the failure of the first defendant to treat the interference with the claimant's solar panels as a material planning consideration was *Wednesbury* unreasonable, having regard to what is said in the relevant provisions of the local plan and the NPPF. The need to mitigate climate change by, amongst other things, promoting the use of renewable energy technology was, he argued, not a private interest matter. He also doubted whether, if 1D had correctly understood the factual position, the same decision would have been reached, given the first defendant's erroneous approach to the issue of solar panels, which 1D continues to follow. For the same reason, C's counsel argued that the recent grant of planning permission in response to 2D's revised application did not render C's challenge academic.

14. Lane J held that the distinction between what materiality means, in a particular planning context, and the weight (if any) to be ascribed to a material consideration is set out in the judgment of Lindblom J (as he was then was) in *Cala Homes (South) Ltd v Secretary of State for Communities and Local Government and Winchester City Council* [2011] 1 P&CR 22, where, at [29], he said this.

> 29. The law has always distinguished between materiality and weight. The distinction is clear and essential. Materiality is a question of law for the court; weight is for the decision-maker in the exercise of planning judgment. Thus, as Lord Hoffmann stated in a well-known passage of his speech in *Tesco Stores Ltd v Secretary of State for the Environment* [1995] 1 W.L.R. 759; (1995) 70 P. & C.R 184 (at p.657G–H):

> This distinction between whether something is a material consideration and the weight which it should be given is only one aspect of a fundamental principle of British planning law, namely that the courts are concerned only with the legality of the decision-making process and not with the merits of the decision. If there is one principle of planning law more firmly settled than any other, it is that matters of planning judgment are within the exclusive province of the local planning authority or the Secretary of State.
>
> So long as it does not lapse into perversity, a local planning authority is entitled to give a material consideration whatever weight it considers to be appropriate. Under the heading 'Little weight or no weight?' Lord Hoffmann observed (at p.661B–C):
>
> > … If the planning authority ignores a material consideration because it has forgotten about it, or because it wrongly thinks that the law or departmental policy (as in *Safeway Properties Ltd v Secretary of State for the Environment* [1991] JPL 966) precludes it from taking it into account, then it has failed to have regard to a material consideration. But if the decision to give that consideration no weight is based on rational planning grounds, then the planning authority is entitled to ignore it.

15. Accordingly, Lane J held that, in appropriate circumstances, an LPA in the reasonable exercise of its discretion may give no significant weight or even no weight at all to a consideration material to its decision, provided that it has had regard to it. The question therefore is what is capable of being a material consideration for the purposes of a planning decision? Although he considered that the concept of materiality was wide, in principle it encompasses any consideration bearing on the use or development of land. Whether a particular consideration is material in a particular case will depend on the circumstances. In the context of development plan-making and development control decision-taking, Lane J considered that the test of materiality formulated by Lord Scarman in his speech in *Westminster City Council v Great Portland Estates Plc* [1985] AC 661 (at pp. 669H–670C–E) is whether the consideration in question 'serves a planning purpose', which is one that 'relates to the character and use of land'. Where, however, the statutory scheme does not make a particular matter a material planning consideration, either expressly or by implication, the element of discretion enters the picture. At this point, the test becomes one of rationality.

16. Lane J considered that both the local plan and the NPPF recognise the positive contribution that can be made to climate change by even small-scale renewable energy schemes. That point was driven home by section 19(1A) of the Planning and Compulsory Purchase Act 2004. He considered that what emerges from section 19(1A) and the NPPF is that mitigation of climate change is a legitimate planning consideration. He found that the stance of 1D, in rejecting as

immaterial, the effect that another development proposal may have upon a renewable energy system (such as C's solar panels) was irrational and one which no reasonable authority could take. Obviously, the claimant's solar panels relate to the use of his land and are not solely for some other purpose. 1D failed to appreciate that interference with the solar panels is a material planning consideration by reason of the part played by them in addressing (however modestly, on an individual scale) issues of climate change. Insofar as the officer's report was based on the categorisation of the claimant's solar panels as a purely private interest, the conclusion was flawed. No consideration was given to why a person's ability to use the sunlight reaching his property to generate electricity falls into a materially different category from the same person's ability to enjoy sunlight falling into his living room or garden which 1D's officers treated as a material consideration, albeit finding that the interference was not such as to make it appropriate to refuse permission. This is not to say that, when it comes to ascribing weight, a planning authority may not legitimately conclude that reduced sunlight to a living room deserves greater weight than interference with solar panels; or vice versa. The problem lies in the *in limine* rejection of interference with solar panels as having any material bearing. Lane J also found against 1D on the issue of whether relief should be refused pursuant to section 31(2A) of the Senior Courts Act 1981 which depended upon the court finding that it was 'highly likely that the outcome for the applicant would not have been substantially different if the conduct complained of had not occurred'). It was the view of the judge that the issues required – but did not receive – proper consideration by 1D. For instance, 1D's conclusion that the effect of the proposed development on the solar panels would be 'negligible' lacked any reasoning. In the result, the court quashed the grant of planning permission of 6 December 2018.

Comment

17. It seems plain that an owner of solar panels may find support in planning law where his building is liable to be overshadowed by nearby development. While *Medway* concerned only solar panels, the question begs as to the extent to which, in the future, decision-makers would be bound to recognise climate change as a material consideration when it comes to applications for renewable energy development.[1] It might be added that it is open to debate whether a right to light to solar panels could be acquired as a prescriptive easement, seeing as the measure of light which can be acquired by prescription is limited to the light required for the beneficial use of the building for its ordinary purposes, although the principle has been extended to a greenhouse.[2]

---

1 See 'Is Climate Change Now a Material Planning Consideration?' by Raymond Cooper in JPL, Issue 10 [2019].

2 *Allen v Greenwood* [1980] Ch 119.

CASE STUDY II

Large Solar Farm in Green Belt Rejected on Landscape Grounds by Secretary of State on Recovered Appeal – Appeal Dismissed

Planning appeal reference APPC3620/W/3000674 (24 November 2015)

1. In a decision letter from the SoS dated 24 November 2015 the operator was notified that its recovered appeal from the refusal of Mole Valley District Council to grant planning permission for the construction of a 32.5 hectare solar park (with an estimated lifespan of 25 years) under application reference MO/2014/0061/PLAMAJ, dated 10 January 2014, at Mynthurst Farm, Mynthurst, Leigh, Surrey was dismissed. The appeal had been recovered for the SoS's determination because the proposal was considered to be significant development in the Green Belt. The SoS agreed with the recommendation of the inspector, Phillip Ware, that the appeal should be dismissed.

2. The appeal site was set in largely undeveloped countryside within four fields currently in arable production forming part of an overall landholding extending to some 312 hectares. The site is within the Low Weald National Landscape Character Area, which is an area of broad low-lying gently undulating clay vales comprising a generally pastoral landscape with arable farming and characteristic field boundaries. The Surrey Hills AONB is around 3.8km to the north-west of the appeal site.

3. The solar panels were going to be located in four adjoining fields. The panels would be 2.2m at the highest point, would have a gap of around 5m between rows and would be mounted on steel frames. They would be set back from the boundaries. The proposal would retain and enhance existing boundary vegetation and there would be a buffer zone alongside a watercourse. In addition, there would be a number of related structures including nine inverter stations (each 3.6m high and sited in 0.6m depressions), a grid connection building, 2m high deer fencing between 2.5m high posts, closed-circuit television (CCTV) cameras on 2.5m high galvanised poles and a number of access tracks.

4. The appeal site lay within the Metropolitan Green Belt. The development plan comprises the Mole Valley Core Strategy (2009) and the saved policies of the Mole Valley Local Plan (2000). The policies of the Core Strategy included policies which directed development towards built-up areas and refers to (amongst other matters) then-extant national policies relating to Green Belts,

landscape and sustainable development which have since been superseded by the NPPF.

5. The appellant accepted that although the development amounted to inappropriate development in the Green Belt, very special circumstances existed to outweigh the limited harm which was recognised by the officer's recommendation for approval. As there were no extant development plan policies relating to the development in the Green Belt, the NPPF was the basis for the assessment. The appellant contended that the impact on the openness of the Green Belt would be mitigated by two factors. First, the development would be limited in height with the solar panels at 2.3m and no other structures taller than 3m. This meant that the development could be effectively screened by existing vegetation and the proposed mitigation planting. Second, the proposal was for a limited period of 25 years after which the site would be returned to open agricultural land. The installed capacity of the solar farm would be 13.5MW which was estimated to produce electricity to power 3,060 average homes. It was argued that the NPPF provided strong support for renewable energy development and also gave rise to a diversification of the farming enterprise, which was particularly important owing to the fall in milk prices and the general volatility of the market. The solar farm would provide a consistent income to support the operation of the wider farm and enable the development of new facilities for which planning permission had been given. These matters were addressed in the Agricultural Assessment submitted with the application.

6. The appellant argued that the proposal could be accommodated in landscape and visual terms. Whilst there would be a change in land use for the time-limited operational phase of the development, it was claimed that there would be an overall net benefit on trees and hedgerows. All the existing hedgerows and the majority of trees and woodland on and surrounding the site would be retained and enhanced by way of infill and reinforcement hedgerow and tree planting. It was claimed that whilst the appeal site was set within a pleasant environment, it was unremarkable in scenic quality terms and had a capacity to accommodate a solar farm without causing unacceptable harm. For instance, the enclosed nature of the landscape would help to diminish the perceived size of the development by restricting views so that only discrete sections of the solar farm would be seen. Further, except from limited locations and at very close quarters, the proposal would not be seen against the skyline. Where views of the development were gained, these would be largely confined to areas in close proximity to the boundary, particularly from the footpaths and bridleways to the north and south. Overall, it was contended that the proposed development would not materially change the perception of the Open Weald Landscape Character Area, mainly due to the layering effect of surrounding vegetation and the existence of other forms of infrastructure such as roads, buildings and settlements.

7. In terms of visual amenity, it was claimed that the harm would not be unacceptable. For instance, the appreciation of users of the road network would not be so great as to significantly change the users' appreciation and enjoyment of the rural character of the countryside through which they were passing. Views of the development from public rights of way would be constrained by topography and vegetation and the only significant visual effect would be limited to locations in the immediate vicinity of the site – and these views would be mitigated by planting. The Ecological Appraisal submitted with the application also demonstrated that there would be no harmful impact on any designated sites or protected species and the proposal included a number of habitat enhancements, including an apiary. There were no heritage assets within the site and the Heritage Assessment demonstrated that there would be no harmful effect on the setting of any asset. If there were any archaeological assets this could be addressed by a condition. The Flood Risk Assessment also showed that the site was in Flood Zone 1, which meant that there was a low risk of flooding. The site is Grade 3b agricultural land and was therefore outside the NPPF definition of best and most versatile (BMV) agricultural land. Conditions would also mitigate the negative effects arising during the construction phase and during the operational phase traffic would be very limited. No properties would be subject to an overbearing impact and the Residential and Visual Amenity Study demonstrated that only limited views of the development would be possible from the nearest property. A planning condition could also deal with decommissioning. Overall, it was contended that there were very special circumstances which meant that planning permission should be granted.

8. The case for the planning authority was that the proposal was inappropriate development in the Green Belt which is, by definition, harmful. The scope of the proposed development was such that it would have a major adverse impact on the openness of the Green Belt and be contrary to two of the purposes of the designation of the area – safeguarding the countryside from encroachment and assisting in urban regeneration (in that the development could be located on the roofs of existing commercial properties). It was also argued that national policy was moving away from large-scale solar projects towards smaller schemes associated with brownfield sites and existing buildings. In other words, national policy was that the appellant should demonstrate a need, not for the renewable energy generation, but for development of this particular location. It was also argued that little weight should be given to the proposed 25-year lifespan of the proposal: unacceptable development is not rendered acceptable simply because it will only be in place for 25 years. Further, allowing sheep to graze amongst the panels would do little to maintain the character of the area. In the result, it was claimed that very special circumstances to justify the harm to the Green Belt in principle and by reason of impact on openness and the purposes of the designation had not been demonstrated. It was argued that the development would be

perceived as a single large scheme due to its unnatural and homogeneous form, colour and materials stretching across the site and the degree of visibility would vary through the seasons. There were also a number of potential public viewpoints from nearby bridleways and footpaths as well as from residential properties. It was not accepted that the rows of solar panels would be visually comparable with the appearance of crops in fields. Overall, it was claimed that the development would have an adverse impact on the character and appearance of the site and the surrounding area. A number of written objections were received from local residents and organisations such as the Campaign to Protect Rural England (Surrey Branch), the Surrey Wildlife Trust, Reigate and Banstead Borough Council, the Ramblers Association, Newdigate Parish Council, Charlwood/ Leigh/Salfords and Sidlow Parish Council, the Norwood Hill Residents Association, the Charlwood Society, and Crispin Blunt MP. Those respondents who objected to the proposal raised the following main matters in addition to Green Belt and landscape impact: (a) lack of continuing demand for solar power; (b) the unsuitability of the land for sheep grazing; (c) the loss of agricultural land; (d) the safety of users of the footpaths and bridleways during the construction period; (e) the length of the proposed temporary period and the uncertainty that the land will eventually revert to agriculture; (f) ecological impact; (g) the effect on neighbouring properties; (h) health issues; (i) impact of construction traffic; and (j) precedent for other similar proposals.

9. The inspector accepted that developers needed to demonstrate very special circumstances if development was to take place in the Green Belt. He also accepted that very special circumstances could include the wider environmental benefits associated with the increased production of energy from renewable sources. He said that substantial weight should be given to the fact that the proposal represents inappropriate development which was, by definition, harmful to the Green Belt. The inspector said that openness was an essential characteristic of the Green Belt. In this instance, the scale of the development, comprising arrays of solar panels and related fencing and other structures, across a site of over 30 hectares, was, as the inspector found, such that it would clearly have an impact on the openness of the area and could not be effectively screened by existing vegetation and proposed mitigation planting.

10. Although the inspector accepted that the harm to the openness of the area would be time-limited, he considered that the period involved was such that the effect of the reduced openness would still last for about a generation and did little to reduce the harm to openness. He went on to say that the NPPF sets out a number of purposes related to the designation of a Green Belt and the proposal would conflict with one of these, namely safeguarding the countryside from encroachment, seeing as the proposal would introduce an essentially manufactured form of development into the largely natural environment.

Accordingly, the proposal was conflicted with the development plan (which contained a number of policies aimed at the protection of the countryside in general) and national policy in relation to the Green Belt even though the site is not within an area specifically protected at national or local level for its landscape beauty. The area is part of the Low Weald National Landscape Character Area and is described as being broad, low-lying, gently undulating clay vales, comprising a generally pastoral landscape with arable farming, with field boundaries of hedgerows and remnant strips of cleared woodland. This is also reflected in the more localised Open Weald Landscape Character Area (assessed in the Council's 2013 Landscape SPD) which emphasises the small scale of the landscape and the importance of the patchwork of fields and hedgerows. The inspector considered that the appeal site is typical of this landscape character in terms of field size, shape and landscape elements.

11. The appellants argued that the enclosed nature of the landscape (i.e. the patchwork of fields and hedgerows) would help to diminish the perceived size of the solar farm. However, the inspector found that although the field boundaries and planting would be retained and enhanced, this overstated the softening effect brought about by the retention of the field boundaries and additional planting. It was his view that the solar farm would be perceived as one single development, albeit divided by hedges, stretching over a wide area. The horizontal extent of the scheme, allied to its not inconsiderable height, would, as he found, make it appear as a single large development stretching over a wide area of the landscape in place of the current agricultural landscape and would be seen as man-made and alien to their rural surroundings. The fence, CCTV cameras and poles, and associated structures would add a further sense of urbanisation in this isolated rural area. It was the inspector's assessment that the landscape was incapable of absorbing the development without changing and harming its essential character. In addition, he found that the visual amenity of receptors using the public footpaths and bridleways would be significantly affected to such an extent as to be unacceptable. He found that although the effect would reduce over time as the proposed planting matured, the experience of those using this route would be materially harmed by the proposal. He did, however, accept that although residents might find the change unwelcome, the visual element of residential amenity would not be affected to such a degree that the properties concerned would come to be regarded as unattractive and thus unsatisfactory (but not uninhabitable) places in which to live. Overall, it was the inspector's view that the proposal would harm the character and appearance of the surrounding landscape and conflict with landscape policies. The visual amenity of the area, as experienced by receptors on the footpaths, would, as he found, also be significantly harmed.

12. The inspector accepted that the benefit arising from the provision of renewable energy (the proposal would have an installed capacity of 13.5MW)

added weight to the case in favour of the scheme and it was unnecessary for the appellants to demonstrate the overall need for the proposal. However, the support for renewable energy is generally caveated by the need for siting of developments to be appropriate and for the impacts to be acceptable or capable of being made so. The inspector also accepted that the fact that the development could be decommissioned after 25 years and the land returned to its former state could not be ignored, although it still meant that the development and its effects would be in place for a significant period.

13. Although the inspector considered it arguable that the current trend in this sector was to move away from large-scale solar developments, the application and appeal still had to be determined in accordance with the development plan and other material considerations and the current policy is generally supportive of renewable energy projects subject to the caveats above (i.e. where developments were appropriately sited and where environmental impacts were acceptable or could be satisfactorily mitigated). Although the provision of renewable energy was considered to be a matter that attracted significant weight in favour of the proposal, the issue between the parties is the weight to be ascribed to this factor and other positive and negative aspects of the scheme. On the question of securing the decommissioning works, the inspector found that, consistently with the recommended approach in the NPPG, a condition could address the removal of the installation and the reinstatement of the land although, as he found, this matter did not add any weight to the arguments against the proposal.

14. Other matters, such as objections involving the loss of agricultural land, are covered by the NPPF which provides that the economic and other benefits of the BMV agricultural land should be taken into account. Where significant development of agricultural land is demonstrated to be necessary, areas of poorer quality land should be used in preference to that of a higher quality. This approach has been reaffirmed by the WMS entitled 'Planning Update March 2015' of 25 March 2015. The definition of BMV land is found in the Framework, and comprises land in Grades 1, 2 and 3a of the ALC. The appeal site was shown as Grades 3 and 4 on the 1979 land classification map and the appellant's uncontested survey shows it to be Grade 3b. It was therefore outside the type of agricultural land which national policy seeks to protect and this matter did not weigh against the proposal.

15. The inspector also found that although the proposal included the intention that sheep would graze between and beneath the solar arrays, there was no mechanism to ensure that this took place throughout the lifetime of the development, and, in his view, this intention carried very little weight. He also mentioned that the appellant's unchallenged Ecological Appraisal conclusively

demonstrated that there would be no harm to designated sites or protected species. The inspector also accepted that the proposal included the retention and strengthening of existing hedgerows, along with other planting including a buffer zone by Deanoak Brook and that an area of land would be used as an apiary. However, he said that although no designated sites or protected species were identified as being affected, the construction of the solar farm would be, as he found, a significant undertaking and there would be inevitable harm caused to the existing ecology of the site and the immediate area. Some aspects of the ecological enhancements can fairly be regarded as mitigation for this harm, and other elements as mitigation in relation to landscape harm. However, he considered that these matters added very limited weight to the arguments in favour of the proposal. On the issue of farming diversification, the inspector accepted that, partly due to the fall in milk prices and for other reasons, the farm needed a reliable source of income, and that, in part, would fund other farming projects which have received planning permission. These matters were in line with local and national policy aimed at supporting a prosperous economy and promoting the development and diversification of agricultural enterprises. The inspector accepted that this factor added some weight to the arguments in favour of the development. In terms of vehicle movements, he considered that once the solar farm was built, the number of vehicle movements would be very small and even though the access at that time would be shared with a public bridleway, this was the case with the existing farm access and there was no reason to suppose that the addition of limited vehicles accessing the solar farm along this route would lead to any problems. The inspector considered that there was no evidence that the proposal would harm vehicle or pedestrian safety and this matter was neutral in the planning balance.

16. In the event that planning permission was granted, conditions were set out in the council's committee report and a further set was included in the appellant's appeal statement. The two sets of conditions were generally similar, but the parties had not commented on the limited differences between the two versions. These conditions had been slightly modified in the light of the NPPG and are set out in the Annex to the report. Aside from a condition specifying the approved plans, a number of details of the development would need to be submitted for approval in the interests of the appearance of the area. Given that the proposal was for a period of 25 years and the land would then be restored, a range of conditions would be necessary to ensure the long-term clearance and remediation of the site. The hours during which construction could take place should be limited in order to protect residents' amenity. Both parties had put forward a condition prohibiting the use of floodlights or other external lighting during the operation of the solar farm. The inspector considered this reasonable in the interests of the amenity of the area and the need to avoid light pollution. However, the council's condition would have extended this to include the construction

phase – but, given that the permitted working hours include some hours of darkness, this additional control would be unreasonable. A temporary access road would be necessary during the construction phase and conditions were necessary in the interests of highway safety and the appearance of the area to ensure the provision and subsequent removal of this access. To protect the watercourse and promote biodiversity, a buffer zone would be necessary alongside Deanoak Brook together with a further condition to implement the recommendations of the appellant's Ecological Appraisal. It would also be necessary to require a programme of archaeological investigation to evaluate any heritage assets which may be present. A landscaping scheme would also need to be submitted and implemented in the interests of the appearance of the development.

17. It was the inspector's conclusion that the proposal amounted to inappropriate development in the Green Belt and would harm its openness. It would also conflict with one of the purposes of designating the Green Belt in the first place. This, he found, weighed heavily against the proposal. In terms of the economic dimension of sustainability, he found that there would be a short-term employment benefit during the construction phase but, of greater significance, a benefit to the diversification of the farm holding. However, as against this benefit, he found that there would be significant harm caused to the natural environment in terms of the landscape and visual amenity of the area, albeit that there would be some very limited ecological enhancements. However, he did find that the proposal would be sustainable in terms of the need to mitigate and adapt to climate change, including moving to a low carbon economy. The fact that the proposal was to be only temporary in nature (albeit for a long period) also weighed in favour of the proposal as it would limit the harm both in terms of Green Belt policy and in relation to landscape impact.

18. At the end of the day, the inspector considered that the case was one where the balance was clearly against the development due to the significant weight which, as he found, should be accorded to the harm to the Green Belt and the character and appearance of the area. Despite the acknowledged benefits, these harms outweighed the benefits, even the weight to be accorded to the production of renewable energy. He reiterated that national policy advises that renewable energy proposals should be located where impacts are, or can be made, acceptable. However, he considered that this was not the case with the current proposal which he said could not be sustainable when assessed against the NPPF as a whole. As he put it: the level of harm significantly and demonstrably outweighs the benefits of the proposal in terms of paragraph 14 of the NPPF. It followed that very special circumstances sufficient to justify inappropriate development did not exist and he accordingly recommended to the SoS that the appeal be dismissed, a recommendation which was accepted.

Comment

19. This was a recovered appeal involving a very large site in the Green Belt where the inspector appears to have had little difficulty in finding that very special circumstances had not been made out despite the generation of energy from renewable sources. His view was that the scale of the development across a site of over 30 hectares was clearly going to impact on the openness of the area and could not be effectively screened by existing vegetation and proposed mitigation planting. Although the scheme would be time-limited (25 years), he still considered that this period involved was long enough and did little to reduce the harm to the character and appearance of the area contrary to a number of local policies aimed at the protection of the countryside in general as well as national policy in relation to the Green Belt. In his view the development (along with its associated paraphernalia) would appear as a large development stretching over a wide area in place of the current agricultural landscape and would be seen as man-made and alien to its rural surroundings. This failed application demonstrates the trend away from large-scale solar applications in the countryside unless, of course, the environmental impacts are acceptable or can be satisfactorily mitigated, although, having said that, the scope for using previously developed land and large buildings in the countryside is usually limited in practice.

CASE STUDY III

10MW Solar Farm Rejected because of Harm to Landscape – Appeal Refused

Planning appeal reference APP/D3125/W/16/3158494 (16 August 2017)

1. In a decision dated 16 August 2017, under planning appeal reference APP/D3125/W/16/3158494, Neil Pope, an inspector appointed by the SoS, refused an appeal against the decision of West Oxfordshire District Council to refuse planning permission for the construction of a solar PV park to include the installation of solar panels with a control room, transformer housings, inverters, security system (fencing and infrared cameras), underground cabling, landscaping, access tracks and other associated works under application reference number 15/04003/FUL.

2. The potential capacity of the redesigned solar farm would be in the region of 7MW, whereas when determined by the LPA it had been around 10MW. By the time of the appeal the application had been revised by the retention and reinforcement of a hedgerow across the site and the provision of semi-mature mitigation planting. The layout of the proposed panel area had also been reduced by around 25%. Further amendments involved the use of 'grass-crete' in lieu of crushed aggregate along part of the access track, the removal of part of the mitigation hedgerow and additional off-site mitigation on the eastern side of the site. Even though the extent of the proposed development had been reduced by the time of the appeal, the inspector ruled that he had to determine the matter on the basis of the plans which were considered by the LPA in March 2016, more than a year earlier. The reason for this was that although he was dealing with a reduced level of proposed development, pre-application consultation had taken place on the basis of the original plans and interested parties, especially neighbouring residents, might be aggrieved if a decision were made on appeal on the basis of details which they were previously unaware of. There had been no consultation by either the LPA or the appellant in respect of the final design layout and the further landscaping amendments. The inspector said that he was mindful of the need for flexibility in the planning system yet noted the Planning Inspectorate's Procedural Guide which advised that the appeal process should not be used to evolve a scheme and that it was important that what was considered by the inspector was what was considered by the LPA and on which interested people's views had been sought.

3. The inspector said that the main issue on the appeal was whether the benefits of the proposal, including the production of electricity from a renewable source, outweigh the adverse impacts upon the character and appearance of the area, including any cumulative impact arising with two nearby approved solar farms.

4. Relevant local policies concerned local landscape character and renewable energy. He also noted relevant national policies in the NPPF and national guidance which gave advice on and general support for renewable energy schemes. He also took into account the Climate Change Act 2008, the government's commitment to renewable energy and the legally binding targets affecting the reduction in the UK's emissions which he said did not automatically override environmental protection.

5. The inspector, in considering the benefits of the scheme, noted that the appellant had calculated that the maximum output from the development would be 9,510MWh per annum which would be the equivalent annual electricity needs of 2,304 typical households. It had also been calculated that the proposal would result in carbon savings (i.e. if displacing electricity generated using the standard fuel mix) of up to 6,105 tonnes of CO_2 per annum if the maximum output was achieved.

6. The inspector also noted that the proposal would include new/strengthened hedgerow planting within the site and some semi-mature mitigation planting. Grass underneath the solar PVs would also provide for foraging birds. These things, the appellant claimed, would make a positive contribution to the character and appearance of the area and, to a limited extent, would be likely to enhance nature conservation. Moreover, as Grade 3b agricultural land, the site did not comprise BMV agricultural land, which meant that the proposal would not harm the agricultural industry and would also provide some limited support for the construction industry. The inspector accepted that these environmental and economic benefits could be given considerable weight in the overall planning balance.

7. The appeal site lay within the Cotswolds National Landscape Character Area (LCA) and was only 1.8km south of the Cotswolds AONB. One of the key characteristics of the LCA are the dry stone walls that define the pattern of fields. At local level, the site lies within the Shilton Downs LCA and the Open Limestone Wolds Landscape Character Type (LCT). The description of this LCA included a reference to its attractive and largely unspoilt rural character. The LCT is described as large-scale, smoothly rolling farmland occupying the limestone plateau and dipslope, with large or very large fields and a very open and exposed character. The inspector noted on his extensive visits the unspoilt open attributes of the farmland that makes up the appeal site and the dry stone walls and boundary

vegetation that define the field edges which he said were attractive rural qualities that reflected some of the key characteristics of the LCAs and LCT. However, the proposal site was not itself a designated landscape and already includes solar farms. The area was, however, popular with visitors and residents, many of whom were likely to derive considerable enjoyment from the pleasing views across the rolling farmland and limestone plateau.

8. It was the view of the inspector that the appellant had underestimated the value of the views, scenic quality and amenity of the area. He considered that the site and surroundings were of medium sensitivity to the type of development proposed. He noted that the development would involve erecting a considerable number of ground-mounted PV panels in very many arrays, each having a maximum height of 2.2m across much of the appeal site. There would also be transformer and control buildings, infrared lighting poles, access tracks and a security fence around the proposed panel area. This would not be small-scale development and would give rise to a dramatic change in the rural character of the site and would detract from the unspoilt open qualities of the site. The inspector's finding was that the proposal would result in 'a high magnitude of change to the character of the site and a major adverse effect'.

9. The inspector considered that the scale, colour, form and texture of the man-made development would compromise a discordant element within the Cotswold landscape. He did, though, accept that the low profile of the development, the semi-enclosed character of elements of the wider landscape and the dry stone walls and vegetation that defined the field boundaries would, to some extent, limit the landscape impact. The inspector considered that the cumulative effect upon the character of the local area arising from the number of solar farms within the landscape around Shilton would be limited as they would be adequately separated by the smoothly rolling farmland and established intervening vegetation.

10. The inspector also accepted that the adverse landscape impacts would be time-limited and reversible and that, as a result, there would be no material harm to the setting of the village. Overall, he considered that the harm to the landscape character should be given moderate weight. He also accepted that the limited height to the development and intervening landform, vegetation, walls and buildings would largely screen the proposal from views beyond a distance of about 1.5km from the site. However, until the landscape mitigation became effective (and during winter months), parts of the development would still be seen from the public realm to the east and north. He said that some of the arrays and the dark coloured solar PV panels set in their metal frames would be very different to the appearance of the surrounding fields and landscape. He thought that this would catch the eye and stand out as a conspicuous addition to the landscape. It was his view that the proposal would have a medium magnitude of impact on

views and would be likely to result in a medium adverse effect upon the quality and enjoyment of these views which, he considered, weighed against granting planning permission.

11. It was the view of the inspector that as the proposal would harm the character and appearance of the area, it would conflict with local policies and that the proposed mitigation would not satisfactorily address the adverse landscape and visual impacts. He considered that this carried considerable weight in the planning balance.

12. On the face of it, the inspector's finding that the proposal was going to result in 'a high magnitude of change to the character of the site' made it inevitable that he was going to find that the benefits of the proposal were not going to outweigh the adverse impacts which he identified. He considered that the impact would be unacceptable upon the local environment and the quality of the landscape would not be conserved. As a consequence, he found that the development would not satisfy local policy NE12 or emerging policy EH4 (both of which deal with renewable energy) and would also fail to satisfy the environmental objective when it came to achieving sustainable development under the NPPF (paragraph 8(c)). In the circumstances, he concluded that the appeal should not succeed.

Comment

13. The interesting feature of this application was that by the time of the appeal the scheme had been revised resulting in a panel area reduction of around 25%. There were also landscaping and other improvements. Despite these revisions the inspector considered that he had to determine the appeal on the basis of the plans considered by the LPA more than a year earlier. The reason he gave for this was that although he was dealing with a reduced level of development, pre-application consultation had taken place on the basis of the original plans and there had there been no consultation by either the LPA or the appellant in respect of the final design layout and the further landscaping amendments. The inspector referred to the Planning Inspectorate's Procedural Guide, which discouraged the use of an appeal to evolve a scheme which might be acceptable. It was a case where the planning balance again went against the appellant despite the benefits of renewable solar energy. As the inspector put it, the proposal would result in 'a high magnitude of change to the character of the site and a major adverse effect'.

CASE STUDY IV

Solar Farm Rejected on Landscape and Heritage Grounds – Appeals Refused

Planning appeal references APP/U2235/W/16/3155702 and APP/M2270/W/16/3155716 (25 August 2017)

1. In a decision dated 25 August 2017, under planning appeal references: (a) APP/U2235/W/16/3155702; and (b) APP/M2270/W/16/3155716, Keith Manning, an inspector appointed by the SoS, refused appeals against decisions of, in the case of (a) Maidstone Borough Council (MBC) (Appeal A), and, in the case of (b) Tunbridge Wells Borough Council (Appeal B), to refuse planning permission for the construction of a solar farm and associated works including fencing enclosure, transformers, switch gear housing, substation (i.e. the Appeal A works) and a temporary construction access (i.e. the Appeal B works) under application reference numbers 15/503884/FUL (Appeal A works) and 15/505149/FUL (Appeal B works).

2. The appeal sites exceed 20 hectares although the fenced area containing the solar panels is around 15 hectares. The solar panels were proposed to be in place for 35 years. Appeal site A straddled a meandering watercourse within a gentle valley separating the proposed northern and southern installations. The area is crossed by a number of public rights of way (mainly footpaths) following the higher ground above the valley. The landscape is undulating and largely open and pastoral in nature with generally medium-sized fields, hedgerows with occasional trees and scattered copses associated with ponds. These solar panels were to be located in two fields which are larger than is typical in the immediate vicinity.

3. The inspector identified a number of local policies within the relevant local and emerging plans, along with policies in the NPPF and in various Ministerial Statements. It is unnecessary for the purposes of this summary to say anything other than that the general objective of the relevant policies is to protect the countryside (i.e. that due regard must be had to landscape quality and character as a central tenet of local policy as expressed in adopted and emerging plans) particularly policy ENV34 of the Maidstone Borough-Wide Local Plan (MBLP) which concerns the protection of Special Landscape Areas (SLAs) including the 'Low Weald' which encompasses the larger southern installation within the site of Appeal A. It is worth noting that EWNV28 does not even anticipate renewable energy developments in the countryside and tended to be absolute in resisting harm, as opposed to balancing harm against benefits and, as the inspector found, a lack of consistency with the approach in the NPPF reduced the weight which

could be accorded to the policy, although it did not mean that it was irrelevant. In considering the quality of the landscape, the inspector noted that whilst valued landscapes within the meaning of the NPPF (formerly paragraph 109) are not designated landscapes, it is clear, as the inspector so found, that valued landscapes do not preclude landscapes which have been formally recognised in the development plan. In other words (as the emerging MBLP recognises) that the 'Low Weald' is a landscape of local value and that decisions on renewable energy should take into account the landscape and visual impact of the proposal (albeit that the extent of the SLA stops at the watercourse separating the southern array from the northern).

4. As for the NPPF, whilst protection of the countryside for its own sake is not an expression used in the NPPF, the concept is, as the inspector found, not wholly incompatible with its core principle that incorporates recognition of its intrinsic quality and beauty, albeit that this must plainly involve the balanced approach to sustainable development. As the inspector also indicated, the recognition of the importance of renewable energy is a feature of national policy which addresses the impacts of climate change. The inspector also emphasised that the importance of landscape considerations in the balanced approach to renewable energy has been repeatedly emphasised in Ministerial Statements and advice, namely that the promotion of renewable energy should not automatically outweigh local environmental concerns including those relating to landscape quality and character, a message reinforced through the NPPG, which indicates a preference for the use of buildings and previously developed land for solar power projects in preference to agricultural land, albeit that there is no sequential test required and that the most compelling justification for its loss is only required in the case of BMV land. However, the inspector accepted that renewable energy projects had to be developed in a large range of situations with varying degrees of inherent environmental sensitivity and where there was capacity in the National Grid. In the circumstances, the scope for using previously developed land and large buildings was necessarily limited in practice.

5. Although the LPAs raised no particular concerns in relation to heritage issues, the inspector considered that local residents had put forward sufficiently cogent reasons for him to identify heritage impact as an issue of potentially decisive importance and he cited local policies (and referred to relevant legislation) which were relevant for these purposes.

6. The inspector's determination on landscape character was fatal to the success of the appeals. He found that the quality of the landscape overall was reflected in its partial inclusion within the MBC (Low Weald) SLA. He attached no weight to the fact that the boundary of the SLA corresponded to the water course between the two arrays, thereby formally excluding the proposed northern

array from its purview. The fact was, as he put it, that there was no discernible change in landscape quality or character across that boundary. The two fields are integral and directly contribute to the character, appearance and quality of a relatively discrete but undulating tract of countryside within the circumference of the higher ground which tended to accommodate the network of paths and scattered elements of rural settlement. The inspector said that from all points on this network 'the overall pleasantness of the largely pastoral scene is very apparent as is its timeless sense of tranquillity and sense of remoteness from the pressures of the modern world'. He said that these were distinctive attributes which created a sense of place of a particular type, whether formally designated or not, and he said that he had no doubt that the appeal site could properly be regarded as a valued landscape for the purposes of the NPPF. As he put it, the SLA qualifies by reason of its designation and in view of its particular attributes, whereas the area outside it shared those qualities in any event.

7. The landscape character SPD places the appeal site within the Staplehurst Low Weald with a guideline to conserve and the 2015 Maidstone Landscape Capacity Study assesses this as being of high overall landscape sensitivity and sensitive to change. The inspector did not doubt the correctness of this. It was his view that the area would be transformed by the installation of the proposed solar arrays and associated equipment. As he put it, 'They would be fundamentally incongruous relative to that character'. In terms of visibility, the inspector also found that the centrality of the proposed solar arrays on undulating land would, in the absence of mitigation, ensure that the negative change in character would be more or less continuously apparent. He considered that the appellant had underestimated the potential visual impact of the arrays on users of the footpath network. The inspector placed little weight on the temporary nature of the adverse landscape and visual effects 'as 35 years is effectively a generation at least'. In terms of mitigation, the inspector expressed concern that a significant volume of the proposed planting was to take place outside the appeal site on land which was not controlled by the appellant (but for which a relevant consent – described by the inspector as 'a letter of good intent' – had been given) and would be subject to enforcement difficulties. The inspector found that the relevant consent did not constitute an enforceable agreement and in his view there was a risk that attitudes and ownership might change over time. It was, therefore, doubtful whether, as the LPA had suggested, a long-term management agreement could be introduced as a condition which could be built into an off-site scheme of measures. Quite apart from this, the inspector also doubted whether the anticipated rate of growth of appropriate native species was such as to make it sufficient as a visual barrier over eight to ten years. In the inspector's view it was probable that more growth would be required to screen the development effectively from significant parts of the public realm. This would of itself introduce uncharacteristically uniform

vegetation at height so as to draw attention to the existence of the development behind what would comprise an incongruously thorough and substantial screening within what he described as a pastoral landscape which gained much of its character from open views across fields and hedgerows. In the result, the inspector did not think that the site readily lent itself to effective mitigation by screening the solar arrays from view. The inspector duly found that there would be harmful conflict with, as he put it, the 'weighty intentions' of the existing development plan insofar as the effect of the proposed development on the character and appearance of the area, with particular reference to the landscape, would be very significantly detrimental. That outcome, he considered, in combination with the temporary construction works, would be contrary to the overall thrust of both existing and emerging development plan policy across the administrative boundaries and relevant national policy.

8. The question of heritage impact arose for consideration as there were a number of Grade II listed buildings in the wider area (nine within 500m of the development site, plus three buildings from the Kent Historic Buildings Index plus farm workers cottages, barns and oasthouses) and it was contended that the development would impact on the significance of such assets, including any contribution made by their setting. In fact, one of the objectors argued that the development would be damaging to the totality of the setting of the historic agrarian landscape of which the listed and non-listed assets formed part. It was, however, the view of the inspector that any harm to the significance of the designated assets was less than substantial and although a factor to be weighed in the balance, he did not consider it to outweigh the benefits of the scheme which were significant. However, it clearly added weight in the balance to the principle harm to the character and quality of the local landscape which encompassed heritage assets, both designated and non-designated.

9. The inspector took into account the economic and social benefits, including some employment at the time of construction but, as he said, these could be realised elsewhere as a consequence of comparable projects. However, even though the appellant had sought to minimise impact through the choice of the location, there would still be clear conflict with the policies of the development plan and emerging policies of varying but of generally substantial weight. He also accepted the environmental benefits arising from solar energy and of the importance of such projects but, in the circumstances, he did not consider that these benefits outweighed the overall harmful conflict with aspects of the development plan and NPPF. He considered that the 'local environment would be severely compromised and the impacts would not be acceptable' and that the scheme did not represent sustainable development.

Comment

10. This was yet another case where the adverse landscape impacts proved fatal to the success of two appeals in what was a large site in the countryside. The inspector also thought that the limited life of the scheme (35 years) would be 'effectively a generation at least'.

CASE STUDY V

Domestic Solar Energy Proposal on Land Just Outside a National Park Rejected on the Basis of Green Belt Harm – Appeal Dismissed

Planning appeal reference APP/B1740/W/18/3199671 (7 February 2019)

1. The appeal decision is dated 7 February 2019 under planning appeal reference APP/B1740/W/18/3199671. It was an appeal against the decision of New Forest District Council (NFDC) refusing permission for the installation of 27 ground-mounted solar panels around two sides of the rear garden (which had an outlook over open fields) of what was described as a substantial modern dwelling having a very high electricity demand. Although the dwelling lay within the Green Belt, the panels would be located on the edge of the garden which was just outside the National Park boundary.

2. The Inspector determined that the installation was large enough to comprise an engineering operation. It was proposed that the solar panels would be close to ground level with planting to restrict visibility in order to minimise their effect on the openness of the Green Belt. However, the Inspector found that the number and spread of the solar panels would affect the openness of the Green Belt and would result in development encroaching into the countryside and would result in conflict with the NPPF.

3. On the National Park issue, the Inspector stated that the NPPF required great weight to be given to conserving and enhancing the landscape and scenic beauty in the National Park. Although the Inspector considered that the application site was a sensitive location where development would have an effect on the surrounding landscape and scenic beauty of the National Park, he felt that the ground-mounted panels would have only a limited effect on the surrounding landscape. Accordingly, he found that the solar panels would conserve the landscape and scenic beauty of the National Park. In the circumstances the Inspector determined that there would be no conflict with NFDC's local policies which took effect outside the National Park, which sought well-designed development which would protect or enhance the environment, including indirectly minimising the risk of damage to areas of landscape value and having regard to energy efficiency. Indeed, the proposal was one which was supported by a local policy where the benefits of renewable energy schemes had to be given significant weight.

4. The Inspector also considered whether very special circumstances could be shown under Green Belt policy which might allow such development. However, while he conceded that renewable energy should be accorded significant weight under local policy, he was still not persuaded that the effect of the low level of the panels on the openness of the Green Belt and on the National Park was such as would give rise to very special circumstances. He therefore found that the proposed solar panels would comprise inappropriate development which harmed the openness of the Green Belt. In short, while accepting that the production of renewable energy should be accorded significant weight, the Inspector nonetheless took the view that it still did not outweigh the substantial weight which had to be given to Green Belt harm, which meant that the proposal was contrary to the NPPF which sought to protect the Green Belt from inappropriate development, and he accordingly dismissed the appeal.

Comment

5. This was a surprising outcome as the proposal site lay outside the National Park and the ground-mounted panels would be well screened. Moreover, the number of panels did not appear to have been excessive in what was described as a substantial modern dwelling. Local policy was also supportive of renewable energy schemes subject to their not having unacceptable effects on various matters including the National Park which, as the Inspector found, would not be materially affected by the installation. At the end of the day, the Inspector considered that while the installation may have been compatible with local policies, it was still precluded by the rigours of Green Belt national policy.

CASE STUDY VI

Solar Panels Not Allowed on Grade II Listed Church – Appeal Partly Allowed

Planning appeal reference APP/Q3115/W/19/3234356 (18 November 2019)

1. In a decision dated 18 November 2019, under planning appeal reference APP/Q3115/W/19/3234356, Neil Pope, an inspector appointed by the SoS, partly allowed an appeal against the decision of South Oxfordshire District Council to refuse planning permission for the installation of 36 black solar panels on the south-facing aspect of the main church roof and 16 black solar panels on the south-facing aspect of church outbuildings.

2. The church and outbuildings were at Henley-on-Thames and were located in a conservation area. The church was a 1907 Grade II listed building with special architectural qualities, which included its Gothic style, brick walls and stone dressings, steeply pitched traditional plain clay tiled roofs, tower with octagonal lantern and spire and Art Nouveau stained glass windows. The listing included the Manse and garden wall, the Church Hall and churchyard wall, gates and railings. The significance of the heritage asset included its riverside location, the contribution made by its numerous listed buildings and its medieval street layout and burgage plots. The church was a prominent and attractive feature within the conservation area, whereas the outbuildings were hidden from public view. There were numerous development plan policies relevant to the appeal involving the historic environment and renewable energy. The proposal involved the installation of 36 solar panels on the church's south-facing main roof slope and would contrast awkwardly with the shape/form and appearance of the existing plain clay tiles. The inspector considered that the addition of solar tiles would comprise a discordant addition to a main roof slope on an important building which would markedly detract from an appreciation of the architectural interest and special qualities of the church. Even though the panels would be temporary and reversible, they would remain on the roof for many years and would appear as an incongruous and harmful addition to the local landmark. The inspector considered that when the conservation area was considered as a whole, the adverse impact would be between the middle and lower end of the sliding scale of harm.

3. Although the 16 solar panels proposed on two roof slopes of the single-storey 20th-century outbuilding would also contrast awkwardly with the shape/form and appearance of the clay tiles on the roof of this building, the panels

would not occupy a prominent position on a listed building or intrude into any important views of the church. The inspector found that the impact of these panels upon the significance of the conservation area as whole would be almost imperceptible.

4. It was the inspector's finding that the proposal would not preserve the special architectural interest of the church and would harm the character and appearance of the conservation area and would conflict with development plan policies. However, as these policies did not contain the 'public benefits' balance contained in the NPPF, paragraph 196, this limited the weight which could be given to any conflict with these policies. In weighing the harm with any public benefits arising from the proposals, the inspector noted the advantages of even small-scale renewable energy projects in cutting greenhouse gas emissions. In this instance, the appellant calculated that the proposals would generate 13,500kWh of electricity per annum and would lower the carbon footprint of the church as well as reduce the overheads of the building. However, the inspector did not consider that this lent any weight to the planning merits of the scheme. It was his view that the public benefits outlined did not outweigh the identified harm from 36 solar panels on one of the church's main roof slopes. However, the much lower public benefits in the case of the 16 solar panels on the outbuildings were sufficient to outweigh the lesser harm in respect of this part of the appeal site and made it possible for a split decision allowing for the 16 solar panels on the outbuildings and refusing permission for the 36 panels on the main roof of the church. The conditions should also be addressed insofar as they prescribed a temporary permission for the intended 25 years of the installation and for the pre-commencement approval of the proposed solar limpets which were intended to be attached to the panels in order to minimise disturbance to the fabric of the roof.

Comment

5. This was always going to be a challenging appeal in view of the prominence of so many solar panels on one of the main roof slopes of a Grade II listed church with special architectural qualities, despite a consequential reduction in the overheads of running the building. The inspector considered that the panels would be a harmful addition to a local landmark.

CASE STUDY VII

Free-standing Solar Panels Not Allowed in Grounds of Country House in National Park – Appeal Dismissed

Planning appeal reference APP/Y9507/W/3233900 (27 November 2019)

1. In a decision dated 27 November 2019, under planning appeal reference APP/Y9507/W/3233900, Julia Gregory, an inspector appointed by the SoS, dismissed an appeal against the decision of South Downs National Park Authority to refuse planning permission for the installation of a free-standing solar array on a large country house known as Fittleworth House near Pulborough.

2. The inspector noted that the first statutory purpose of the National Park was to conserve and enhance the natural beauty, wildlife and cultural heritage of the area. NPPF, paragraph 172 also identifies the great weight which should be given to conserving and enhancing the landscape and scenic beauty in National Parks.

3. The solar array in this instance was to be away from the built development. It was to be sited in a field comprised within rising land which had a wide hedgerow to the south. The array measured 18.3m x 3.3m and was mounted so that the panels would each reach some 2.3m in height. The panels were to extend along much of the southern boundary, some 6m away from the hedgerow. The panels would be unlike any other feature in the vicinity seeing as they would be rigid geometric features with metal and reflective panels. The inspector found that they would appear incongruous in the landscape and would also be clearly visible from a public footpath. The inspector found that they would erode the character of the countryside and effectively extend domestic clutter onto an agricultural field. The inspector was also unsure whether the hedgerow would be maintained at a sufficient height and thickness for its entire length to screen solar array from land to the south. In addition, the native mixed hedge planned to the north of the proposed arrays would take a significant number of years to become well established and to provide any screening, nor would it be effective in the autumn and winter. There would also be gaps to the hedgerow where it would be closest to the public footpath to allow access through which the arrays would be apparent. Although the inspector conceded that a new hedge might have some small wildlife benefit, it would create an enclosed developed area of land that would not replicate the local field pattern. Her finding was that the array would be visually incongruous with its surroundings which is open fields.

4. The inspector acknowledged that there was a need to achieve net-zero greenhouse gas emissions by 2050. The NPPF also sought to increase the use and supply of renewable energy, recognising that even small schemes provide a valuable contribution to cutting greenhouse gases but, as she found, it requires adverse impacts to be addressed satisfactorily. The inspector noted that there was support for renewable energy in the South Downs National Park Partnership Management Plan 2014–2019 (PMP), but South Downs Local Plan 2014–2033 (LP) policy SD51 required proposals for solar energy to be suitably sited and clearly associated with buildings or properties they were intended to serve. In this instance, the solar panels would be well away from Fittleworth House and would not be suitably sited and would thus be contrary to LP policy SD51. The inspector found that the proposal would also be contrary to policy SD4 of the LP, which states that development proposals would only be permitted where they conserved and enhanced landscape character. It would also be contrary to LP policy SD5, which required all development to be of the highest possible design quality which reflected and respected the exceptional quality of the natural, agricultural and built environment of the National Park. Proposals should adopt a landscape-led approach and respect the local character through sensitive and high-quality design that made a positive contribution which sought to enhance local character and distinctiveness of the area. The proposal was also found to be contrary to LP policy SD6 in which proposals would only be permitted where they preserved the visual integrity and scenic quality of the National Park, in particular by conserving views from publicly accessible areas which were within, to and from settlements and contribute to viewers' enjoyment of the National Park and included views from public rights of way, open access and other publicly accessible areas. The inspector also found that the proposal would breach policy 1 of the PMP which related to sustainability whose purpose was to conserve and enhance the natural beauty and special qualities of the landscape and its setting in ways that allowed it to continue to evolve and become more resilient to climate change and other pressures.

5. In the result, the inspector dismissed the appeal, concluding that the development would fail to conserve and enhance the natural beauty of the National Park contrary to the development plan and the PMP.

Comment

6. The difficulty with this proposal is that the free-standing array was neither suitably sited nor satisfactorily screened in what was a National Park setting. For instance, development plan policy required proposals for solar energy to be suitably sited and clearly associated with buildings or properties they were intended to serve, whereas it was proposed that the solar array would be sited well away from the built development in a field on rising land. It meant that the panels would be unlike any other feature in the vicinity and would also be clearly visible from a public footpath.

CASE STUDY VIII

Free-standing Solar Panels for Domestic Use Not Allowed in Green Belt and Area of Outstanding Natural Beauty – Appeal Dismissed

Planning appeal reference W/4000264 (29 January 2020)

1. In a decision dated 29 January 2020, under planning appeal reference W/4000264, H Miles, an inspector appointed by the SoS, dismissed an appeal against the decision of Tunbridge Wells Borough Council refusing planning permission for the installation of 60 solar panels on mounted frames for domestic use.

2. The inspector identified the main issues on the application to be these: (a) whether the proposal would be inappropriate development in the Green Belt; (b) the effect of the proposal on the openness of the Green Belt; (c) the effect of the proposal on the character and appearance of the surrounding area including the High Weald AONB; and (d) if the proposal was found to be inappropriate, whether any harm by reason of inappropriateness, and any other harm, would be clearly outweighed by other considerations. If so, would this amount to the very special circumstances required to justify the proposal.

3. The inspector noted from the NPPF that the fundamental aim of Green Belt policy was to prevent urban sprawl by keeping land permanently open; and that the essential characteristics of Green Belts were their openness and permanence. The NPPF goes on to state that inappropriate development is harmful to the Green Belt and that all proposals for development in the Green Belt should be treated as inappropriate and thus should be approved only if very special circumstances exist (unless they come within one of the categories in the closed list of exceptions in either NPPF, paragraph 145 or paragraph 146 and the inspector found that none of the exceptions arose on the application). It followed that the proposal would be inappropriate development to which the inspector was required to attach substantial weight as set out in NPPF, paragraph 144.

4. The inspector dealt with openness in this way: he said that the effect of development as encroachment on the countryside may be in the form of visual intrusion or loss of openness. The appeal site was currently open grassed land with no notable buildings although there was some fencing, planting and an access drive. The inspector found that the appeal site had 'an open feel, characteristic of the Green Belt'. He noted that the proposed solar panels would result in a development covering a large area of what is currently open land, with

panels of up to 2.6m in height which he considered was not insubstantial. It was his finding that the proposal would have a harmful effect on the spatial openness of the Green Belt. He found that engineered solar panels would be at odds with, and harmful to, the open rural landscape. They would also be visible in public viewpoints and, owing to the topography of the land, may be visible from some distance including the High Weald Landscape Trail. Although the inspector conceded that it may be possible to screen the panels with some additional landscaping, he said that he had not been provided with the details relating to this, including the size or location of the proposed landscaping that would be required to demonstrate that the proposed solar panels would not be visible. Accordingly, the inspector found that the proposed development would result in 'notable harmful intrusion into the Green Belt'. It meant that the proposal would have a significantly greater effect on the openness of the site in comparison to its mainly undeveloped nature.

5. In terms of character and appearance, the inspector noted that the appeal site was outside the limits to built development (LBD) for the purposes of the development plan. Local plan policies seek to direct new development within the LBD with a view, amongst other things, to maintaining the rural countryside landscape character of the areas outside the LBD. The appeal site also lies within an AONB where the NPPF advises that great weight should be given to conserving and enhancing landscape and scenic beauty. These issues enjoy the highest status of protection. The inspector found that the appeal site was 'pleasant undeveloped open grassed land and as such it makes a positive contribution to the landscape and scenic beauty of the AONB and the surrounding countryside area'. In other words, the site was not a traditional domestic garden area but had a more rural character.

6. The inspector found that the development would result in the introduction of large synthetic solar panels which would result in built development covering a notable area of attractive land, which would not be in keeping with the rural character and appearance of the area whether or not the proposal was prominent or in public view. It meant that the proposal would have a harmful effect on the character and appearance of the area including the AONB contrary to local policies and policies within the Core Strategy.

7. In dealing with material considerations, the inspector noted, in relation to renewable energy projects in the Green Belt, that NPPF, paragraph 147 explained that developers would need to demonstrate very special circumstances if projects were to proceed. These may include the wider environmental benefits associated with increased production of energy from renewable sources. The scheme in this instance was predicted to enable the host property to gain independent renewable power for 80% of its needs and would reduce CO_2 emissions. The inspector

agreed that this was a notable benefit but would be limited as the proposal would only generate energy for a single property.

8. The inspector dismissed the appeal on the ground that the proposed development was inappropriate development within the Green Belt. It was his view that the considerations in favour of the proposal did not give rise to the very special circumstances necessary to justify a development which was not only contrary to local policies and to policies in the Core Strategy but would also give rise to harm to the character and appearance of the area including the AONB.

Comment

9. The location of the 60 solar panels on mounted frames on grassed land in an open rural and highly protected landscape (Green Belt and an AONB) meant that this was always going to be a very challenging appeal.

CASE STUDY IX

13.6GWh Solar Farm on 16 Hectare Site Rejected because of Adverse Visual and Heritage Impacts – Appeal Dismissed

Planning appeal reference APP/D1265/W/19/3241953 (23 July 2020)

1. In a decision dated 23 July 2020, under planning appeal reference APP/D1265/W/19/3241953, Neil Pope, an inspector appointed by the SoS, dismissed an appeal against the decision of Dorset Council (the LPA) to refuse planning permission for the construction of a solar farm and associated development, including perimeter fencing, CCTV cameras and landscaping in accordance with the terms of the application (albeit subject to multiple revisions) under reference number 2/2019/0470/FUL. The appeal site lay within the North Dorset Limestone Ridges LCA and the Upper Stour Valley LCA.

2. The area inside the proposed perimeter fencing comprised approximately 16 hectares (or 40 acres) and the proposed height of the solar panels above ground level was 2.6m. The appeal site formed part of the settings of a number of listed buildings and three conservation areas. It was accepted by the appellant that the proposal would harm the settings of four heritage assets. The main issue on the appeal was whether the benefits of the proposal (in terms of contribution to electricity generation from a renewable source) outweighed its harmful impacts on the character and appearance of the area and the significance of designated and non-designated heritage assets.

3. After dealing with numerous local and national planning policies (as well as the UK Solar PV Strategy) the inspector referred to local landscape character assessments and to the former district's Landscape Sensitivity to Wind and Solar Development document that was published in 2014 which, although not forming part of the development plan, were nonetheless considered to be material considerations. The inspector's attention was also drawn to the Bournemouth, Dorset and Poole Renewable Energy Statement published in 2013, another local non-statutory document which, in his view, carried limited weight.

4. In terms of benefits, the inspector was told that the anticipated output from the proposed development would be circa 13.6GWh which would be sufficient to power 4,387 homes annually (although using Ofgem's latest Typical Domestic Consumption Value the proposal could power 4,689 homes annually). The contribution was one which the appellant claimed would assist the government in meeting its commitment to achieving 'net-zero' carbon emissions by 2050 and make a valuable contribution towards cutting greenhouse gas emissions. In

combination with other renewable and low carbon energy schemes it would assist in tackling climate change. The inspector gave these wider environmental benefits substantial weight in the planning balance. In addition, tree planting and general landscaping would enhance the landscape qualities of the area together with proposed bird and bat boxes which would provide new and improved wildlife habitats. The proposal would accord with the duty to preserve biodiversity (section 40 of the Natural Environment and Rural Communities Act 2006).

5. The inspector also considered that the proposal would provide some support for the construction industry and could assist in helping to create and sustain employment during the economic downturn. Some construction workers could also use some local services and the development would generate additional income for the landowners, enhancing farm incomes and possibly diversifying some farm businesses which would accord with the government's objective of promoting a strong rural economy. In addition, the inspector accepted that the proposal would assist in increasing the security and diversity of electricity supply. He considered that these economic benefits were important and could be given moderate weight.

6. The appeal site comprised three adjoining pasture fields with boundary hedgerows and trees within part of an elevated open plateau of undulating farmland. One of the fields sloped gently downwards in an easterly direction towards the River Stour. The site and surrounding landscape were also crossed by several public rights of way. The appeal site did not form part of a designated landscape and, other than the corridor along the River Stour, this part of the countryside was not considered by the inspector to be especially tranquil. Nevertheless, he took the view that the appeal site lay within an intimate valley landscape and was an attractive rural area and he considered that it formed part of a 'valued landscape' to which NPPF, paragraph 170(a) applied (the LPA had assessed the site's attributes having regard to the widely used guidance contained in Box 5.1 of the Guidelines for Landscape and Visual Impact Assessment produced by the Landscape Institute and Institute of Environmental Management and Assessment, which the inspector considered was helpful in identifying a 'valued landscape').

7. The inspector accepted that the development would introduce 'very many rows/arrays of solar panels' within the site along with associated infrastructure (numerous metal clad inverter cabins, a substation, communication buildings, storage battery containers, a switchgear building, 4m wide access track, 2m high perimeter fencing and CCTV cameras all set within a fenced compound). Although the new tree and hedgerow planting would reduce the impact, the inspector considered that the proposal would markedly change the character and appearance of the site. The inspector determined that the 'overtly utilitarian form of development would considerably erode the rural and pastoral character' of the

appeal site and 'would diminish their contribution to the key landscape characteristics of the North Dorset Limestone Ridges LCA and the Limestone Hills LCT' (referring to LCAs). This change of character, he found, would also 'contrast sharply with the key characteristics of the Upper Stour Valley LCA' and 'would be adverse and weighs against granting planning permission'.

8. The inspector also considered that the proposed development would be seen from many sections of the public rights of way and would still be prominent even if some sections were diverted, which would give rise to a serious loss of amenity when using the public rights of way across the site. The inspector considered that given the limited height of the solar panels it was unlikely that the proposed development would give rise to any significant adverse visual impacts beyond a distance 1km from the site. Within this radius the impact would be serious and conspicuous and would 'considerably' detract from the appearance of this part of the countryside. These adverse visual impacts weighed against granting permission even though the scheme was only planned to continue for 40 years and would be experienced by many people in that time (it appears that limiting the development to 25 years would render it unviable). In the result, it was the view of the inspector that the proposal would result in harmful cumulative landscape or visual impacts and led him to find that it conflicted with local and national planning policies and the management objectives for one of the LCTs affecting part of the site's eastern boundary which harm carried considerable harm in the overall planning balance.

9. The proposal site also formed part of the countryside setting to a number of designated heritage assets from which elements of the proposed works could be seen although this would not of itself amount to an adverse impact upon their heritage significance or interest. The inspector identified a local Grade I listed church where, from a small section of the churchyard, there would be only glimpsed views of part of the appeal site, which he considered would amount to less than substantial harm (towards the lower end if there was a sliding scale of harm within this category). However, it would, as he found, still harm the significance of what he called a 'high grade designated asset' which carried 'considerable weight in the planning balance'. The inspector also identified a Grade II listed rectory dwelling from which many rows of the proposed solar panels and some inverter buildings could be seen in one sector which, as he found, would, to a limited extent, erode the contribution which the appeal site makes to the historic landscape setting and to an appreciation of the significance of the listed building. Although he found that the harm would be less than substantial if there was a sliding scale of harm within this category, it would be towards the middle and carried considerable weight in the planning balance. Other heritage assets included a Grade II listed dwelling and the remains of a mill which would be visible from the same sector of the solar farm and where the inspector considered the harm would be between the middle and upper

end of the less than substantial category and which carried considerable weight in the planning balance.

10. The appeal site also lay within 500m of three conservation areas whose significance was derived primarily from their architectural interest and links to the various listed buildings and the arrangement and layout of buildings and spaces within the streets and the association with their rural surrounds. The appeal site formed part of the extensive countryside and settings of the conservation areas. In the case of two of these areas the inspector considered that there would be no adverse impacts to their significance or to their extensive rural settings. In the case of the third conservation area the proposal would result in a moderate level of harm in that the same section of the proposal site would 'markedly' intrude and detract from the unspoilt rural setting of the area, which also carried considerable weight in the planning balance. In terms of the heritage balance as a whole, the inspector considered the matter to be finely balanced. However, his view was that as the development would be reversible and temporary in nature the heritage balance 'just tips' in favour of granting permission.

11. In the view of the inspector the overall planning balance led him to find that the benefits of the proposal (including the production of energy from a renewable source and the wider environmental benefits from a reduction in greenhouse gas emissions) were insufficient to outweigh the totality of the harmful impacts to the character and appearance of the area and to the significance of the various designated and non-designated assets. As he found, the development would not be appropriately sited and would conflict with local policies and would also conflict with the government's objectives for renewable and low carbon development which required applications for such development to be approved but only where their impacts were or could be made acceptable which, in this instance, the inspector found would not be the case.

Comment

12. This failed appeal demonstrates just how difficult it is to obtain permission for large solar farms in attractive rural areas. It is worth noting that certain parts of the country, such as the south west, have a higher incidence of solar radiation than other areas and a greater theoretical energy potential. As a result, areas such as Dorset are likely to experience greater pressure for accommodating solar farms. In a number of such cases appellants point to the time-limited nature and reversibility of such developments, yet inspectors will often say that these periods are still long enough to give rise to impacts which justify dismissal. In truth, if the UK is to realise its legally binding target of 'net-zero' emissions by 2050 then the planning balance will surely have to change to accommodate an increasing number of larger solar farms in the countryside. It is certainly not going to happen if energy production is concentrated offshore.

CASE STUDY X

The UK's Largest Solar Farm Obtains a Development Consent Order

DCO reference EN10085 (28 May 2020)

1. On 28 May 2020 the SoS for the DBEIS granted a DCO known as the Cleve Hill Solar Park Order (reference EN10085) to the operators of the 490 hectare Cleve Hill Solar Park on the North Kent coast approximately 2km from Faversham and 5km from Whitstable within the jurisdiction of Swale Borough Council (SBC). This will be the UK's largest solar farm (and largest battery energy storage system) with a predicted generating capacity of 350MW (enough to power over 91,000 homes and save 68,000 tonnes of CO_2 emissions per annum) comprising 880,000 ground-mounted solar panels on a site said to be as large as 600 football pitches. The project is due to begin electricity generation by 2023 and is clearly well in line with the UK's zero emissions target.

2. The SoS accepted the report dated 28 February 2020 of the ExA, a panel comprising three members of PINS, which conducted an Examination into the application submitted on 15 November 2018 by Cleve Hill Solar Park Limited (the applicant) for a DCO under section 37 of the PA 2008 for the Cleve Hill Solar Park and associated development. The application was accepted for Examination on 14 December 2018. The Examination began on 30 May 2019 and was completed on 30 November 2019. The ExA's Report to the SoS is found on the NSIP website, alongside a letter containing a statement of reasons for the SoS's decision for the purposes of section 116 of the PA 2008 and the notice and statement required by regulation 31(2)(c) and (d) of the 2017 Infrastructure Regulations.

3. The DCO would grant development consent for the construction, operation, maintenance and decommissioning of an electricity generating station comprising a solar farm with the option of an additional energy storage facility with a total capacity of around 350MW. The development would include: (a) a ground-mounted solar PV generating station with a gross electrical output capacity of more than 50MW comprising arrays of panels fitted to mounting structures fixed to the ground by piles, inverters, transformers, and a network of underground cables; (b) the option of an energy storage facility with a gross storage capacity of more than 50MW, along with a flood protection bund, transformers, switch gear, underground cables, a construction compound and landscaping; (c) a substation enclosed within a flood protection bund, with a network of underground cable circuits to connect the substation to the arrays, the storage

facility and an existing substation; (d) a network of cable circuits, construction compounds, landscaping, earthworks, drainage, and the undergrounding of existing overhead line; (e) a means of access to an existing highway; (f) habitat management areas; and (g) maintenance of an existing coastal flood defence.

4. The principal issues considered during the Examination are set out in the ExA Report under the following broad headings: (a) energy need; (b) landscape and visual effects; (c) biodiversity and nature conservation; (d) cultural heritage; (e) agricultural land; (f) traffic and transport; (g) noise and vibration; (h) socio-economic effects; (i) water environment (including flooding and coastal defence); (j) safety and security (particularly in respect of the proposed battery storage element); and (k) compulsory acquisition.

5. A summary of the decisions which led the SoS to grant development consent (in respect of which a total of 867 representations were made by statutory authorities, non-statutory authorities and local residents and businesses) are set out below.

Need for the development

6. Although the application was an NSIP by virtue of being an onshore generating station with a generating capacity of greater than 50MW, there is no NPS for energy infrastructure covering solar-powered electricity generation or battery storage such as that at Cleve Hill Solar Park.

7. In the absence of a specific NPS applicable to the proposed development, section 105(2) of the PA 2008 provided that the SoS was required to have regard to any matters considered important and relevant to his decision. Even though NPS EN-1 applied to electricity generating stations with a generating capacity of more than 50MW but did not apply to this particular type of generating station, the SoS still considered that its policies were important and relevant to his decision on whether to grant or withhold consent for a DCO. The SoS accepted that the development was compatible with government policy and would contribute to the delivery of low carbon and renewable energy in line with legal commitments to *net zero* and the need to address climate change. The SoS considered that the development would generate low carbon electricity with a net saving in greenhouse gas emissions over the course of its life, notwithstanding the loss of a carbon sink in the form of salt marsh. The SoS also agreed with the ExA that the battery energy storage system was a factor of significant additional weight.

Landscape and visual effects

8. The total area of land that would be occupied by the development was around 490 hectares. This included land set aside for energy storage, land set aside for habitat mitigation purposes, flood defences, internal tracks and a relatively small area occupied by the existing London Array substation. The actual land area that would be covered by the solar panels was only around 176 hectares.

9. The site was described in the ExA's Report as being a flat and featureless coastal plain, interrupted by drainage ditches, borrow pits, reed beds and the 5m high coastal flood defence bund/embankment. The site also contained a 400kV overhead line on lattice towers, a short distance of overhead line on wooden poles and the London Array substation mentioned above. The ExA noted that the 400kV line introduced incongruous vertical structures in a predominantly flat landscape.

10. The solar panels themselves would rise to a maximum vertical height above the ground of 3.9m and would be aligned in an east–west direction (in contrast to many solar farms which orientate the arrays to the south). The applicant chose the east–west alignment as it claimed that while this resulted in more panels being needed because the load factor was reduced, the layout offered a better electricity generation profile than south-facing panels.

11. Landscape and visual impacts were a major concern. Although the applicant accepted that there would be significant adverse effects from the development, it considered that these would be limited to viewers over a relatively small area and would affect only a small number of receptors (although including some properties). In considering this issue, the ExA noted that NPS EN-1 sets out that:

> [v]irtually all nationally significant energy infrastructure projects will have effects on the landscape (paragraph 5.9.8). They should be designed carefully to minimise harm to the landscape, providing reasonable mitigation where possible and appropriate. The existing character and quality of the local landscape, how highly it is valued and its capacity to accommodate change should all be considered in judging the impact of the Proposed Development.

12. The ExA's report also states that: 'the relatively low, horizontal development is largely visually contained within the Order limits because of the enclosing influence of the existing flood defences and the topography and the vegetated character in the higher ground to the south'. The ExA also noted that the impacts of the development were reversible on decommissioning (whilst acknowledging that this might not happen for a considerable length of time – possibly 40 years). The SoS accepted the ExA's key conclusions on landscape and visual effects, namely: (a) that there would be no significant effects on

AONBs; (b) that there would be major and significant effects on an Area of High Landscape Value (as designated in a local development plan); (c) that there would be adverse effects on landscape character, scenic value, recreational value, landscape quality and condition, rarity and representativeness; and (d) that two residential properties would experience major and significant long-term impacts on some views, as would two public rights of way locally, including the Saxon Shore Way.

13. The ExA's report also sets out that while the development has a considerable footprint, changes to views away from the immediate area would be reduced by the visual containment of the solar panel arrays within the site and, from elevated viewpoints further away, by the effect of distance, topography and the visual context. The ExA also noted that views from the Saxon Shore Way across the Swale Estuary would not be affected, but walkers on that path would be aware of the development behind them. The SoS considered that all these adverse effects on landscape and visual effects should be given moderate weight in the planning balance.

14. The SoS also noted the strength of feeling that local residents had expressed about the potential adverse impacts of the development on the landscape of the Graveney Marshes. However, it also noted that NPS EN-1 sets out that the nature of energy NSIPs meant they were very likely to have a negative effect on landscape and visual perception and that these effects may be hard to mitigate. Nevertheless, the SoS accepted that these adverse effects would be minimised as far as possible.

Biodiversity and nature conservation

15. This was acknowledged to be a major consideration on the application. Natural England, the Kent Wildlife Trust (KWT) and the RSPB took part in the Examination. KWT and the RSPB both objected to the proposal because of its potential adverse impacts on wildlife – principally in relation to a number of bird species – where they felt that adequate mitigation could not be put in place to prevent significant impacts. The key wildlife species that were considered during the Examination were ground-nesting birds – particularly Brent geese, lapwing and golden plover – marsh harriers, dormice and European eels. The ExA considered the information provided by the applicant, the methodology it had used to compile the information, the proposals for mitigation and enhancement and the conclusions it had drawn in assessing the potential impacts of the proposed development.

16. The applicant considered that there would be no significant adverse impacts arising from the development on ornithology or on other important ecological features, either alone or in combination with other plans or projects. The applicant

also considered that the change of use from agricultural land to a solar farm would mean a benefit to invertebrates as there would be no use of pesticides.

17. In considering the issues raised, the ExA noted the contents of the Local Impact Reports submitted by SBC, Canterbury City Council and Kent County Council (KCC). The Local Impact Report from SBC considered that 'there is no certainty that effect [sic] on wildlife will be neutral or positive, or that the aims of the Development Plan policies will be met'. In its Local Impact Report, Canterbury City Council stated that biodiversity impacts were a key issue. Lastly, KCC's Local Impact Report raised concerns about impacts on ground-nesting birds and the use of the development site by birds from adjacent designated areas. KCC suggested that habitats would be managed during construction. It also noted that the removal of over-wintering and breeding bird habitat was potentially the biggest loss from the development but deferred to Natural England on the details.

18. On specific issues, the ExA noted representations in respect of ground-nesting birds (including lapwing, skylark and yellow wagtail), 'letters of no impediment' from Natural England in respect of water voles and great crested newts, insects (the possible use of the solar panels by aquatic insects as places to lay their eggs), the disturbance of birds by piling noise, the establishment, management and adequacy of the proposed Arable Reversion Habitat Management Area (including when it would be sown), the adequacy of the mitigation proposed, especially in relation to the capacity of the Arable Reversion Habitat Management Area to support populations of lapwing, golden plover and Brent geese. There were also concerns about the impact of the development on marsh harriers.

19. In relation to possible impacts on lapwing, golden plover and Brent geese, the SoS noted that there was considerable discussion during the Examination about mitigation measures that might be put in place to minimise the potential impacts of the development on these species. In particular, there were discussions about the ability of the Arable Reversion Habitat Management Area to support the birds, including the use of manure to fertilise the area and improve its capacity to provide the necessary food for the species. There were concerns the manure that might be used on the site would be from animals that had been given Ivermectin, a chemical that inhibits worms, but which could potentially harm the ability of the land to be used for food supplies for the birds. While Natural England was content with the proposed mitigation measures, the KWT maintained its concern that the necessary outcome, in terms of the ability of the land to support the three bird species, would not be achieved.

20. As indicated, there were concerns about the impact of the development on the ability of marsh harriers to continue to forage on the site once the solar panels

were in place, with consequent displacement of birds if food sources were no longer available. The applicant's case was that the arrangement of the solar panels along with the maintenance of drainage ditches would provide suitable space for marsh harriers to continue their foraging activities once the development was operational. While Natural England was content that the impacts of the development on the marsh harrier population could be managed effectively, the KWT took a different view. In respect of potential impacts on European eels, the ExA noted that mitigation measures proposed by the applicant were agreed with the Environment Agency as being in compliance with the Eels (England and Wales) Regulations 2009 (SI 2009/3344). The Environment Agency was content that impacts on European eels would be kept to an acceptable level.

21. The ExA was content with the applicant's approach to biodiversity surveys. It was also content that, by the end of the Examination, the evidence presented to it allowed it to consider that the information requirements in relevant policy documents, including the Marine Policy Statement and NPS EN-1, had been satisfactorily met.

22. The ExA sets out that it had given great weight to the potential effects of the development on internationally designated sites. The ExA was satisfied that golden plover, lapwing and Brent geese from the Swale SPA and Ramsar sites would receive suitable protection from measures in the DCO it recommended to the SoS and the associated habitat management plans to ensure that the sites would be protected from significant effects. The ExA noted that there was a general consensus (albeit with some reservation from KWT) that that was a reasonable conclusion on the evidence.

23. In respect of the potential impacts on and mitigation for marsh harriers, the ExA noted that Natural England was content that the interests of the species would be protected. The KWT and other parties did not agree. On balance, the ExA was content that the development would not cause any significant adverse impacts on marsh harriers. The ExA was also satisfied that nationally designated sites of ecological importance – the Swale SSSI – could exist alongside the proposed development and that relevant policy requirements (including in NPS EN-1) in respect of protected species – European eels and hazel dormice – had been met. The ExA also attached little weight to the concerns of KCC about the loss of habitat for ground-nesting birds which it considered would not be significant when considered against the benefits. The ExA was therefore content that the development would provide opportunities to conserve and enhance biodiversity.

24. The ExA noted that NPS EN-1 sets out a need for mitigation and enhancement to form part of any project. By the close of the Examination, there was nearly consensus (with KWT a dissenter) that the mitigation proposed was

appropriate for displaced birds from the Swale SPA and Ramsar site flocks. There was a range of views on whether mitigation proposed for marsh harrier would be effective. The ExA noted the lack of empirical evidence one way or another in this matter and that concerns were raised about whether the solar panels would dissuade the species from foraging. However, taking account of Natural England's evidence the ExA considered that, on balance, the proposed mitigation measures were sufficient to mitigate any likely significant effects. The ExA was also satisfied that mitigation proposals for other species – including hazel dormice and European eels – would provide suitable protection.

25. In conclusion, the ExA was content that the proposed programme of mitigation and monitoring would ensure there were no significant adverse effects from the development either on its own or in combination with other plans or projects and was in accord with relevant policy requirements and that there was no reason to withhold consent under this head. In the result, biodiversity and nature conservation was given neutral weight in the ExA's assessment of impacts. The SoS drew the same conclusion as the ExA in relation to protected species and as to the suitability of the mitigation measures that would be put in place which Natural England accepted would have a positive impact.

Cultural heritage

26. The proposed development was going to have a potential impact on a number of heritage assets. While there were no designated cultural assets within the development site (although there is an undesignated Second World War pillbox), there are a number of assets whose 'setting' (i.e. the surroundings in which a heritage asset is experienced) would be affected (All Saints Church, Graveney (Grade I listed), Graveney Court (Grade II listed), Sparrow Court (Grade II listed) and the Graveney Church Conservation Area which lie within 1km of the site boundary for the proposed development). The applicant also identified further heritage assets within 5km of the site boundary (ten Grade I listed buildings, 34 Grade II listed buildings, 13 scheduled monuments, one Grade II Registered Park and Garden and 15 conservation areas), but predicted that there would be no significant effects on those assets.

27. SBC agreed with the applicant's assessment that there would be no direct impact on heritage assets and with the assessment of significant effects as set out above. The Graveney Rural Environment Action Team (GREAT – which represents Graveney residents opposed to the development) and KCC felt that the impacts of the development would be greater than those identified by the applicant.

28. In considering impacts on heritage assets, the ExA assessed the requirements and advice set out in the NPSs, the NPPF and in relevant legislation (the Infrastructure Planning (Decisions) Regulations 2010 (SI 2010/305)). The ExA

considered the position in relation to the specific heritage assets that the applicant, GREAT and SBC had assessed would be significantly impacted by the development and concluded as follows.

29. All Saints Church, Graveney – the solar panels closest to the church would be 500–600m distant. Mitigation planting might provide some help, but the development would 'seriously erode the rural character of the area and the contribution of setting to the significance of All Saints Church'. The ExA concluded that the less than substantial harm should be weighed as moderate in the planning balance.

30. Graveney Court – a house with 15th-century origins which owes its significance to its special historic and architectural interests and its setting alongside All Saints Church. The ExA concluded that, as with the church, the less than substantial harm should be weighed as moderate in the planning balance.

31. Sparrow Court – the southern boundary of the development site would be located some 250m from the court – a farmhouse with 15th-century origins. Its significance drives from its special architectural interest and historic links with the church and Graveney Court. Despite some vegetation cover, the siting of the solar panels would erode the open landscape from which the court, in part, derives its significance. The ExA concluded that this would be less than substantial harm with moderate weight in the planning balance.

32. Church of St Thomas the Apostle, Harty – this small and isolated church would lie about 2km north of the proposed development site across the Swale Estuary. There would be views from the church across to the development site but the solar farm would appear relatively small in extensive surroundings. The ExA referred to the applicant's view that the existing sea wall around the development site would substantially screen the solar farm from the church leaving a band of silver above the sea wall while elements of the development higher up would be seen against the backdrop of the existing substation for the operational London Array Offshore Wind Farm. The ExA concluded that less than substantial harm would result from the development in the case of this asset.

33. The Shipwright Arms – much of its historic interest is linked to its remote location and links to the Faversham and Oare Creeks. The coastal defences on the north-east side of Faversham Creek would offer substantial screening of the solar panels, the impact of which would be insufficient to amount to harm.

34. Other listed buildings – the applicant identified a number of heritage assets within 5km of the proposed development, but detailed assessments were carried out only on those sites within 1km following consultation with KCC and Historic

England. The ExA also viewed four other heritage assets which had been suggested by GREAT as it felt they had been omitted from the list of sites assessed by the applicant in its application. The ExA concluded that the impact of the development was so minor that it would not harm the significance of the heritage assets.

35. Graveney Church Conservation Area – a small, isolated group of buildings which are linked to Graveney Church and Graveney Court. Though the proposed development would have an adverse impact on the significance of the church and the court, the overall effect on the conservation area would be more benign. The ExA concludes there would be less than significant harm.

36. Other heritage assets – there are a number of conservation areas in neighbouring towns. None of these would be affected by the development. Although there would be no physical change to the Second World War pillbox, the ExA found that its significance would be diminished and that this carried moderate weight in the planning balance.

37. In respect of 'historic landscape character', the ExA found that the development would dilute the essence of the grazing marshes although retention of the drainage ditches would retain the historic legibility of the landscape and the ExA concludes that this matter should be given moderate weight in the planning balance.

38. The SoS accepted the conclusions of the ExA in relation to the level of harm that was likely to be caused to the various named heritage assets and concluded that, overall, the adverse impacts had to be weighed against the wider benefits of the development in the planning balance.

Agricultural land

39. NPS EN-1 sets out that energy NSIPs should aim to minimise impacts on best quality agricultural land (classified as Grades 1, 2 and 3a under the ALC) and should instead use land of poorer quality (Grades 3b, 4 and 5 under the ALC). In addition, the NPPF sets out that development should contribute to the protection of soils and respect the economic benefits of the most valuable categories of agricultural land.

40. SBC's Local Plan seeks to prevent development on agricultural land unless there is an overriding need that cannot be met elsewhere. The Local Plan sets out restrictions on the development of better quality land, including that classified as Grade 3a under the ALC. The applicant's assessment was that the development would affect approximately 370 hectares of arable land of which 2 hectares would be ALC Grade 2, 9 hectares of ALC Grade 3a and 360 hectares of ALC Grade 3b

(approximately 97% of the site). SBC accepted that more than 90% of the land would be ALC Grade 3b, but questioned whether any agricultural land should be used for solar power as opposed to rooftops and brownfield land. Other witnesses claimed that a far higher proportion of the development site should be classified as being of higher ALC grading than that stated.

41. The ExA's conclusion in respect of agricultural land was that the vast majority of the land that would be used for the proposed would be ALC Grade 3b, which meant that the development would be in accordance with the relevant policy set out in NPS EN-1 and that little weight should be given to the loss of agricultural land in the planning balance. The SoS saw no reason to disagree with this assessment.

Traffic and transport

42. NPS EN-1 sets out that transport impacts related to national significant energy infrastructure are an important consideration in assessing applications for development consent. NPS EN-1 also sets out mitigation options to minimise impacts from traffic and recommends that where the project in question is likely to generate a large increase in HGV movements, then measures to limit impacts should be included in any DCO that might be granted.

43. The NPPF requires applicants to consider transport issues at an early stage but notes that development should only be prevented or refused on highways grounds if there would be an unacceptable impact on highway safety, or the residual cumulative impacts on the road network would be severe. The ExA noted that SBC's development plan contained provisions in relation to assessment of traffic impacts that placed great store on maintaining the safety of road users and preserving the character of rural lanes in particular. The SBC impact report highlighted the fact that construction traffic would affect local residents and, in relation to cyclists, would result in harm in relation to road safety and recreational amenity. As the main construction traffic route would be along rural lanes, the impacts of this would mean that policy DM 26 of the SBC Local Plan would not be met. The KCC Local Impact Report indicated that the operation of the development would result in few road traffic movements. KCC was also satisfied that the impacts of traffic movements during construction (and decommissioning) could be mitigated through the Construction Transport Management Plan submitted by the applicant as part of its application. The applicant provided information about traffic and transport assessments in the ES submitted with the application. A pre-application scoping opinion from PINS indicated that significant traffic and transport effects during operation of the development were unlikely which meant that a detailed assessment of traffic movements during this phase of the development was not needed. The Application also proposed that a number of mitigation measures should be agreed with relevant local planning

authorities as part of any Construction Traffic Management Plan or Construction and Environmental Management Plan and included provisions for these in a draft DCO submitted as part of the application.

44. The ExA was satisfied that the main source of any impacts would be during the construction of the development rather than during its operation and that a detailed assessment of the latter was not required. The ExA was also satisfied that appropriate mitigation would be put in place to ensure there would be no significant residual impacts arising from the development. The ExA also assessed that impacts during the decommissioning of the proposed development, potentially in around 40 years' time, would be no worse than those likely to arise during construction. The ExA's overall conclusions were that the temporary but significant effects of the development during construction would be mitigated to an acceptable level by measures in the Construction Traffic Management Plan which would meet the relevant provisions in NPS EN-1 for energy NSIPs. In the same way, the development would be in accordance with relevant local plans in respect of road user safety and there would be no permanent damage done to the character of rural lanes. The absence of any significant impacts meant that the provisions of the NPPF had also been met. The ExA's overall conclusion was that traffic and transport do not weigh heavily against the making of a DCO and the temporary effects on the local population were a minor negative effect to be weighed in the planning balance. The SoS agreed with this assessment, citing the fact that mitigation measures would be put in place to minimise any impacts as much as possible.

Noise and vibration

45. NPS EN-1 and NPS EN-5 acknowledge that excessive noise can have adverse impacts on human health and quality of life. The scope of the applicant's noise assessment (covering construction, operation and decommissioning phases) was agreed with SBC which seeks to avoid or minimise harm from noise impacts. The main effects during the construction phase were anticipated to be from piling of the posts that would support the solar panels and transformers and vehicle noise on site, noting that daytime noise criteria would be exceeded for no more than one month at the closest point to each receptor. Vibration levels were assessed as being less than perceptible while noise increase from traffic movements on local roads would be minor. The applicant considered that these effects would not be significant.

46. As far as operational impacts were concerned, the applicant assessed that some daytime and night-time noise limits would be exceeded by noise from the installed plant and there would be significant impacts on the small number of properties affected. The decommissioning impacts were assessed as being similar to those that would arise during construction. The ExA noted that mitigation

measures would be incorporated into the Construction Environment Management Plan and the Construction Traffic Management Plan and that the applicant had concluded that there would be no significant effects at the properties included in its assessment of impacts.

47. The ExA noted that in the Statements of Common Ground signed between the applicant and SBC and Canterbury City Council (CantCC), both authorities confirmed that the applicant's approach to methodology, assessment, the identification of receptors and proposed mitigation was acceptable. The ExA accepted that piling activities would lead to instances of noise exceeding daytime noise criteria at eight properties in the vicinity of the proposed development, but considered that this would represent a worst case and that the exceedances would be by only a small amount.

48. The ExA also considered that vibration levels from on-site activities would be below noticeable levels except at one and possibly even two properties. Overall, it considered that the impacts during construction would be limited and of short duration. During operation, noise levels would be above daytime criteria for some properties so further mitigation measures would be needed to alleviate any impacts. The ExA considered that the Construction Environment Management Plan and the Construction Traffic Management Plan, which would be secured in any DCO, would provide adequate mitigation. The ExA therefore agreed with the applicant's conclusions on impacts. The ExA considered that the decommissioning of the development would generate similar impacts to those produced during construction and with mitigation measures in place the ExA agreed with the applicant's assessment of impacts.

49. In summary, the ExA considered that mitigation measures would be acceptable to alleviate any significant adverse impacts. Overall, the construction impacts would only be temporary and any adverse noise and vibration during operation could be mitigated and so be in compliance with NPS EN-1 and NPS EN-5, the NPPF and the Local Plans of SDC and CantCC. In the result, the ExA concluded that noise and vibration did not weigh against a DCO and was neutral in the planning balance. The SoS agreed with this analysis.

Socio-economic effects

50. This covers a broad range of issues – the social, economic and land use effects of the development, which includes tourism, recreation, land use, employment, human health, public access, health and safety at work, electric, magnetic and electromagnetic fields, telecommunications, television reception, and utilities and waste issues. The ExA considered the development against the policies set out in the NPS EN-1, in the NPPF and in the development plans for SBC and CantCC.

51. It was the view of the applicant that there would be positive, though not significant, increases in local employment while there would be minor negative impacts on tourism during construction and operation of the development. The applicant assessed that there would be significant effects on users of the Saxon Shore Way during construction operations but this would affect only a short section of the route, be temporary (for a period of 12 months) and only when those operations were taking place within 500m of the route. Also, construction would not take place after 13.00 on Saturdays and not at all on Sundays or Bank Holidays. During the operation of the development it was predicted that there would be a significant adverse effect on a public right of way though impacts on other public rights of way were assessed as being not significant. The applicant concluded that there would be no significant cumulative effects on the socio-economics of tourism in Swale Borough, the City of Canterbury or Kent more generally arising from the proposed development. In addition, the applicant concluded that no significant effects had been identified in relation to human health, electric, magnetic and electromagnetic fields, telecommunications, TV reception, utilities or waste management. The applicant also stated that mitigation measures had been incorporated into the design of the development.

52. The applicant's Equality Impact Assessment considered whether the impacts of the development would discriminate against people with characteristics defined in the Equality Act 2010. It concluded that there was the potential for impacts from the traffic and access during construction in relation to children attending the Graveney Primary School (which sits alongside the construction traffic route) but that mitigation in the Construction Traffic Management Plan would minimise the potential for inequality or discrimination.

53. Socio-economic issues were raised in many relevant representations with the main areas of concern being impacts on public footpaths, the local economy, tourist numbers, human health and well-being and the loss of agricultural land. The absence of any direct local benefit arising from the development was also raised. SBC's Local Impact Report noted that potential impacts on tourism and on the economy through reduced visitor numbers would mean it would not be in compliance with parts of the Borough's Local Plan in respect of tourism and recreational activities. CantCC's Local Impact Report set out that the development would have limited economic benefit. KCC's Local Impact Report considered the proposed development would transform the character of the landscape from arable to industrial and deter the use of public rights of way. KCC did, however, welcome the applicant's proposed permissive path that would connect two public rights of way but was also keen to see the creation of a new off-road path between two existing footpaths.

54. A considerable number of representations were submitted throughout the Examination in relation to potential socio-economic impacts arising from the development. There were also concerns about the loss of recreational space on physical and mental well-being of local residents and on visitor numbers to the area (which would have consequential impacts on local businesses). There were also concerns that the development would bring no benefits to the local economy. Questions were also raised about the potential for health impacts arising from electromagnetic fields, the potential security issues and the applicant's Equality Impact Assessment. There were also discussions about improvements to existing cycle routes and proposals for new cycling routes. The use of agricultural land for solar energy farms was also raised. The ExA considered all these issues.

55. The applicant contended that the development had the potential to create 750 full-time equivalent jobs in Kent and 4,725 in England and would generate £120 million gross value added in Kent and £670 million in England.

56. On tourism, the ExA noted figures for tourist visits to the Swale region and the income it generated which had been provided by the applicant. It concluded that while there would be impacts arising from the construction of the proposed development, these would be temporary and would not be in one fixed place through the construction programme. The ExA considered that there was the possibility that the economic impacts of spending by construction workers working on the development would offset any impacts from loss of visitor numbers. Its overall conclusion was that it had seen no evidence that the proposed development would lead to a reduction in visitor numbers.

57. In respect of recreational amenity, the ExA noted that the applicant proposed to upgrade a number of public rights of way in and around the site of the development site. The ExA did consider that there would be adverse impacts on recreational users of the various footpaths but that these would be temporary and reversible. The ExA also noted the mitigation measures proposed in the applicant's Public Rights of Way Management Plan which would be appended to the Construction Traffic Management Plan.

58. As far as land use issues were concerned, the applicant proposal would see 370 hectares of arable crop production be taken up with solar panels and sheep grazing of which 97% would be Grade 3(b) under the ALC. Land around or under the panels would be seeded with grass and wildflower mix which would be grazed by sheep which the ExA considered would improve biodiversity. It was the view of the ExA that the development would not result in any significant land use

effects. As far as matters relating to human health were of concern to interested parties, the ExA was satisfied that a package of mitigation measures in the Construction Traffic Management Plan and the Construction Environmental Management Plan would minimise any risks to local people or contractors working on the site of the proposed Development. The ExA was also satisfied in relation to other matters raised by interested parties in relation to human health that suitable mitigation would be put in place – through the Construction Traffic Management Plan and the Construction Environmental Management Plan and the Battery Safety Management Plan – to avoid negative impacts on the health and well-being of local people.

59. On equality issues, the ExA noted that the applicant's Equality Impact Assessment recorded that construction traffic for the development had the potential to result in inequality and discrimination to pupils at Graveney Primary School. However, the ExA noted that there were already in place a footbridge linking the school car park with the school to obviate the need for pupils and their parents to cross the construction route. While this bridge would not allow access to the school playing fields from the school, the ExA was satisfied that the frequency of HGV traffic along the construction route was not of such a magnitude as to make supervised crossing of the road to be unsafe. Mitigation measures in the Construction Traffic Management Plan and the presence of the existing footbridge would therefore minimise the potential for discrimination and inequality to the children.

60. The ExA's overall conclusions on socio-economic impacts were that these were significant impacts for consideration in the Examination but that the applicant had met the relevant provisions in NPS EN-1 for energy NSIPs, including what was required in the way of mitigation measures. In terms of conclusions on specific socio-economic issues arising from the development, the ExA noted the minor economic benefits, the minor and reversible impacts on tourism and the mitigation measures which would mean inequality and discrimination would be minimised. In addition, the ExA concluded that there would be harm to users of a number of public footpaths near or running through the development site. The ExA's view was that the development would accord with the relevant local plan as far as safeguarding tourism and providing some local employment opportunities. The ExA's overall conclusion was that the impacts identified were of limited harm and this position would be carried through into the final planning balance. The SoS saw no reason to disagree with the ExA's conclusion under this head.

Water environment (flooding and coastal defences)

61. The questions of the susceptibility of energy NSIPs to flood risk and whether such infrastructure could cause or aggravate flooding are matters covered in the NPS EN-1 and in the NPPF. Changes to water quality resulting from energy NSIPs are also subject to policy drivers. The Swale Borough and Canterbury City Development Plans are also relevant to the application, as is the Medway Estuary and Swale Strategy, which sets out a strategy for managing flood and coastal erosion risk over a 100-year period and includes a specific proposal for coastal realignment at Cleve Hill. The applicant's case in relation to the water environment was that with mitigation measures in place there would be no adverse impacts arising from the proposed development either alone or in combination with other plans or projects. The applicant asserted that there would be a potential improvement in surface water quality at the development site because of a reduction in the use of pesticides and fertilisers. The applicant's Flood Risk Assessment also set out that the development site lies in Flood Risk area 3a, that is land which has a 1 in 100 annual probability of river flooding year risk or 1 in 200 annual probability of sea flooding. The conclusion of the applicant's Flood Risk Assessment was that the existing flood defences around the site would protect it up to the 1 in 1,000 year event. It should be noted that the applicant is seeking powers in the DCO to take over the maintenance of the flood defences in and around the development site from the Environment Agency if the development went ahead.

62. The applicant also asserted that the solar arrays and the related transformers and connecting cables had been designed with additional above-ground clearances to ensure that they were able to withstand a 1 in 1,000 year wave overtopping event. Given these design features, the applicant considered the risk from tidal flooding to be low. The applicant also took the same view in relation to risks from river, rain and groundwater flooding, concluding that these would be negligible.

63. The applicant's Flood Risk Assessment applied both the 'exception' and 'sequential' tests to the proposed development as required by NPS EN-1 and the NPPF and concluded that it passed both. The Environment Agency also confirmed that the latest predictions on climate change impacts supported the modelling impacts contained in the applicant's Flood Risk Assessment which did not require updating.

64. The Environment Agency and the applicant submitted a joint paper which set out how the ongoing maintenance of the flood defences would be undertaken in the event that the development went ahead and gave an analysis of why the powers available to protect the development during its operation would be needed. The joint paper also explained the marine licensing position in relation to

those maintenance works below Mean High Water Mark. The MMO had queried why there was no assessment of likely significant effects in the ES submitted with the Application. The applicant explained that there would be no change to the baseline so it was unnecessary to undertake such an assessment. The applicant also explained that in the event any more extensive works were needed in the future then it would take these forward under separate consent processes.

65. The ES submitted by the applicant set scenarios included in the Medway Estuary and Swale Strategy at a draft stage and exchanges with the Environment Agency about the managed retreat of the coastline at the site of the development site. The ES noted that the Environment Agency had taken the presence of the development into account in finalising the Medway Estuary and Swale Strategy.

66. The ExA noted that many representations raised concerns about the potential flooding and coastal defence risks and about the responsibility for maintaining flood defences being transferred from the Environment Agency to the applicant. However, the Environment Agency was content that future maintenance of the flood defences could be passed to the applicant and had agreed that the flood mitigation measures included in the development's design were suitable.

67. The ExA also noted that the development site was of strategic importance to the Medway Estuary and Swale Strategy which aimed to protect 17,000 homes in its area over a 100-year life cycle. The Cleve Hill site is one of eight that would collectively meet this obligation. The lifetime of the solar park would be 40 years and the proposed delivery programme in the Medway Estuary and Swale Strategy had been adjusted to delay the managed realignment of the site from 2039 to 2069.

68. The MMO had discussed with the applicant its proposal to include powers for maintaining the flood defences in its draft order. The MMO had suggested that a deemed marine licence would be the most appropriate way to deal with those parts of the development – the flood defences – that extended below the Mean High Water Mark rather than pursuing the option of transferring existing marine licence exemptions held by the Environment Agency to the applicant. The signed Statement of Common Ground between the applicant and the MMO reflected that position and amended wording for the deemed marine licence had been agreed.

69. Flood risk was mentioned in the Local Impact Reports for both CantCC and KCC (the lead local flood authority), with the former indicating the key issue was flood risk in its area and the latter noting that the development could lead to an increase in flood risk elsewhere. KCC's Local Impact Report also highlighted the need for an effective mitigation strategy to deal with surface water run-off to avoid sedimentation of watercourses.

70. Several of the interested parties disagreed with the applicant's Flood Risk Assessment and there were concerns about potential flood impacts in Faversham and Whitstable. In addition, concerns were raised about responsibility for maintaining the existing coastal flood defences passing from the Environment Agency to the applicant. The applicant contended that the managed realignment set out in the Medway Estuary and Swale Strategy would increase the flood risk at Faversham rather than decrease it.

71. The ExA noted the representations made to the Examination about the opportunity cost of cancelling or delaying the Medway Estuary and Swale Strategy's approach to managed retreat at the Cleve Hill site in respect of flood relief, carbon sequestration and ecosystem services. In response to the point about carbon sequestration, the applicant claimed that data in the ES predicted that there would be a 59,000 tonnes of CO_2 per annum offset arising from the development while a managed retreat approach would offset only 1,500 tonnes of CO_2 per annum.

72. In respect of flood relief, the Environment Agency indicated that it was content with a flexible approach to the implementation of the Medway Estuary and Swale Strategy. The applicant reviewed the Medway Estuary and Swale Strategy and noted two options – the managed realignment at the Cleve Hill site from year 20 or managed realignment in the longer term (with earlier re-alignments taking place at other parts of the Strategy area). The ExA noted that the original Order drafted by the applicant did not include a fixed timescale for the life of the development. However, changes were made to the Order during the Examination to limit the lifetime of the proposed development to 40 years if the Environment Agency was ready to implement managed realignment at that time. These changes were incorporated into the Order submitted to the SoS by the ExA. The Environment Agency duly confirmed that the applicant's proposed decommissioning proposals would leave the Cleve Hill site in a suitable condition for managed retreat to be undertaken thereafter.

73. The ExA had asked both the applicant and the Environment Agency to comment on matters related to the Water Framework Directive (which aims for 'good status' for all ground and surface waters (rivers, lakes, transitional waters, and coastal waters) in the EU). The applicant claimed that the development would give rise to negligible effects on the water environment and that the development was in compliance with the Directive. The Environment Agency indicated it had no concerns about the Water Framework Directive providing the construction, operation and decommissioning of the development were undertaken in a responsible manner. In light of this, the ExA concluded that the development would be in compliance with the Water Framework Directive (and thus comply with NPS EN-1) subject to all proposed mitigation measures being secured in the DCO.

74. As far as flood risk was concerned, the ExA concluded that the applicant's Flood Risk Assessment was appropriate and met the requirements of NPS EN-1. The ExA also concluded that the applicant has designed the development in such a way as to protect the equipment most at risk of flooding. The ExA accepted that the risk of flooding in Faversham and Whitstable was not materially increased by the presence of the development. In relation to coastal change and management, the ExA concluded that the risks and issues have been adequately addressed. With regard to impacts on the water environment, the ExA concluded that the applicant had set out measures to control pollution in its ES. However, there were two outstanding issues, namely: (a) the possible contamination from batteries and solar panels; and (b) sediment pollution resulting from water run-off from the solar panels. The ExA concluded that both of these matters had been satisfactorily addressed by the applicant. The ExA's overall conclusion was that construction and operational risks have been identified and properly managed and it was satisfied that there would be no adverse effects on water quality, water resources, water bodies or the wider water environment and that the development would be compliant with the Water Framework Directive and relevant policies on flood risk. In fact, the ExA agreed with the applicant that water quality locally was likely to improve. It is plain that matters arising under this head had engaged the intense interest of local people. The SoS noted the ExA's conclusions that the risk of flooding as a result of the development was unlikely to be materially different to a scenario without the development. He also noted that there were concerns about the responsibility for the flood defences along the river boundary of the development being transferred from the Environment Agency to the applicant but that the Agency itself was content. In the result, the SoS considered that the ExA's conclusions were robust and that this was a matter which did not weigh against the grant of consent.

Safety and security

75. EN-1 does not make specific reference to battery storage nor are there any relevant Development Plan policies. However, paragraph 3.3.31 of NPS EN-1 provides: 'The Government expects that demand side response, storage and interconnection, will play important roles in a low carbon electricity system …'.

76. The applicant's ES concluded that it was unlikely the development would cause a significant accident, but it acknowledged there were risks, principally in relation to possible fires in the battery storage facility. However, the ES set out mitigation measures in the facility that would detect and suppress fires.

77. In relation to security, the applicant stated it would be protected by perimeter fencing, CCTV, lighting with sensors and restrictions on who would be able to access the site.

78. The applicant's ES set out various measures that could be taken to minimise risks of accidents. The applicant also provided an outline Battery Safety Management Plan which was reviewed by the Health and Safety Executive and Kent Fire and Rescue Service. The applicant's Air Quality Impact Assessment considered possible outcomes in the event of a battery fire.

79. The SoS noted that there were a number of concerns from interested parties about the safety of the battery storage facility. These concerns were exacerbated by the new technology that the battery storage facility represented. For instance, the Faversham Society expressed strong concerns about the safety of the batteries that would be utilised in the development's energy storage facility, stating: (a) that there had been no proper testing of this matter; (b) that there was no track record of such large installations in the UK; (c) that lithium-ion batteries could catch fire and explode; (d) it was unclear who would be responsible for assessing the safety of the installation; and (e) there was uncertainty about access arrangements for emergency personnel. GREAT also raised concerns about the safety of the energy storage facility in respect of the possibility of explosion, fire and the threat of terrorism.

80. One of the interested parties, Dr Erasin, expressed concerns about the effects of a fire in lithium-ion batteries with the possible release of toxic fumes – specifically, hydrogen fluoride gas – with potential serious risks for the populations in the vicinity of the development such as at Seasalter, Graveney, Faversham and Whitstable. Dr Erasin suggested that there should be a 15km safety zone from any population around the battery storage site. He also raised the possible environmental risk of copper leaching from the solar panels. He also suggested that it would cost around £40 million to dispose of the batteries as part of any decommissioning and expressed concern about the possible use of Vanadium Redox flow batteries which he considered posed an unacceptable risk given their constituent parts.

81. GREAT also made representations about the lack of early engagement with the Kent Fire and Rescue Service which had led to the Service not being registered as an interested party to the Examination of the Application. GREAT also raised the point that some correspondence between the applicant, Kent Fire and Rescue Service and the Health and Safety Executive had not been disclosed to the Examination. GREAT also highlighted that the proposed battery storage facility at the proposed Development would be seven times larger than the current largest similar facility in the world. It also highlighted that battery energy storage fires were more likely to occur in coastal and mountain areas and that they had occurred across a range of battery usage. Faversham Town Council also raised concerns about the scale of the battery storage element and about fire and toxic risk. At a later stage in the Examination the Faversham Society disclosed

conclusions in a report into two fires at battery storage facilities in Arizona which reinforced their views on the dangers of the proposed storage facility. The applicant's response to this was that suitable mitigation measures had been built in to the proposals for the battery storage facility.

82. The ExA held a special session on battery storage issues to reflect the level of interest in this topic. The session heard from interested parties who had concerns about the battery storage facility as well as from a company, Leclanche, which appeared at the invitation of the applicant in an independent capacity (although the ExA considered that Leclanche could not be counted as truly independent as it provided energy storage systems). Leclanche had installed battery storage systems worldwide, but not on the scale as the one that would form part of the development. However, the company explained that the principles for incorporating safety features into these designs were well-established and applied irrespective of scale. Leclanche said lessons had been learned from battery fires, including those in Arizona, and noted that all of the fires had started at the construction stage of the development cycle.

83. The ExA noted the protective measures that would be in place during the operation of the development and that inspections could be undertaken by the Health and Safety Executive and Kent Fire and Rescue Service. The ExA asked about battery leakage and was told that the management systems would be able to detect leaks and initiate automatic shut-down. The ExA was content that any leakage would be small and confined within the affected container. The ExA also noted that the outline Battery Fire Safety Management Plan set out the minimum information that would need to be included at the detailed design stage for the proposal. Indeed, Requirement 3 of the proposed draft order required the approval of a Battery Safety Management Plan which would set out minimum requirements for safety matters. The ExA was happy that in setting out minimum requirements for information, the relevant LPA or Kent Fire and Rescue Service would be able to ask for more information to allow them to fulfil their duties. It was the view of ExA that there would be no material threat to health arising from a battery fire at the development and it was satisfied that the applicant's engagement with the Kent Fire and Rescue Service had informed the outline Battery Safety Management Plan. Once a DCO had been made, the LPA and relevant consultees would need to be given details of the proposed installation. The ExA was satisfied, therefore, that this process would make available all the information that the Kent Fire and Rescue Service would need to be able to fight a fire in the battery storage facility.

84. So far as site security was concerned, the ExA was satisfied that the measures proposed to protect the site were reasonable. ExA acknowledged that fear of criminal activity was capable of being a material consideration in the

determination of the application, although it went on to conclude that no party had provided any evidence that measures additional to those proposed by the applicant were necessary.

85. The ExA acknowledged that because of the scale of the proposed battery storage facility (which was a new technology) there was risk of fire or an explosion. However, it took comfort from the legislation and guidance and the Battery Safety Management Plan which would be subject to consultation with relevant bodies and the ExA was, therefore, confident that the risks could be managed or mitigated appropriately. The ExA noted that the measures proposed by the applicant might be viewed as minimal but there was no evidence before it that anything else was needed. The ExA's overall conclusion was that there was nothing of weight under this head to carry into the overall planning balance. The SoS noted that the concerns from interested parties about the potential health risks of a fire or explosion within the battery storage facility that formed part of the development but he did not see any reason to disagree with the conclusions reached by the ExA.

Habitats Regulations 2017

86. The Habitats Regulations 2017 require the SoS to consider whether the project is likely, either alone or in combination with other plans and projects, to have a significant effect on Natura 2000 sites (namely protected European sites (PES)). If likely significant effects cannot be ruled out, then an Appropriate Assessment of the implications of the project for that site in view of its conservation objectives must be undertaken by the SoS pursuant to regulation 63(1) of the Habitats Regulations 2017. The SoS must therefore determine whether the project will have an adverse effect on the integrity of the site. Consent may only be granted if the project will not adversely affect the integrity of a PES.

87. In the case of the development, the SoS notes that the applicant and other parties including Natural England and non-governmental organisations provided information to assist in the consideration of habitats impacts. The ExA produced a report on the implications for PES arising from the application and it took account of representations in its report.

88. The boundary of the development site overlaps to some extent with the boundaries of two PES – the Swale SPA and the Swale Ramsar site. The ExA records that the applicant carried out a study of PES that could potentially be affected by the development. It concluded that there would be no likely significant effect on most of those sites (the Outer Thames Estuary SPA, the Blean Complex Special Area of Conservation, or the Thanet Coast and Sandwich Bay SPA and Ramsar Site). These conclusions were agreed with Natural England and KWT. None of the interested parties disputed this conclusion.

89. The applicant did, however, conclude that there was the potential for likely significant effects on the Swale SPA and Swale Ramsar site. The applicant set out a range of factors arising from the development that had the potential to lead to a likely significant effect on these sites: loss or change of habitats; noise and visual disturbance; hydrological changes; and deposition of dust.

90. The ExA considered all these matters with particular attention being focused on the potential for displacement of four species of bird that formed part of the interest feature of the Swale SPA and Swale Ramsar site: Brent goose, lapwing, golden plover and marsh harrier due to loss or change of habitats.

91. The SoS noted that the ExA's overall conclusion was that the development would not lead to an adverse effect on the integrity of the Swale SPA or Ramsar site due to noise and visual disturbance, loss or change of habitats, hydrological changes or deposition of dust. The ExA considered that there was sufficient information available to the SoS to be able to (if necessary) undertake an appropriate assessment of the effects of the development on PES. The SoS's HRA accompanies the decision letter and concludes that a likely significant effect could not be ruled out in respect of the Swale SPA and Ramsar site due to the effects of noise and visual disturbance, loss or change of habitats, hydrological changes or deposition of dust. The SoS therefore had to consider whether the development would have an AEoI on those sites, either alone or in combination with other plans or projects. An HRA was therefore carried out to assess the implications of the development in relation to the conservation objectives of those sites to ascertain whether it would adversely affect the integrity of the PES. The overall conclusion of the Assessment was that there would be no AEoI of either the Swale SPA or the Swale Ramsar site either alone or in combination with other plans or projects subject to the mitigation secured in the DCO.

Compulsory acquisition and temporary possession

92. The applicant is seeking powers for the compulsory acquisition of freehold interests and private rights and for the acquisition of temporary possession of land. The PA 2008, together with related case law and guidance, sets out that compulsory acquisition can only be granted if certain conditions are met. Such documentation was provided by the applicant who reported to the ExA that it had reached agreement with 91% of all parties in respect of obtaining agreement for access to land.

93. The reasons given by the applicant for wanting the powers requested were: to secure land, new rights over land, the imposition of restrictions and the temporary use of land required to enable the applicant to construct, operate and maintain the project within a reasonable commercial timeframe. The inclusion of

powers of compulsory acquisition in the DCO was to ensure that these steps could be achieved.

94. The ExA considered the applicant's case for securing these powers by reference to the key tests set out in the Compulsory Acquisition guidance issued by the Department for Communities and Local Government (now the Ministry of Housing, Communities and Local Government), *Compulsory Purchase Process and the Crichel Down Rules*, July 2019. The applicant considered that the approach it had adopted and the information it had provided met the key issues set out in the guidance, namely: (a) whether reasonable alternatives had been considered; (b) whether the applicant had a clear idea about how it would use the land; (c) whether the proposed action was legitimate, proportionate and necessary; (d) whether there was a compelling case in the public interest to grant the powers requested; and (e) whether the applicant had appropriate funding available for the payment of compensation.

95. As far as the availability of funds was concerned, the ExA was content with the applicant's funding arrangements for the development.

96. The ExA questioned the applicant in relation to its request for powers of compulsory acquisition and temporary possession in respect of the flood defences and the proposed Habitat Management Areas. In relation to the flood defences, the ExA was happy that these were correctly categorised as associated development as their purpose was to protect the proposed development. That being the case, the ExA concluded that the test for granting compulsory acquisition powers over them had been met.

97. In respect of the Arable Reversion Habitat Management Area and the Freshwater Grazing Marsh Habitat Management Area, the ExA was also content that these constituted associated development, and that the compulsory acquisition powers sought were therefore justified in this case as well. The ExA was not, however, convinced that a case had been made for the inclusion of the whole of Plot No 5/03 in the provision granting compulsory acquisition powers. A major portion of Plot No 5/03 comprised the Lowland Grassland Meadow Habitat Management Area with the remainder occupied by solar arrays and bordered by proposed native species hedging (forming Works 1 and 4). The applicant said that the main aim of the Lowland Grassland Meadow Habitat Management Area was to establish a grassland sward and scrub with greater ecological value than the existing land. It meant that no physical works were proposed within the Lowland Grassland Meadow Habitat Management Area. The ExA took the view that the primary mitigation of impacts had already been achieved by deleting solar panels from the part of the site that would be used for the Lowland Grassland Meadow Habitat Management Area. The ExA was not,

therefore, convinced that the case had been made out for the inclusion of the whole of Plot No 5/03 in the provision granting compulsory acquisition powers, other than for Works 1 and 4 (though powers of Temporary Possession would still be in place for all other relevant Works).

98. The ExA considered the effects on statutory undertakers and others with protective provisions in the proposed DCO and concluded they were acceptable. The ExA further considered that Crown Land had suitable protection subject to the inclusion of provisions acceptable to TCE in the DCO. Lastly, the ExA was content that section 132(3) of the PA 2008 in respect of Open Space Land had been satisfied. The ExA also considered that the provisions of the Human Rights Act 2008 had been met.

99. The ExA considered that there would be significant benefit from the grant of the DCO which would only be realised if the requested compulsory acquisition and temporary powers were granted (except for those relating to the Lowland Grassland Meadow Habitat Management Area in Plot No 5/03 (other than in relation to Works 1 and 4)). By the end of the Examination there were no outstanding objections to the grant of compulsory acquisition and temporary possession powers.

Conclusions on compulsory acquisition and temporary possession

100. The ExA considered that all legislative and policy requirements had been met (subject to the qualification in relation to the Lowland Grassland Meadow Habitat Management Plan in Plot No 5/03). The ExA's specific conclusions were: (a) there was a compelling case for the powers requested; (b) the proposed development was in accord with NPS EN-1 and NPS EN-5; (c) the land in question was needed to secure the proposed development (except for Plot No 5/03); (d) there would be a public benefit from the proposed development; (e) any private loss would be mitigated or minimised; (f) the applicant had explored reasonable alternatives; (g) there were no alternatives which ought to be preferred; (h) secure funding for the proposed development was available; and (i) in relation to human rights, the ExA was satisfied that: (1) the Examination ensured a fair and public hearing; (2) any interference with human rights arising from implementation of the proposed development was proportionate and struck a fair balance between the rights of the individual and the public interest; and (3) that compensation would be available in respect of any quantifiable loss.

101. The SoS sees no reason to disagree with the ExA's conclusions under this head and was satisfied that there were no outstanding issues or reasons to refuse the compulsory acquisition and temporary possession powers as recommended by the ExA. However, in respect of the ExA's consideration of the request for compulsory acquisition powers in relation to Works other than 1 and 4 over Plot

No 5/03, the SoS took the view that in accordance with section 122 of the PA 2008, the land was required and that there was a compelling case for its inclusion, particularly in view of the additional benefits in respect of biodiversity net gain that the development would be able to deliver if the Lowland Grass Meadow Habitat Management Area could be implemented in full.

SoS's consideration of the planning balance

102. The SoS considered that decision-making in PA 2008 cases was a balancing exercise and the weight afforded to different elements of the matrix of impacts and benefits will affect the overall conclusion. In the absence of a type specific NPS for solar power or for battery storage, the SoS considered that he was required to determine applications for DCOs for NSIPs against the criteria laid out in section 105 of the PA 2008.

103. Section 105(2) requires the SoS to have regard to: (a) any local impact report (within the meaning given by section 60(3)) submitted to the SoS before the deadline specified in a notice under section 60(2); (b) any matters prescribed in relation to development of the description to which the application relates; and (c) any other matters which the SoS thinks are both important and relevant to the SoS's decision.

104. The SoS considered that there was a strong case in favour of granting development consent for the development. NPS EN-1, which gives support to renewable electricity generating NSIPs, was relevant and important to the consideration of the application. This support must, however, be considered in the context of the planning balance.

105. In addition, the SoS acknowledged the substantial weight given by the ExA to the contribution to meeting the need for renewable energy infrastructure given by the proposed solar farm element of the proposed development on its own account and the further weight in favour of the proposed development's battery storage facility.

106. The SoS also noted that the ExA identified that the development would, in addition to meeting demand for electricity, also do so in a way which would be consistent with the Climate Change Act 2008 (2050 Target Amendment) Order 2019 (SI 2019/1056), which amended the Climate Change Act 2008 to set a legally binding target of a 100% reduction in greenhouse gas emissions (compared to 1990 levels) in the UK.

107. However, a number of adverse effects were identified by the ExA in respect of landscape, visual, recreational and cultural heritage impacts, and also limited weight was attributed by the ExA to temporary transport and traffic impacts. In

addition, local residents and some local organisations raised various concerns, including about the proposed battery storage facilities, citing the risk of fire, explosion and the release of poisonous gases and the impacts on amenity, wildlife and general well-being.

108. In his consideration of all the merits and dis-benefits of the proposed development the SoS concluded that, on balance, the benefits of the development outweigh its negative impacts. He also considered that his decision did not adversely impact on the public sector 'general equality duty' contained in the Equality Act 2010. He also considered his duty in section 40(1) of the Natural Environment and Rural Communities Act 2006 to have regard to the purpose of conserving biodiversity, and in particular to the United Nations Environmental Programme Convention on Biological Diversity of 1992, when granting development consent. The SoS was of the view that the ExA's report, together with the environmental impact analysis, considered biodiversity sufficiently to inform him in this respect. In reaching the decision to give consent to the development, the SoS considered that he had due regard to conserving biodiversity.

109. The SoS received a considerable amount of correspondence after the close of the Examination raising concerns about the potential impacts of the development. However, he did not believe that they raised any new issues that were not considered by the ExA in its Report.

SoS's conclusions and decision

110. For the reasons given, the SoS considered that there was a strong case for granting development consent for the Cleve Hill Solar Park. Given the national need for renewable energy infrastructure and the substantial weight the SoS attaches to the contribution of this development to meeting that need, he did not believe that this was outweighed by the development's potential adverse impacts, as mitigated by the proposed terms of the Order.

111. The SoS therefore accepted the ExA's recommendation to make the DCO granting development consent (albeit with various modifications which do not materially alter its effect). In reaching this decision, the SoS acknowledged that regard had been given to the ExA's Report, the Local Impact Reports submitted by SBC, CantCC, KCC and to all other matters which considered important and relevant to the SoS's decision as required by section 105 of the PA 2008. The SoS also confirmed for the purposes of regulation 4(2) of the 2017 Infrastructure Regulations that the environmental information as defined in regulation 3(1) of those Regulations had been taken into consideration.

Comment

112. In the absence of a specific NPS for solar power or for battery storage, the application was addressed against the criteria laid out in section 105 of the PA 2008. It was also recognised that NPS EN-1 gives support to renewable electricity generating NSIPs. The SoS acknowledged the substantial weight which the development would make to meeting the need for renewable energy infrastructure consistently with the legally binding target of a 100% reduction in greenhouse gas emissions (compared to 1990 levels) in the UK. The decision in this case has been given some prominence as it also contains areas of interest common to many solar applications and these matters were identified under a number of broad heads which serve as reminders for the range of impact and other assessments required in dealing with both small-scale and large-scale solar projects, namely: (a) energy need; (b) landscape and visual effects; (c) biodiversity and nature conservation; (d) cultural heritage; (e) agricultural land; (f) traffic and transport; (g) noise and vibration; (h) socio-economic effects; (i) water environment (including flooding and coastal defence); (j) safety and security (particularly in respect of the proposed battery storage element); and (k) compulsory acquisition. Indeed, such a checklist would also apply in the case of wind power. This application was a benchmark decision for the SoS in what will be the UK's largest solar farm (and largest battery energy storage system) when it comes online in 2023 and clearly represents a serious declaration of intent when it comes to the UK's zero emissions target. This was a large-scale project in a suitable location and when it came to biodiverstity and nature conservation it is to be observed that there were objections to the scheme from the KWT and the RSPB because of its potential adverse impacts on wildlife, principally in relation to a number of bird species, where they felt that adequate mitigation could not be put in place to prevent significant impacts. Despite the objections of these bodies the applicant's proposals for mitigation and enhancement were accepted and the finding was that there would be no significant adverse effects from the development. It meant that a formidable objection, acknowledged by the parties to be a major consideration on the application, was overcome.

CASE STUDY XI

Renewable Energy and Climate Change Benefits of Solar Farm Sufficient to Justify Additional 10-Year Period of Operation

Planning appeal reference APP/X6910/A/3257588 (1 December 2020)

1. In a decision dated 1 December 2020 (under planning appeal reference APP/X6910/A/3257588) an inspector appointed by the Welsh Minsters allowed an appeal against the decision of Blaenau Gwent County Borough Council (under application reference C/2019/0280) refusing planning permission for a 30MW solar park, access and ancillary development without compliance with a condition previously imposed under an earlier planning permission (reference DNS/3213639 dated 31 July 2019), the effect of which was extend the life of the 2019 permission from 30 to 40 years.

2. It appears as though the 30-year limit was imposed in the interests of the area's character and appearance and the preservation of historic assets, namely the Tredegar Cholera Cemetery Scheduled Ancient Monument (SAM). The application site falls within an SLA in what is a remote agricultural landscape of uplands punctuated by valleys with isolated farms and dwellings. It is also within the rural setting of the SAM, which lies on elevated land. The original permission was allowed on the grounds: (a) that the impact of the development would be temporary and fully reversible; and (b) that the benefits of the proposal in generating an anticipated 30MW of electricity annually from a renewable source, for a period of 30 years, would outweigh the identified harm.

3. The reason for the new application was that the operator wished to amend the time limit for operating the solar farm due to advances in solar panel technology. The issue was whether the benefits of extending the life of the development for a further 10 years outweighed any harm. There had been no material alteration to the landscape in the limited time since the grant of the original permission and the extended period would not be of a wholly different order of magnitude to the period of 30 years. It was also estimated that the additional 10-year period would result in a saving equivalent to 160,000 tonnes of CO_2, which was one-third greater than the extant permission and would, as the inspector found, contribute to a sustained offsetting of carbon emissions and to energy security during the 10-year extended period. The inspector attached significant weight to these energy and climate change benefits.

4. Despite the adverse landscape, visual and heritage impacts, the inspector concluded that the benefits of the proposal in generating 30MW of renewable electricity per annum over an additional 10 years significantly outweighed the conflict with the development plan.

Comment

5. This was an entirely sensible outcome where the inspector clearly attached significant weight to energy and climate change benefits over the additional life of the solar farm. It is also noteworthy that the inspector (as had the Minister in granting the original permission) attached weight to the fact that the harmful impacts of the development on the landscape and on the setting of the SAM would remain time-limited and fully reversible. This is invariably an argument of great weight in applications involving wind and solar farms.

Index

References are to page numbers.